Teaching *New* Patriotism
in the 21st Century

Teaching *New* Patriotism In the 21ˢᵗ Century

Errol Putman, EdD
Jeffrey Ginger
Matthew Schultz
Amy Rivenburgh

Emily Dague, editor

PUTMAN PUBLISHING LLC.
Geneseo, New York 14454

Putman Publishing was created initially to guarantee the publication of *Teaching New Patriotism in the 21st Century*, after numerous larger publishing houses turned down our efforts to rejuvenate and re-imbue the word patriotism with current and heartfelt meaning. Putman Publishing makes it our personal mission to enlighten the citizens of the United States to basic human rights needs in the United States and around the world.

Publication of *Teaching New Patriotism in the 21st Century*

Published in the United States by Putman Publishing, Geneseo, New York

Putman Publishing, LLC
Box 427 Geneseo NY, 14454
www.teachingnewpatriotism.com

Library of Congress Cataloging-in-Publication Data

Putman, Errol et. al, *Teaching New Patriotism in the 21st Century* (Geneseo, New York: Putman Publishing, 2004)

ISBN 0-9759316-0-1
Library of Congress catalogue number

Printed in the United States of America

—Dedicated to the children of the United States of America in the hopes that one day we will live in a world where there truly is liberty and justice for all.

The word patriotism has been much abused; but it is a good word. Instead of avoiding it because of its abuse . . . every effort should be made to imbue it with real meaning and make it a potent influence in the development of a sound national life.

REPORT OF THE COMMITTEE
ON SOCIAL STUDIES — 1916

Contents

Foreword

True patriotism hates injustice in its own land more than anywhere else.
CLARENCE DARROW

The terrorist attacks on the World Trade Center, Pentagon, and Flight 93 that occurred on September 11, 2001 were the first direct attacks on the United States that most Americans could remember. In many ways the impact was astronomical and with consequences that reverberated through the American psyche. Over the weeks immediately following, in an effort to measure this impact on the American spirit, we asked friends and acquaintances, and acquaintances of friends, to respond to the following question: In what way(s) has your definition of patriotism been impacted by the events of September 11, 2001?

As one might expect under the circumstances, responses varied considerably. While some individuals focused directly on the tragic events, others attempted to look at and analyze the larger picture to discern a deeper meaning of the events, resulting in a significant contrast of the perspectives presented. Nevertheless, for the most part one theme was repeated in almost all the responses: the feeling of betrayal. Each entry included in *Teaching New Patriotism in the 21ˢᵗ Century* is reprinted exactly as it was received, completely unedited, from every profound thought through every imperfect sentence. Although the large number of replies were too numerous to permit printing them all, the following collection represents the variety of regional and philosophical responses received.

A Sense of Pride

I have always loved my country and what it represents and have felt a sense of pride in being a citizen, calling this land my home. But life in today's world is hectic, with so much daily stress, that these feelings have been forgotten—I've taken my country for granted. The terrorist attacks of September 11th have not only brought these feelings to the forefront in my life, but have strengthened them. I realize now what being a US citizen really means. It's not merely enjoying the freedoms we have, but also being part of a greater family. Loving my country means loving fellow Americans. Now more than ever I appreciate and respect people for who they are, and value their worth as human beings. I feel a need to participate and help when and where I can. Patriotism is love and support for one's country—I guess that really means love and support for its people.

Cindy
Administrative Assistant
New York

Patriotism Had Infected Everyone

It was Thursday September 13. We had a game at home against Attica. We warmed up, and just had gone through introductions. A student was introduced, and was going to sing the Star Spangled Banner. The color guard was at the 50, and the student walked out with the microphone. When she started singing, I zoned out. I looked at everyone around me, and we all had this blank look on our faces. We all just stared at the flag like we had never done this before. You must keep in mind that we had all done this pre-game ceremony thousands of times. I looked at the head coach, and he looked at me. By now, the singer was half way through, and the coach and I just looked at each other and the team. I looked at the biggest, strongest, most well respected kid on our team, and he had tears in his eyes. Looking back at the flag, and seeing it blowing in the wind, and realizing EVERYTHING that the flag stood for, I myself got chills and felt the hair on my arms stand up. By the time she had finished singing, I had tears in my eyes too.

Justin
High school history teacher
New York

During a Time of Need

I am pleased to see that so many people are now proud to display their patriotism, and that it is now the "politically correct" thing to do. I was disappointed when our Supreme Court ruled that our freedom of speech as guaranteed by the First Amendment allowed us to burn our own flag or to display it inappropriately. It angered me more that our own people would do this than when it was done by members of another country.

Tim
Undersheriff
New York

National Pride Has Been Focused

Patriotism it self hasn't changed. Just shall we say the number of people actually showing it has changed. Now as I go through airports and other cities I see more US Flags then I have seen (other than July 4th). The lack of tolerance for non-patriotic actions, politically correct is now taking a back seat to United We Stand and the rest be darned. But to the point of the definition of Patriotism— "Love or loyal, or zealous support for one's own country, especially in all matters involving other countries, nationalism" (Webster's Unabridged Dictionary). Perhaps there in itself is the difference. Since the days of Nixon there has been a low level of national pride. With the events of 9–11 the national pride has been focused. The target, the enemy is no longer something inside our borders, instead it is something outside our own country.

Chris
Manufacturing Systems Consultant
New York

Make Sure It Is Not at the Expense of too Many Liberties

At the time of the attacks, I was teaching an American history class the reasons for the American Revolution. How could a question of taxes bloom into a fight for liberty? This was the center of my approach. We explored the concept of liberty and what it meant to the 'aristocracy' of the colonies and to the common people of the colonies. This led to the look at such documents as the Magna Carta, the English Bill of Rights, and the writings of John Locke. The culmination of this was Jefferson's wording in the Declaration of Independence.

When the attacks happened two words form both Locke and Jefferson came front and center. The purpose of government is to protect "life, liberty. . . ." Life is listed first by both. Liberty is listed second by both. At this point all students agreed that protection of "life" is the most important thing this government can do at this time. "But at what cost to 'liberty'?" was my question back. Another question to the students and to myself, "Do we take the extreme of a Patrick Henry statement, 'Give me liberty or give me death'?" Another question to the students and myself, "Do we give the president virtual dictatorial powers as we have in the past during war?" Where does life, where does liberty stand in these extremes?

My change in what patriotism really is was shaped by what I was teaching in the classroom at the time. Before I was vaguely familiar with liberty. Teaching the concept at the time of the attacks made me painfully aware of that term and what it fully means. One view that has not changed is that flying flags without knowing what those colors truly represent is only chauvinism, not patriotism. I'm afraid we have had way too much chauvinism in the last month.

Dave
High school history teacher
Nebraska

America Will Prevail

The meaning of Patriotism, "the love for my Country," has not changed. What has become more evident and maybe taken on a different perspective since September 11, 2001, is that the 'idea' of patriotism portrays an open praise and display of love for our Country and the American people. Patriotism is shown daily in the support and solidarity for America. In the past, I have probably been among the 'guilty' of taking freedom and democracy for granted. I have always participated in patriotic customs, traditions, and activities, such as displaying the flag, patriotic songs, National Anthem, and support for America. Since the September 11 tragedy, not only do I participate, but I have a feeling of unity and membership in America.

By demonstrating love and respect for each other, we can overcome the trials that we continue to face. The act of terrorism made me realize the importance of love, family, and friends and that we need to look at life and freedom as a precious 'gem.'

I am optimistic in the belief that America will prevail and eventually we will experience the feeling of freedom that we once knew. To quote Eleanor Roosevelt, "True patriotism springs from a belief in the dignity of the individual, freedom and equality not only for Americans but for all people on earth, universal brotherhood and good will . . ."

Mariah
Public School Administrator
Tennessee

Really Stressed Over All This

I have a friend at ground zero (works 2 blocks from the Capital—her law firm just moved there from 2 blocks from the White House) who is really stressed over all this. Says it is getting harder and harder to go to work each day.

My four-year-old was drawing a flag yesterday—all on her own—and when I noticed and commented on it, she said yes, but it needs two more colors. I got her the red and the blue, and she finished it, cut it out, and we taped it to our sliding glass door. In her own little way, she's absorbing some of this.

Loss of innocence is even harder to withstand when it happens with one's children.

Mary Lynne
Attorney
New Mexico

Where Freedom Rings Every Day

I don't think that my view of patriotism has really changed that much from September 11th on. I think when you really get down to it, Americans are a truly patriotic people anyway. Just listen at a ball game when the national anthem is sung or played. Everyone gets into it. When Kate Smith sang God Bless America, long before Whitney Huston did it, everyone sang along and some even teared up.

The Pledge of Allegiance is still a very big thing in schools and elsewhere. No one turns their heads or grumbles because of it. They say the words in unison because everyone knows the words and feels the words deep down. It's our land, our country, our anthem, and our song. And I feel that every true American keeps these things close to their heart whether they express it openly or not. I think too that TV has given us all a glimpse of what other countries are like today and how much better we have it than most other people on this place we call Earth. We may take advantage of it, bitch about it, complain that things don't always go our way when it comes to the government, but all in all, over the past 225 years, it is the only place on the planet where freedom rings everyday.

Leon
Supervisor
Maryland

To Salute the Flag While in Uniform is a Privilege

After 5 long grueling months spent in the Mediterranean Sea onboard the strike destroyer USS Thorn DD-988, every sailor's thoughts about patriotism changed drastically after the events that occurred on September 11, 2001. What once was taken as a simple gesture of saluting the national ensign turned into an undeniable act of utmost respect and pride. The honor of being able to salute the flag of the United States of America while dressed in a military uniform is a privilege that I had often overlooked in the past. Every time that I see an American flag flying, whether at half-mast or at full mast a feeling of pride overpowers me.

Onboard my ship, almost every American sailor went to the ship's store and bought a small American flag pin, and proudly wears it over there heart in their Navy coveralls, the underway uniform. What most people in this world cannot understand is how we as Americans can respond to such a devastating and horrific act with so much honor and pride, but they do not know Americans obviously. When Pearl Harbor, Hawaii was bombed on December 7, 1941 by the Japanese Zero wing fighters, Americans came together and supported their country and their troops as they prepared for war. The same type of maniacal act was repeated on September 11, 2001 when two civilian airliners were flown deliberately into the North and South towers of the World Trade Center, and another airliner was flown into the Pentagon.

Although military units were not targeted and battleships were not taken out of commission, innocent peoples' lives were lost forever. It is this most devastating act against innocent lives that is the most disturbing of all. Who would dare to take innocent lives with no regard to human life and societies values? Obviously, this is the work of crazy and deranged individuals. After 225 years of declaring our independence from Great Britain, this country has been through so many changes that have affected peoples' lives. World War I, World War II, the Korean War, the Vietnam War, and finally the Gulf War in the early 90's.

Unfortunately many people opposed the Vietnam War, yet the troops were praised when they came home from the Gulf War. Patriotism is something that we as Americans often take for granted, and overlook daily. Before the events of September 11, 2001 when was the last time that anyone took the time to actually look at our National Insignia and realize what it stood for? The American flag is flown all over the world, in hundreds of countries, millions of people viewing it, and still none of those people can experience the pride and honor that I feel every morning when "colors" is sounded at 0800. In closing, I believe that it is every American's duty to fly their flag in the highest regard for this great nation.

Steve
Sailor
US NAVY

Proud Without Being Blind

As for patriotism, I have always been proud to be an American. I am the first one to get misty-eyed because of a patriotic tune or tear down a person for not knowing the proper means to treat and fold the American flag. It was also an important influence for me to join AmeriCorps. My opinion towards the recent increase in patriotism is not what I expected though. I am sort of disgusted that it had to take such a horrible incident to awaken pride in the American public. It has been extreme here in Delaware, since it is located between New York City and Washington D.C. Sometimes the public becomes overly patriotic and starts to ignore or disregard corrupt or ridiculous actions made by the government. Can't people be supportive of their government and proud without being blind to its faults and mute to making suggestions? Is that not being the best citizen? Sorry I . . . had to get that off my chest.

Cindy
AmeriCorps
Delaware

It's An Emotional Thing

You asked how the meaning of patriotism has changed for me since the September 11 national tragedy. It's an emotional thing, of course. There are no infallible signs of the love or lack of love one has for the Country. I have to say this first: for me it's changed very little. As well you can remember, I was most critical of my country's policy and actions during the war in Southeast Asia. Then and always, however, I've been a patriot, and I believe in making that known. I respect the national symbol—the flag. I've nudged and lectured others at parades and Memorial Day services about standing, removing hats and placing the hand over the heart. I fly the flag at my home on national holidays and special occasions. I continue to criticize national policy but always because I care deeply for our country. Nothing has changed for me. It will be interesting to see if there is a change in public behavior at next weekend's homecoming parade on our campus.

Certainly every citizen must be pleased to see our renewed sense of unity manifest itself in increased donations to the ARC and ad hoc charitable groups. Although I've appreciated the contributions of diversity programs on my campus and elsewhere, I've held the position that "Unum" is more important than "E Pluribus." It seems others are, at least temporarily, thinking that way too.

It's a stretch in reasoning, but I think our pre-attack lack of unity and our lack of a shared belief in a common good are the products of a generation of selfish, inappropriately competitive, and greedy Americans. Perhaps we would have had an efficient federal presence in our airports if we weren't obsessed with tax dollars and the size of government. Surely we've known the security inadequacies since the 70's. Maybe now we are beginning to understand once again that the welfare of our neighbor is intrinsic to our own well being, and we all share the financial responsibility of the common good. Now we are in the process of spending decades of tax saving. "We the people . . ." is at the core of any definition of patriotism.

Seeing a few more flags is a nice change in public behavior. Perhaps I'm not looking, but I don't see people treating their neighbors differently. I commend the President and others for stressing so firmly the official position that our war is not with Islam, Muslims or the people of any one nation. Nonetheless, I'm sure more Arabic persons and Muslims are being detained, questioned, threatened and generally harassed than quieter times would require. But we have not created internment camps. If our nationalism is a little more sophisticated, we've progressed. Yet I do not believe the common man sees the gray areas very well. Patriotism for most is fueled with anger, hatred and a desire for violent revenge. That we could love our country more for all the good it does in the world hasn't occurred to many.

"God bless America" is everywhere. It reminds me of WW II rhetoric. Although a constitutionally secular nation, we tend to look for anything to unite us spiritually when we feel threatened. I wonder if the reference includes the god of American Muslims who outnumber American Episcopalians? (I think Ed Bradley cited the numbers.) We can't wage war without believing God is on our side. Americans believe terrorists go to hell, but Bin Laden has assured his true believer terrorists of a life in Paradise. Is this irony too obvious to mention? Anyhow, God, the flag and a fountain of anger characterize the patriotism of the moment. Sadly, intense patriotism is ephemeral and superficial. When we've bloodied our hands sufficiently, we'll retreat to our obsessions with ourselves.

Bob
Professor
Michigan

Have To Be Willing To Stand Up

I was born a few years after WWII, in an era of prosperity. Although, I'm too young to remember anything about the Korean conflict, I was a young adult and lost many friends and acquaintances to VietNam. Although I lived through the press and publicity of VietNam, the anti-war demonstrations, the marches on Washington, the peace protests, I never feared for my PERSONAL safety. My home territory was never threatened. It was distanced from me in a way that made much of it seem like a product of Hollywood. And that's how September 11th first impacted me, too. This is like watching a disaster movie. But those people whose lives were lost or forever altered by the attacks gave their lives or the lives of their loved ones, even if unknowingly, because of a nation's principles, values and commitments to the way of life that we've all taken for granted for much too long. Watching the news reports about the Anthrax threats and cases, I commented that I am feeling so vulnerable, as are many Americans. This is not something that I've ever dreamed of feeling with respect to my country. NEW YORK CITY WAS CLOSED FOR 3 DAYS! Our collective fear is taking an unheard of toll on our economy. The fact that this fear has SHUT DOWN our government offices, our postal system, the air travel industry points to how vulnerable we are.

The unspeakable attacks of September 11th have brought the people of this nation (and much of the free world) together again. I am awed by the acts of heroism that I've heard and seen reported, the selflessness of ordinary citizens who have stepped forward to help the rescue, the outpouring of financial support from individuals, industry, corporations, entertainers, the courage of our firemen and policemen to put themselves in the path of danger voluntarily and expect no special recognition for it, the valor of our military who stand ready, or are actively kicking back!

God Bless the USA and all her citizens!

Norma
Computer Marketer
New York

Freedom and Opportunity Are Not Without Cost

I grew up in the 60's and 70's when America was re-exploring the meanings of independence and global responsibility. The meaning of patriotism was also in question. Was love of country demonstrated by supporting an armed conflict in a foreign land that had unclear objectives and mixed public opinion or protesting the same? I chose to volunteer my services to my country believing that the gifts provided by this 'land of opportunity' were not without cost. It's what makes us different. Patriotism was a willingness to pay that price. Over the years, those gifts have been looked upon as more of an entitlement. I am an American so am entitled to whatever America has to offer without having to pay for that entitlement. The incidents of 9/11 changed that. They re-acquainted Americans with the fact that the gifts of freedom and opportunity are not without cost. I think that once again, patriotism is a willingness to pay the price that is demonstrated on a variety of fronts. I don't think that the love of country defined by patriotism has changed, but the circumstances surrounding the demonstration of that love are much clearer.

Steve
Materials Manager
Delaware

Patriotism Has Become More Real

For me, patriotism has become more real—less abstract. I'm very proud when I see people displaying flags and wearing red/white/ blue ribbons and pins. It reminds us we can't take our freedoms for granted anymore. We have to be willing to stand up for them and help those who need help. I think the little things like ribbons and pins bring us together and let us know we're all in this together so it's bound to turn out right in the end. Maybe that helps lessen the stress and give us something positive to grasp.

Carolyn
Database Analyst
Florida

Defend Our Right to Choose

How did I happen to be born in America, instead of in a country where basic human freedoms are denied? I have always felt lucky to be an American. Though I deeply regret the loss of life in war, I know we must defend our right to choose the way we, as Americans, live our lives. September 11th made me sharply aware that this country I have felt so safe in is no longer secure. My patriotism has been strengthened by this horrendous assault on our people. We must retaliate, to insure that those who attack us realize they have awakened a sleeping tiger.

Emily
Retired School Teacher
Michigan

Political Correctness of the Right

Patriotism has become the new political correctness of the Right. If you now say "We need to understand why the rest of the world hates us." your comments are interpreted as saying that we deserved the attack. Peace demonstrators are assailed in person, in the editorial pages, and on television as being anti-American. Their motives are inferred to be that WE are the bad person and we should ignore our attackers. I believe it was George Will who wrote of the change in isolationist thinking from the old, "We are too good for the world" to the new, "The world is too good for us to be involved in it." He accuses those who promote restraint or peace as being self-hating, anti-Americans. He gets away with his accusation because this plays on the street as the new political correctness—

Patriotism as it was at the beginning of the Cold War, "America, Love it or leave it."

Dennis
Professor
New York

Don't Think It Changed My Feelings

I was stunned and thought I was going to be sick as I watched the TV news and all the video out of New York. I immediately thought of the people on the planes and the people trapped in the WTC buildings and if I might know any of them as I have friends who work down there. Thankfully they were not among the missing. I thought of my nephew and how it might affect him and his ship. I thought of my kids and the possibility of a draft. I thought how absolutely sick the towel-heads are. They have no respect for life and need to be exterminated. I would be willing to enlist if that is what it might take to put an end to these crazies. I am proud to be an American and always have and always will be. I don't think it changed my feelings of patriotism one way or another.

Charles
CEO
New York

I Am a Strong American Patriot and I Always Will Be

As you might have guessed, the meaning of patriotism hasn't changed much for me. I have always been proud of our country and willing to defend her against all enemies. I get tears in my eyes whenever I hear the Star Spangled Banner or Taps. That doesn't mean that I agree with all of our politicians and/or all of their policies. However, I'm still a captain in the United States Army Reserves (inactive) and if they give me a call, I'll be on my way as soon as I kiss the wife good-bye and hand her the power of attorney form that I keep in the safe. I wanted to get in on the Gulf War, but my contacts in D.C. had all retired, except for one. He said I was crazy and implied that I was too old. I should have court-martialed the son-of-a-bitch when I had the chance in 1967.

I am saddened by the events of September 11th, but I am also saddened by the thought that, for most Americans, the renewed (new?) sense of patriotism will probably not remain strong in the face of a prolonged effort against our enemies. The bills are piling up and after a brief period of mourning, the anti-war groups will be back in the spotlight. The first planeload of body bags to come home from Afghanistan will further weaken our resolve to find and kill the blasphemous (expletive deleted) that brainwash young men into thinking their path to heaven is through the slaughter of innocent people.

The meaning of patriotism has not changed for me. I am a strong American patriot and I always will be. I hope I am wrong about my fellow Americans.

Frank
Jr. Hi Science Teacher
Michigan

Preface

Patriotism consists not in waving the flag, but in striving that our country shall be righteous as well as strong.

JAMES BRYCE

According to Christopher Wheatley, writing in *ELH*, the definition of "patriot" that most closely approximates current thinking first appeared in an English language dictionary in 1676, and was defined in very simple terms as "a benefactor or lover of his country."[1] In the decades that followed, patriotism evolved into a potent political force in England—a watchword of justice. In the hands of its proponents, the definition was broadened to include the "action to withhold loyalty to the state as it existed while proclaiming a 'patriotic' intention of restoring it to its ancient purity."[2] This belief was based on three assumptions: (1) that England was the birthplace of liberty, (2) the English government was susceptible to corruption, and (3) political power was based on a balance between King, House of Lords, and House of Commons.[3]

Since it was widely accepted throughout England that corruption occurred when one of the three branches of government came under the influence of one of the other branches of government, any effort made to correct the balance was deemed appropriate and

---

1. Christopher J. Wheatley, "The Volunteers and the Rhetoric of Honor and Patriotism." *ELH* 60, no. 2 (1993): 397–418.

2. Hugh Cunningham, "*The Language of Patriotism*" in *History and Politics:* Vol.I. "Patriotism: The Making and Unmaking of British National Identity," ed. R. Samuals (London: Routledge, 1989), 53.

3. Ibid., 58.

"patriotic."[4] Considering that the American colonies were deeply rooted in English institutions, it should not come as any surprise that the Founders of the United States labeled their efforts to thwart the abuse of England's power in the second half of the eighteenth century as "patriotic."[5]

---

4. Ibid.

5. James A. Martin, and Mark E. Lender, "A Respectable Army: The Military Origins of the Republic, *1763–178,"* ed. J.H. Franklin and A.S. Eisenstadt, *The American History Series* (Arlington Heights, Illinois: Harlan Davidson, Inc., 1982) 76.

Introduction

Let us remember that our national unity is a most priceless asset.

GERALD FORD

The events of September 11, 2001, will forever be etched in the minds of all Americans everywhere, and, reminiscent of another time and another place, it was a date "which will live in infamy." The real story of September 11th did not end with the attacks, but continued in the manner in which Americans, individually and collectively, responded. Newspaper and magazine columnists and television and radio commentators stood firm in their opposition to hatred and bigotry, and, instead, encouraged Americans everywhere to work through this tragedy, united.

The positive response was most evident in the actions of the service men and women in Washington and New York. They refused to let the enormity of the situation deter them from performing their duties. They raced to the scenes of destruction and carried out their assigned responsibilities to save the lives of as many people as possible; ordinary men and women risking their lives to save others. In the months that followed, police officers, firefighters, paramedics, emergency medical service staff, and other self-sacrificing workers became the heroes of a society that had previously been too quick to make heroes of sports figures and movie stars.

In contrast to the solidarity expressed in the days following September 11, the manner in which patriotism was defined and taught in the United States has undergone changes, often with surprising results. In the not too distant past, for example, while some Americans called themselves patriots because they proudly acknowledged the flag, others used love of country as justification for burning it. Clearly, the issue is complex and involves many emotions and opinions. Just as generations of Americans have wrestled with the role of patriotism in their lives, educators have struggled to include patriotism in school curricula amid ever-changing political and social climates.

Most often the focus of such efforts, especially in the early years of the Republic, involved teaching patriotism in an almost reverent manner. Students were required to accept preconceived values, and to participate in ceremonial rituals such as singing patriotic songs and reciting pledges. Identified in *Teaching New Patriotism in the 21st Century* as "traditional," these methods became the standard in American education for more than its first 100 years of existence.

As the twentieth century approached, however, attitudes and beliefs changed. Teachers began to use methods directly involving students in identifying, analyzing, evaluating and resolving problems with patriotism. Referred to as "non-traditional" methods in *Teaching New Patriotism in the 21st Century*, the innovative strategies were perceived by their proponents as superior methods for teaching an insightful and informed brand of patriotism.

As every generation defined and redefined patriotism, the burden was on the nation's educators to instill patriotism in order to preserve that which the United States identified as the purpose for its existence. As social acceptance of shifting definitions passed from generation to generation, teachers changed the way they taught patriotism, often (but not always) producing positive results. In effect, as a nation, we have progressed enormously in this respect, especially since the last quarter of the last century. No stronger proof can be found than through observance of the more accepting attitudes and behaviors exhibited among America's youth. But the task is far from complete and there remains much to be done.

Ironically, it was the shifting definition of patriotism, and the shifting emphasis of educators throughout history that created opportunities for blending traditional and non-traditional views regarding an expanded definition of patriotism. Among the first to advocate change were Raymond Muessig and Vincent Rogers. In a 1964 article published in *Social Education* titled "Teaching Patriotism at Higher Concept Levels," they explained that efforts must be made to reach a higher level of understanding, something beyond simply "lovin' yer country."[1] Believing that a non-emotional brand

---

1. Raymond Muessig and Vincent Rogers, "Teaching Patriotism at Higher Concept Levels," *Social Education* 28, no. 5 (1964): 266.

of patriotism was also needed, they appealed for a solution that was not overly saturated with chauvinism, but was also not "void of moral intellectual and emotional sustenance."[2] Ultimately, they concluded that the country needed a balanced love of country; one that included an understanding of the underlying meanings of national ceremonies and symbols, and at the same time accepting diversity, pluralism, respect for the rights of others, and fundamental democratic principles.[3] Toward the end of the twentieth century, Jack Zevin also spoke of the need for schools to teach a brand of patriotism that encouraged pride of country and direct involvement in the political process.[4]

Teaching New Patriotism in the 21st Century, however, is the first serious effort at blending the best of traditional and non-traditional methods. Unlike the Ku Klux Klan, neo-Nazis, militia organizations, and others that have misapplied applications of patriotism in a distorted perception of what the United States should stand for, *New* Patriotism is committed to positive change that is both pro-active and egalitarian. In the *New* Patriotism, love of fellow countrymen holds equal importance to love of country, and must include tolerance for diversity of culture and beliefs. To provide real strategies for teaching an enlightened patriotism, these elements must be emphasized with the same fervor generally reserved for teaching patriotism in a traditional format.

This is especially important since we are living in an increasingly complex society that by 2050 will no longer have a single race in the majority.[5] For example, non-Hispanic whites are no longer in the majority in California, and it is projected that Texas will soon follow California's lead (if it hasn't already).[6] Thus, looking to the future, it is imperative that educators at all levels and in all disciplines join in this effort to further define patriotism in broader

---

2. Ibid.

3. Ibid., 266-270.

4. Jack Zevin, "Clashing Conceptions of Citizenship," *Social Science Record* 31, no. 2 (1994): 23.

5. Annalisa Schmitt, *Executive Summery: A Population Perspective of the United States*, [online source] (last accessed 10 June 2004) http://www.predc.org/summaries/uspopperspec/uspopperspec.html; Internet.

6. Todd S. Purdum, "California Census Confirms Whites Are in Minority," *New York Times*, 30 March 2001.; Jim Yardley, "Non-Hispanic Whites May Soon Be a Minority in Texas," *New York Times*, 25 March 2001.

terms, preparing students to become active, accepting, responsible patriots. Students should be encouraged to ask questions about legislative actions at the national and local levels, whether they are liberal or conservative, Democrat or Republican. Perhaps more importantly, they should understand their responsibility to uphold the tenets of democracy and justice through participation, even if that means making unpopular decisions or questioning the status quo. After all, the authors of the 1916 *Report of the Committee on Social Studies* (which established the philosophical foundation for teaching social studies) emphasized that in order to achieve national efficiency, patriotism is "the responsibility of every citizen."[7]

---

7. National Education Association, "Report of the Committee on Social Studies," *The History Teacher's Magazine* 8 no. 2 (1917): 11.

1

Teaching Patriotism:
The Early Years

A free, virtuous, and enlightened people must know full well the great principles and causes upon which their happiness depends.

JAMES MONROE

Just as patriotism became an influential element in American politics from the first volley fired on Lexington Green, patriotism has also been an enduring consideration in American education. It was not by accident that as issues involving patriotism guided political decisions from the onset of the Republic, education underwent requisite transformation to keep pace with changes that occurred. Although something less than well organized, most often this effort involved identifying the most effective, and traditional, methods of applying each new definition of patriotism to the education of America's youth. This had the intent of producing solid support for God, country, and the fulfillment of national objectives.

As the twentieth century approached, however, attitudes among many educators began to change regarding how America's youth should be properly taught patriotism. Believing that the large number of citizens who equated patriotism with mindless xenophobia and chauvinism was evidence of a failure of the system, they called for immediate change. Rejecting outright the then popular traditional methods of patriotic instruction that rarely resulted in genuine sincerity or thought on the part of students, they sought replacement with non-traditional teaching methods that encouraged direct student inquiry.

The New Nation
(1775–1810)

The importance of keeping the citizenry apprised of patriotic events as they occurred was recognized from the earliest days of the American Revolution. Many colonial leaders, for example, believed that the very existence of the nation should be attributed to the celebration of events such as the Boston Massacre and the Battle of Lexington. Even the signers of the Declaration of Independence stood firm in their belief that "the new nation could not exist until . . . evidence of [its] nationwide celebration appeared in print."[1] The message was clear. In order to create enthusiastic and enduring support for the Revolution, there must exist a patriotic bond between its active proponents and education.

In time, schools throughout Revolutionary America rose to meet the challenge, and, in the years that followed came to play a significant role in the effort to preserve and perpetuate knowledge of the patriotic achievements of the Revolution. Interestingly, the need for forging relationships between education and government had actually been suggested by Benjamin Franklin nearly a quarter century earlier. Believing that education helped provide men with the necessary qualifications "to serve the publick with Honour to themselves and their country."[2] Franklin asserted that one of the main purposes for reading history was that men should have the means to "secure their liberties."[3] This early involvement by the schools may well have produced the first objectives in civic education in what was to become the United States, a list that included literacy, patriotic values, moral virtues, national loyalty, loyalty to institutions, and loyalty to freedom.[4]

---

1. David Waldstreicher, "Rites of Rebellion, Rites of Assent: Celebrations of Print Culture, and the Origins of American Nationalism," *Journal of American History* 82, no. 1 (1995): 44.

2. John Best, *Benjamin Franklin on Education* (New York: Teacher's College Press, 1962), 129.

3. Ibid., 149.

4. Freeman R. Butts, *The Revival of Civic Learning* (Bloomington, Indiana: Phi Delta Kappa Foundation, 1980), 54., and Rosh Welter, *Popular Education and Democratic Thought* (New York: Columbia University Press, 1962), 36.

According to Lawrence Cremin, author of *American Educa-tion: The National Experience 1783–1876,* and a noted authority on the history of education, Benjamin Rush and Noah Webster were two of the leading advocates for teaching patriotism in schools from primary through secondary levels. The goal of these early spirited patriots was nothing less than a new republican individual of virtu-ous character, abiding by patriotism and prudent wisdom, fash-ioned by education into an independent, yet loyal citizen. Without individuals of such enduring qualities, Rush and Webster believed the test in liberty would be short-lived.[5]

Reflecting the energy and sheer enthusiasm of the period, Noah Webster accepted the challenge and produced the means to spread the message. Webster's dictionaries and spelling books, writ-ten to produce a distinct American language, included several quota-tions of American origin. His intent, ultimately, was that his books "kindle patriotism in the hearts of youth."[6] Due in large measure to his untiring efforts, Noah Webster enjoyed considerable success dur-ing the period

As the American Revolution drew to a close, other educators, seeking to imitate Webster's success, followed his example. As the rule, not the exception, textbooks began to celebrate patriotic themes proclaiming love of country, unity, and liberty. Each theme was intended to "attach the child's loyalty to the state and nation [because] the sentiments of patriotism, love of country, vie[d] with the love of God as the cornerstone of virtue. Patriotism . . . must be considered as the noblest of social values."[7] Of the early textbooks, the spellers and the readers appeared to have been the most influen-tial sources of civic education.

In the years following the revolution, Noah Webster, increas-ingly popular due to the success of his dictionaries and spelling books, attempted to educate the American public on his beliefs and the place of patriotism in the school curriculum. In addition to mak-

---

5. Lawerence A. Cremin, *American Education: The National Experience 1783–1876* (New York: Harper & Row, 1980), 5.

6. Merle Curti, *The Roots of American Loyalty* (New York: Columbia University Press, 1946), 124.

7. Freeman R. Butts, *The Revival of Civic Learning*, 55.

ing himself available to lecture on the topic of patriotism, he wrote many newspaper and magazine articles, and corresponded with men from all strata of society. In each case, Webster's theme never varied; his mission was to spread the word about the greatness of America.[8] In addition to the commitment shown by educators like Noah Webster, there is evidence to suggest that concerns relating to education and patriotism extended far beyond primary and secondary education. Thomas Jefferson, for example, suggested that a national university be constructed to serve the whole of the fledgling nation. He believed that patriots in a democratic society served their country best by using their critical powers to ensure governmental honesty. He also believed that "it would be a dangerous delusion were a confidence in the man of our choice to silence our fears for the safety of our rights."[9] Concurring with Jefferson in principle, James Madison added that such a broad base of education would "enlighten the opinions, expand the patriotism and harmonize the principles of those who attended."[10]

But the issue of patriotism and its place in the school did not end with platitudes. Ironically, it was Thomas Jefferson, one of the very symbols of fashionable patriotism during the period, who was the first to raise several perplexing questions regarding the teaching of patriotism: (1) Should teachers indoctrinate by advocating a particular political view? (2) Should teachers be selected on the basis of their political beliefs as well as their academic achievements? (3) Can political teaching be value free, or is it inevitably value laden?[11]

It is interesting to note that the definition of patriotism, confirming the right of individuals to directly oppose actions of government, was widely accepted during the period, even among the Founders. Dating back to seventeenth century England, this definition would not survive far into the nineteenth century. Disappearing for about one hundred years, it did not reappear until the turn of the next century and, in order to show substantial impact, would have to wait until the second half of the twentieth century.

---

8. Merle Curti, *The Roots of American Loyalty*, 124.
9. Rosh Welter, *Popular Education and Democratic Thought*, 17.
10. Ibid., 26.
11. Lawrence A. Cremin, *American Education: The National Experience 1783–1876*, 56.

Years of National Trial
(1811–1860)

The five decades preceding the Civil War were conceivably the most divisive and politically trying the United States has experienced throughout its entire history. Nevertheless, prompted by national events that included the War of 1812—the same war that brought the United States the Star-Spangled Banner[12]—the steady stream of wagon trains moving westward, and the Mexican War, efforts by educators to instill the values of patriotism in the minds of American youth continued. Ruth Miller Elson, the highly acclaimed authority on nineteenth century American textbooks, concluded in her book, *The Guardians of Tradition*, that since textbook authors of the period believed patriotism rivaled God as the cornerstone of virtue, it was the responsibility of the school to influence student loyalties to the nation. Elson observed that "patriotism . . . must be considered as the noblest of the social virtues. Every [school book] contained many pieces sustaining the doctrine that one's loyalty to country must be paramount to all other loyalties."[13] Of the textbooks popularized during the period, William H. McGuffey's *Eclectic Readers* stand out as the most widely read.[14]

Although history was generally perceived as a valuable tool for teaching young Americans about patriotism during the early years of the new nation, not a single state required the study of history during the fifty years following the signing of the Declaration of Independence. Efforts to correct this irony were initiated in the second quarter of the nineteenth century when Massachusetts and Virginia in 1827 became the first states to require their students to study history. In subsequent years, state after state passed laws re-

---

12. Originally written as a poem during the bombardment of Fort McHenry in 1814 and published as "The Defense of Fort McHenry," the poem achieved almost instant popularity, sung to the tune of "To Anacreon in Heaven," a popular drinking song. Still, the Star-Spangled Banner would not be adopted as the official national anthem until 1931, 117 years later. Infoplease, The Star-Spangled Banner [online source] (last accessed 12 May 2004) http://www.infoplease.com/ipa/A0194015.html.\; Internet.

13. Ruth Miller Elson, *Guardians of Tradition* (Lincoln, Nebraska: University of Nebraska Press, 1946), 282.

14. Walter Berns, *Making Patriots* (The University of Chicago Press, 2001), 68.

quiring the study of history. By the end of the century, the study of patriotism was deeply intertwined in the study of history in American schools.[15]

Prior to mid-century, liberty continued to be by far the most emphasized of political values. Posters and banners of Miss Liberty were among the most popular patriotic displays. By mid-century, however, the definition of patriotism was altered dramatically, the result of two events that occurred on opposite sides of the country. And in the end, the two events directly impacted perspectives of patriotism in terms of what it meant and to whom it should be taught.[16]

The first development involved Manifest Destiny, the sweeping justification for land acquisition that captured the attention of many Americans during the period. As wagon train after wagon train pushed westward carrying sufficient numbers of new settlers to populate the ever expanding empire, it was only natural that existing definitions of patriotism be altered. Added to the earlier emphasis on liberty and love of country, was the call for an unwavering recognition of, and devotion to, "a great and powerful nation."[17]

The wave of European immigrants that swept to America's shores at mid-century produced the second development. Arriving in startling numbers, this influx of humanity provoked an almost immediate public uproar to create a system of instant Americanization. Apparently concerned with how the current state of affairs interfaced with education, Benjamin Labaree, President of Middlebury College, felt compelled to offer his thoughts on the matter. In a speech before the American Institute of Instruction in 1849, Labaree emphasized the role of the school in patriotic education and affirmed that "a principle task of the school was the inculcation of those values vital to adequate participation in the American community."[18] Conversely, the majority of Americans believed that re-

---

15. Howard L. Hurwitz, "Teaching Patriotism . . . Not Nostalgia, but Necessity" *The American Legion* 109, no. 3 (1980): 216.; Curti, *The Roots of American Loyalty*, 15.

16. Freeman R. Butts, *The Revival of Civic Learning*, 58.

17. Ibid., 62.

18. Lawrence A. Cremin, *The American Common School* (New York: Teacher's College, Columbia University, 1951), 45.

cent immigrants needed to be educated beyond textbooks and demanded outward signs of loyalty, including some kind of pledge to their new country, salutes to the flag, loyalty oaths, and memorization of patriotic songs.[19]

The respected and revered educator Horace Mann, Secretary to the State Board of Education of Massachusetts from 1837–1849, thoroughly understood the integral relationship between freedom and republican government on the one hand, and education on the other. Although perhaps best remembered for advocating an equal and general education for all, regardless of intellectual attributes or economic standing, Mann also supported the inclusion of patriotism as part of school curriculum. As State Secretary for Education, he directed teachers to "exert their best endeavors to impress upon the minds of children and youth committed to their care and instruction . . . love to their country."[20]

Division and Recovery (1861–1885)

As the United States approached 1860, events that for several years had been a cause of friction between North and South began to intensify, causing extensive harm to the patriotic bond that had previously contributed to national unity. Thus, the stage was set for events that would dramatically impact relationships in both the North and South. When it finally came, the Civil War that began in 1861 exacted a toll that was far more costly and with more far-reaching consequences than one could have possibly predicted. Beginning with the first shots fired at Fort Sumter and lasting well beyond Appomattox Courthouse, the meaning of patriotism, and who was qualified to use the label, stood at "the very heart of the cultural struggle over what it meant to be an American."[21] Although it would be many years before the breach between North

---

19. Freeman R. Butts, *The Revival of Civic Learning*, 62.

20. Lawrence A. Cremin, ed., *The Republic and the School: Horace Mann on the Education of Free Men* (New York: Teacher's College Press, 1957), 106.

21. Cecelia O'leary, "Americans All", *History Today* 44, no. 10 (1994): 21.

and South was repaired, patriotism as a viable political and academic force continued to evolve with succeeding interpretations.

According to Merle Curti, author of *The Roots of American Loyalty*, the Civil War produced one of the most significant and lasting interpretations of patriotism since the American Revolution. He believed that while loyalty and patriotism did not necessarily involve everyone deeply, these two concepts did take on new meaning in the form of sacrifice for innumerable Americans. After all, according to Curti, how could one not understand a sense of sacrifice when reminded of the lives lost in that great conflict, with the memorial parades and ceremonies that began to occur at war's end? Ultimately, he concluded, most of the credit for elevating the significance of sacrifice to a level of public conscience belonged to three literary giants of the period: James Russell Lowell, Walt Whitman, and Ralph Waldo Emerson. Curti claimed that these men through their prose and poetry, did more to stir an awakening of principle among Americans than anything else. As an example, he described an American who, after reading Whitman's "When Lilacs Last in the Dooryard Bloom'd," experienced his "first thrill as a patriot."[22]

The impact that Lowell, Whitman, and Emerson had on interpretations of patriotism after the Civil War appears to have been extensive. According to the noted authority on 19th century textbooks, Ruth Miller Elson, many readers and spellers used in schools during the period contained elements of the patriotic belief that one should be willing to lose not only family and friends, but life itself for one's country. The following poem, popular during the period following the Civil War, is one example of the expanded definition of patriotism:

> *"May the hearts of our people re-echo*
> *the cry,*
>
> *'Tis sweet, oh 'tis sweet for our*
> *country to die."*[23]

---

22. Merle Curti, *The Roots of American Loyalty*, 171.
23. Ruth Miller Elson, *Guardians of Tradition*, 283.

Furthermore, according to Elson, there existed several differences between schoolbooks of the period and those of the mid-twentieth century. Most likely, the textbook differences can be attributed to differences in teaching emphasis. Of particular note, nineteenth century authors, making little effort to be neutral, did not identify patriotism as xenophobia, but simply as love of country, a value that should be inculcated in all youth. While they evaded issues that were controversial in their day, they took a firm and unanimous stand on matters of basic belief. Notably traditional, the values that textbooks emphasized as most important were love of country, love of God, duty to parents, honesty, hard work, and the perfection of the United States. Accepted without question, these values provided the basis for teaching patriotism to American school children through the remainder of the century.[24]

Even the National Education Association was not about to be outflanked on the issue of patriotism. Organized shortly after the Civil War, it readily and emphatically stated its belief in the need for an assertive brand of patriotic instruction in America's classrooms. At its initial meeting held in Indianapolis in 1866, it resolved as a body that "our schools must teach children that patriotism is an integral part of a student's education."[25]

As a result, from the era of the American Revolution until the last quarter of the nineteenth century, with few exceptions educators in the United States taught lessons and conducted ceremonies related to patriotism in standard fashion. They paused only long enough to make adjustments in order to incorporate significant changes in definition when deemed necessary, and then retained the old definition as part of the new. For example, love of liberty, became love of liberty and love of country, and, in turn, became love of liberty and love of country and willingness to sacrifice, and so on. Emphasis was consistently placed on rote recitation of patriotic pledges and songs that resulted in little pedagogical variety.

As the twentieth century approached, however, attitudes among many educators began to change regarding how America's youth should be properly taught patriotism. Believing the large

24. Ibid., 338.
25. Howard L. Hurwitz, "Teaching Patriotism . . . Not Nostalgia, but Necessity," 14.

number of citizens produced by the system who equated patriotism with mindless xenophobia and chauvinism was a failure of the system, they called for immediate change. Rejecting outright the then popular traditional methods of patriotic instruction that rarely resulted in genuine sincerity or thought on the part of students, they sought replacement with non-traditional teaching methods that encouraged direct student inquiry.

Challenges to Accepted Pedagogy (1885–1900)

As the nineteenth century drew to a close and the Civil War became increasingly distant, opposition to conventional definitions, interpretations, and practices for teaching patriotism began to emerge. In 1885, Josiah Leeds, a Quaker, led a crusade to remove warlike propaganda from classroom walls and chauvinistic types of patriotic references from textbooks. A few years later, Josephus Nelson, Superintendent of Schools in Buffalo, New York, spoke against history being taught from the perspective of "our country, right or wrong."[26]

Two highly respected blue-ribbon panels lent their support to the positions assumed by Leeds, Nelson, and others. In 1893, The Committee of Ten recommended that history teachers depart from too heavy a reliance on textbooks and, instead, stress the use of primary sources.[27] A few years later, in 1899, the Committee of Seven publicized their hope that patriotism would be toned down and urged, as had their predecessor committee in 1893, the use of primary sources to supplant the textbook in history courses.[28]

Although challenged on several fronts during the waning years of the nineteenth century, the National Education Association stood fast as an ardent and longtime supporter of traditional approaches to teaching patriotism. In 1892, the Resolutions Committee of the NEA reaffirmed its 1866 position and went on record

---

26. Merle Curti, *The Roots of American Loyalty*, 215.
27. Freeman R. Butts, The Revival of Civic Learning, 63.
28. Ibid., 63–64.

that the American school was a unique influence for "patriotism and good citizenship."[29] Three years later, The NEA reaffirmed the 1892 position of their Resolutions Committee when the full convention of the NEA voted "to recommend flag ceremonies and national patriotic holidays to inculcate patriotism [in students]."[30]

Ironically, it was in the midst of this growing controversy concerning patriotism and its place in the classroom that the Pledge of Allegiance was born. The result of a contest in 1892 that originated as somewhat of a gimmick to celebrate the 400th anniversary of Christopher Columbus' first voyage to the New World, the pledge, presented here in its original form, was written by Francis Bellamy and enjoyed nearly instant success.

> *I pledge allegiance*
> *to my Flag*
> *and to the Republic*
> *for which it stands,*
> *one nation,*
> *indivisible,*
> *with liberty*
> *and justice for all.*[31]

Although it would be another fifty years before its formal adoption by Congress as the official pledge of the United States, the words of Bellamy's patriotic verse quickly caught on and was soon recited in classroom after classroom across the country.[32]

While the values and beliefs espoused by the pacifist Leeds and the anti-nationalist Nelson found support among those in education who opposed routine and mechanical instruction in patriotism, the National Education Association boasted strong support for the

---

29. Rosh Welter, *Popular Education and Democratic Thought* (New York: Columbia University Press, 1962), 26.

30. Ibid., 158.

31. John W. Baer, *The Pledge of Allegiance—A Short History,* [online source] (last accessed 11 May 2004) http://history.vineyard.net/pledge.htm, Internet.

32. Margaret Sedeen, *Star-Spangled Banner* (Washington DC: National Geographic Society, 1993), 177. In 1942, Congress formally adopted the Pledge of Allegiance as the official pledge of the United States.

very trappings of a traditional brand of patriotism that their opposition condemned. The die was cast. The two adversaries, and their followers, holding true to their respective philosophies, advanced into the next century looking for converts.

2

Embracing and Challenging
Traditional Patriotism

Cautious, careful people, always casting about to preserve their reputation and social standing, never can bring about a reform. Those who are really in earnest must be willing to be anything or nothing in the world's estimation.

SUSAN B. ANTHONY

The questions posed toward the end of the nineteenth century regarding patriotism and how it should properly be taught in America's schools carried over into the next century. As a result, almost predictably, the twentieth century witnessed a clash between those who accepted traditional approaches and those who advocated non-traditional approaches for teaching patriotism. The single-minded brand of patriotism that had been so popular only a few years before was increasingly challenged by those who disagreed with methods that relied exclusively on recitation of song and pledge, and the study of American heroes.

This competition between opposing philosophies competing for the right to influence the thinking of America's youth presented a dilemma: How should patriotism be taught in America's classrooms in the coming years? As the United States moved through

Parts of chapter two appeared previously in: Putman, Errol. "The Changing Tide of Professional Print Media and Teaching Patriotism: 1916–1956." *Theory and Research in Social Education* 32 no. 2 (2004): 366–380. Copyright 2004 by the College and University Faculty Assembly of National Council for the Social Studies; reproduced with permission from the publisher.

and between two world wars, educators vacillated between traditional approaches for teaching patriotism that held America in its grip for over 100 years and non-traditional perspectives that offered a fresh new look. Interestingly, as history would show, while adherents of non-traditional methods found converts during periods of calm, the country returned to more traditional thoughts on teaching patriotism when the United States was under threat, real or imagined, either from beyond her borders, or from within.

Conflicting Views
(1901–1917)

Probably influenced to a large degree by the position of the National Education Association on such issues, most educators continued to instruct American youth in the traditional patriotic values in the first years of the twentieth century, much as they had throughout the previous hundred years. Characteristically, the period witnessed several efforts to promote open displays of patriotism; public schools began to require flag salutes, loyalty oaths, and patriotic songs.[1] Two of the more popular expressions of patriotism involving students during the period consisted of reciting the relatively new Pledge of Allegiance and singing The Star-Spangled Banner. Although only recently written, the Pledge of Allegiance had gained rapid acceptance and almost overnight was widely adopted as a popular favorite. In time, the Pledge of Allegiance stood with the popular Star-Spangled Banner as favorites in American classrooms. In subsequent years, both played an increasingly important role in the education of American youth.[2]

The surge of patriotism that swept the United States during the period eventually impacted the new wave of immigrants landing

---

1. Dilafruz R. Williams, *Democracy and Civil Education*, Unpublished Ph.D. diss., Syracuse University, 1987.

2. Margaret Sedeen, *Star-Spangled Banner* (Washington DC: National Geographic Society, 1993), 171. Written by Francis Scott Key in 1814, it was not until 1931 that the Star-Spangled Banner was formally adopted by Congress as the national anthem.

on America's shores. Once again, reminiscent of the 1840s, a popular movement to "Americanize" all foreigners emerged. Much like its predecessor movement at mid-century last, its objective was to apply pressure on the educational establishment to teach immigrants to renounce their native culture in favor of vintage, white middle class Protestant, American values, and to affirm their loyalty to the United States. To accomplish this end, a nationwide campaign was initiated to teach English, history, and civics through industrial and community programs. Support for the movement came from the Daughters of the American Revolution, Sons of the American Revolution, Society of Colonial Dames, and the North American Civic League for Immigrants.[3]

While forces were actively promoting a regimented patriotism, a small circle of educators voiced their appeal for teachers to turn their backs on teaching patriotism via conventional regimented methods. They advocated a brand of civic patriotism be taught in schools as opposed to military patriotism which glorified accomplishments in war and relied on salutes to the flag and the singing of patriotic songs. This civic patriotism emphasized the critical importance of the small group, family, school, church, and community, and stressed the concept of sacrifice for the common good. The flag was to represent the best the country stood for, the ideals yet to be fully realized. Rather than a blind devotion to country, they stressed that schools should emphasize an understanding of the country's history, its laws, institutions, beliefs, and values.[4]

Two early advocates of the young movement, Josiah Royce and Mary Follette, notable educators of the period, took the ideas of civic patriotism a step further. They advanced the idea that it was important to have local unity before national unity could be obtained, believing that national unity could only occur after youngsters were taught to have a feeling of loyalty toward something they could understand. Furthermore, they believed that the only way one could foster feelings of service and loyalty to country was to first experience it at the local level amidst the traditions and

---

3. Freeman R. Butts, *Public Education in the United States: From Revolution to Reform* (New York: Holt, Rhinehart and Winston, 1978), 235–236.
4. Merle Curti, *The Roots of American Loyalty*, 216.

mode of thinking one understood. Writing in *The New State*, Follette noted that it was essential feelings of loyalty be understood on a personal level to "avoid a blind herd instinct" and probable failure.[5]

The liberal views of these progressive patriots, as they came to call themselves, attracted the attention of other reformers of the period who enthusiastically extended their support, including the renowned educator John Dewey, who brought added credibility and a strengthened philosophical base to the movement. Believing that fundamental change was in order regarding the manner in which patriotism was taught, Dewey developed several key arguments to support his position. He believed, for example, that existing philosophies of patriotism could no longer do the job as they had in the past, that although, in the past, patriotism was good for knocking down barriers of sectionalism, patriotism had currently set up barriers with other countries. Moreover, he felt that unity, loyalty, and patriotism of individuals could best be obtained through intelligence and education rather than through fear, compulsion, and violence. Finally, he opposed teaching methods that employed elements of indoctrination because "indoctrination is the systematic use of every possible means to impress upon students one set of . . . political views to the exclusion of others."[6]

Perhaps the most influential special interest group to join the movement was the Internationalists. Although they had experienced little success in the previous century, the Internationalists still sought acceptance of a universal view of patriotism and aspired to use the new movement as a forum to achieve this goal. It was their intent to bring pressure on the movement to adopt and act upon the belief that patriotism should not be restricted to the national borders of the United States, but should freely extend beyond.[7]

In time the National Education Association became involved through its research on the place of social studies in school curriculums. Submitted in 1916, the "Report of the Committee on Social

---

5. Ibid., 216–218.

6. John Dewey, *Moral Principles In Education* (New York: HoughtonMifflin Co., 1909), 191.

7. Merle Curti, *The Roots of American Loyalty*, 217.

Studies" produced the first real effort by a sanctioned education body to identify a list of objectives for history and social studies, including the following definitive explanation addressing the question of patriotism as a curricular responsibility:

> The word patriotism has been much abused; but it is a good word. Instead of avoiding it because of its abuse, and instead of consciously giving young citizens the impression that the thing for which the word stands has somehow lost its significance, every effort should be made to imbue it with real meaning and make it a potent influence in the development of a sound national life.[8]

The authors of *The Report* also concluded that: "A primary aim of instruction in American history should be to develop a vivid conception of American nationality, a strong and intelligent patriotism, and a keen sense of the responsibility of every citizen for national efficiency."[9]

One year after the "Report" appeared in print, Herman Ames wrote "How Far Should the Teaching of History and Civics be Used as a Means of Encouraging Patriotism?" Appearing in the *History Teacher's Magazine*, Ames' article was one of the first efforts by an individual to publish on the topic of patriotism in a major social studies journal. Although many of the points raised by Ames also appeared in the "Report of the Committee on Social Studies," his ideas also strongly reflected the wartime mentality of the period. He spoke of an enlightened patriotism; one that could only be widespread if the youth were taught a feeling of pride in the traditions, ideals, and achievements of the United States. He also emphasized that the narrative of history should be permeated with the patriotic spirit, and that it was the teacher's duty to seize the opportunity offered by the war to aid in promoting an intelligent and patriotic public opinion.[10] Interestingly, he also cautioned prophet-

---

8. National Education Association, "Report of the Committee on Social Studies," 11.

9. Ibid., 17.

10. Herman V. Ames, "How Far Should the Teaching of History and Civics be Used as a Means of Encouraging Patriotism," *The History Teacher's Magazine* 8, no. 6 (1917): 188–190.

ically that "the danger of fostering an exaggerated and unwhole-some idea of nationalism must be guarded against."[11]

Resurging Patriotism
(1917–1929)

With the American declaration of war against Germany on April 6, 1917, most Americans, including educators, turned their backs on the various liberal perspectives offered for teaching patriotism. For the war's duration, energies were concentrated on winning the war, even if efforts required a militant brand of patriotism. Responding to the appeal, schools found themselves involved in several ways, with the major effort in soliciting contributions to support the war effort. Although this measure proved productive, it also created problems for schools. Due to a lack of government coordination, for example, so many different groups called on schools to assist in the war effort that schools were overwhelmed. Eventually, the constant disruptions to education provoked an outcry from the National Education Association, forcing the government to streamline its war-time efforts and produce a method of soliciting contributions that was not quite so burdensome to schools.[12]

Nevertheless, ideas still appeared in print from time to time suggesting ways American students could contribute to the war effort, including, of course, the NEA's own bulletins. One such article titled "Thrift, a Patriotic Duty," written by S.W. Strauss, suggested that a single major contribution American students could make to the war effort was by learning to be more thrifty. Strauss admonished teachers that it was their responsibility "to place thrift teaching in the schools on the grounds of pure patriotism."[13] It is important to note, however, that not all NEA articles were devoted to messages concerning ways students could contribute to the immediate needs of the United States required by World War I. Mary Bradford, in an "Open Letter to the Youth of America," suggested that students

---

11. Ibid., 188.
12. "Protect Patriotic Collections," *N.E.A. Bulletin* 6, no. 2 (1918): 16–17.
13. S. W. Strauss, "Thrift, a Patriotic Duty," *N.E.A. Bulletin* 6, no. 1 (1918): 29.

could also demonstrate their patriotism by staying in school "if the expectations of a patriotic America are to be fulfilled."[14]

Schools also found ways to demonstrate their patriotism and, at the same time, show their disdain for the German government and the German people. During the months following the declaration of war, patriotic fervor reached such a high pitch that all too often reason ceased to rule. In the name of patriotism, German books were burned by order of educational authorities, German music ceased to be played in school, and instruction in the German language was dropped from the curriculum of many schools, colleges, and universities. And as nonsense begat nonsense, sauerkraut became "liberty cabbage" and hamburger became "liberty steak."

In the years following World War I, likely as a reaction against the first Red Scare, citizenship education programs involving students, textbooks, and teachers were subjected to influences from a variety of organizations that believed patriotism should be practiced in the open for everyone to see. As a result, the role of civic education in the 1920's was greatly simplified; students were taught they were to rally around the flag, emphasize the merits and successes of the United States, and say nothing derogatory about the "greatest country on earth."[15] Not too surprisingly, most of the advocacy for the effort, except for the recent addition of the American Legion and the Ku Klux Klan, came from the same patriotic organizations that supported the "Americanization" movement at the turn of the century. The American Legion, for example, led the fight to get Congress and State Legislatures to pass laws requiring flag salutes, military training and loyalty oaths.[16]

The American Legion, joined by the Daughters of the American Revolution, also led the effort to change the wording of the Pledge of Allegiance at the 1923 and 1924 National Flag conference. Fearing that immigrants would, unless properly coached, think about their native flags when reciting the Pledge of Allegiance, the words "my Flag" were dropped from the Pledge of Al-

---

14. Mary C. Bradford, "An Appeal to the High School Young People of the United States," *N.E.A. Bulletin* 6, no. 3 (1918): 16.

15. Freeman R. Butts, *The Revival of Civic Learning*, 67–68.

16. Ibid., 68.

legiance and in their place was substituted "the Flag of the United States of America," to produce the following:

> *I pledge allegiance*
> *to the Flag*
> *of the United States*
> *of America*
> *and to the Republic*
> *for which it stands,*
> *one nation, indivisible,*
> *with liberty*
> *and justice for all.*[17]

Although Francis Bellamy, the author of the original Pledge of Allegiance disagreed, the changes remained, thus producing the first significant change in the pledge since it was written in 1892.

As the decade drew to a close, Edgar Dawson, author of *Teaching The Social Studies*, departed from prevailing opinions and practices and suggested that it was entirely possible history should NOT be taught for the purpose of inculcating patriotism. Furthermore, he believed that teaching patriotism might arouse contempt for, or a hatred of, other nations, and that "it has never been proved that disparagement of others or praise for ourselves produce[d] a sane and wholesome patriotism."[18] Dawson added that the best way to instill patriotism was to teach it impartially and recommended relating to students the general story of the struggles against special privilege that ran through the history of mankind and to fit American history into this story with absolute truth.[19]

---

17. John W. Baer, The Pledge of Allegiance—A Short History, [online source] (last accessed 11 May 2004) http://history.vineyard.net/pledge.htm; Internet. This change came about because many, driven by the 1st Red Scare, were fearful that immigrants would misunderstand the meaning of "my flag" and would continue to swear allegiance to the flag of their previous homeland.

18. Edgar Dawson, *Teaching the Social Studies* (New York: The MacMillan Company, 1928), 284.

19. Ibid.

The Decline of Patriotic Values
(1930–1940)

As the twenties passed into history, thoughts regarding patriotism continued to depart from an emphasis on the value of teaching a traditional form of patriotism, and influences on classroom instruction once again experienced a change in direction. As the new decade was ushered in, a group of noted educators (social critics, labor leaders, philosophers, and political left-wing activists), initiated a ten-year debate concerning "indoctrination" in American education. In the course of the distinguished groups' correspondence and communication, they came to accept two assumptions: indoctrination in American education is morally reprehensible, and the only viable alternative to indoctrination is the serious study of social problems.[20]

In 1933, for example, Paul Limbert, writing in *Progressive Education*, asserted that parents and teachers must present the facts about war and its probable consequences by tracing the roots of conflict back to competition over trade and raw materials. He emphasized that the true relationship between war and imperialism must be taught, including imperialism in their own country, and that the issue of denying national recognition to the "colored" peoples of the world must be addressed. That is, he concluded, if teachers and parents wish "to develop a higher type of patriotism in their children, a patriotism which will know no narrow national boundaries."[21]

Two years later, S.P. McCutchen, also writing in *Progressive Education*, suggested that patriotism was a good word that over time had been soiled by "flag-wavers, one-hundred-per-centers, and professional guardians of political morals."[22] He believed that patriotism should mean a loyalty to the ideals of the nation includ-

---

20. Samuel S. Shermis and James L. Barth "Indoctrination and the Study of Social Problems: A Re-examination of the 1930's Debate in the Social Frontier," *Social Education* 49, no. 3 (1985): 190–193.

21. Paul M. Limbert, "What Children Think About War," *Progressive Education* 10, no. 2 (1933): 71.

22. S.P. McCutchen, "The Real Task of Social Studies," *Progressive Education* 12, no. 8 (1935): 544.

ing "the tradition of government and society based on . . . popular democracy and personal liberty and dignity."[23] He also stressed that government existed to promote the highest welfare of all, including recognition of the innate moral worth and dignity of every man, woman, and child.[24]

During the mid-thirties, in this same changed (and charged) atmosphere, *The Social Frontier* printed a series of articles by noted educators and others critical of indoctrination that was likely influenced by, or a direct reaction to, events abroad. According to Harry Gideonse, one of the leading critics, efforts to inculcate students with social, commercial, or patriotic values "smells like propaganda—and a viciously untruthful sort" that must have originated with the American equivalents of Moscow or Dr. Goebbels."[25]

Although united in their appeal, individually the group of critics expressed their views on a variety of related issues. The following examples provide some insight into their respective views: They defined indoctrination as those "practices which deny the individual the right to choose for himself."[26] They were adamant that "the attempt to influence one's pupils in the school to accept one particular solution to a problem where there is difference of opinion among intelligent, thoughtful, informed, and right-minded persons" was totally unacceptable.[27] They believed that it was teachers' responsibility to develop the child's *own* thinking rather than to impose their viewpoints on the child, and that "indoctrination is the antithesis of education."[28]

Theirs was not simply an effort to exchange ideas, theirs was a mission to bring about change. They sought to "make the school independent of reactionary forces, to prepare the individual to resist the insidious effects of propaganda appeared to be ventures

---

23. Ibid.

24. Ibid.

25. Harry D. Gideonse, "Non-partisan Education for Political Intelligence," *The Social Frontier* 1, no. 4 (1935): 17.

26. B.H. Bode, "Education and Social Reconstruction," *The Social Frontier* 1, no. 4 (1935): 22.

27. C. Washburne, "Indoctrination Versus Education," *The Social Frontier* 2, no. 3 (1936): 212.

28. Ibid., 213.

worthy of an educator's effort."[29] Finally, they also believed that a school "free from indoctrination could bring into being a generation of socially thoughtful men and women willing and able to change the pattern of social living."[30] Theirs was truly a hope for the future. In the course of the debates, several definitions of indoctrination were offered and numerous perspectives presented regarding the study of social problems. The single issue that appeared to generate the most discussion involved good indoctrination as opposed to bad indoctrination.[31] Although many of the discussions were pointedly relevant to the issue of patriotism, they died with the advent of World War II—short of anything being resolved.

There was also, however, a caveat. While responding to the McCutchen article appearing in *Progressive Education* the previous year, Margaret Willis made an astute observation. She advised that "calling attention to a more rational sort of patriotism will not be effective unless it can offer active outlets which are somewhere near as satisfying as the emotionalism of the superheated, flag-waving patriots."[32] With this single remark, Willis identified the biggest problem that adherents to a non-traditional perspective regarding patriotism had to deal with in years past and would have to deal with for years to come. In the larger picture, as history recorded and continued to confirm, non-traditional philosophical perspectives or interpretations of patriotism were accepted most when they mattered least. Except for the exchanges appearing in *The Social Frontier* and *Progressive Education* that placed special emphasis on concerns regarding indoctrination and social problems, social studies journals were all but silent on issues relating to teaching patriotism for most of the thirties.

This omission was probably due in large measure to the attention given domestic and foreign events of the period that included

---

29. Unsigned Editorial, "Introductory Remarks on Education," *The Social Frontier* 1, no. 4 (1935): 9.

30. Ibid.

31. Samual S. Shermis and James L. Barth "Indoctrination and the Study of Social Problems: A Re-examination of the 1930's Debate in the Social Frontier," 190–193.

32. Margaret Willis, "The Real Task of Social Studies: Some Implications," *Progressive Education* 13, no. 4 (1936): 284.

the depression and the New Deal, the rise of Fascism and Communism in Europe, and the military successes of the Japanese in the Far East. In particular, the activities of Germany, Italy, Japan and the Soviet Union commanded considerable attention in social studies journals of the period. Inasmuch as little attention was extended to patriotism directly, it is important to note that opposition to the actions of totalitarian governments such as Germany, Italy, the Soviet Union, and Japan did, in fact, receive attention in social studies journals. In large measure, this opposition was often in response to the exaggerated and distasteful forms of patriotism displayed by the totalitarian governments.

Virtually any action taken by Germany, Italy, the Soviet Union, and Japan in the name of patriotism was viewed as reprehensible. During this period social studies journals experienced a significant shift from focusing on an American brand of patriotism to describing patriotism as it appeared in countries that did not enjoy the fruits of democracy. Although evidence of this contempt appeared as early as 1921, probably influenced by the first Red Scare, with the Timothy Beresney article titled "History in the Russian Schools Before the Revolution," most of the disdain was reserved for the thirties. Examples from the period included "The Nazi Revolution and Its Influence on the Teaching of History in Germany," by Richard Bover and "A Formula for Citizenship," by Abram Brubacher.[33] Brubacher was particularly descriptive. In a pointed reference to the Soviet Union, Italy, and Germany of 1938, he wrote that "from our point of view there are so many evil or undesirable characteristics connected with those systems that even the pronounced patriotic fervor which they attain cannot have our full approval."[34] As a result, with the attention of professional social studies journals focused on events beyond America's borders, teachers who relied on professional journals for direction on issues involving patriotism in the United States did not fare well.

---

33. Timothy A. Beresney, "History in the Russian School Before the Revolution," *The Historical Outlook* 22, no. 7 (1921): 324–328.; Richard Bover, "The Nazi Revolution and Its Influence on the Teaching of History in Germany," *The Historical Outlook* 24, no. 8 (1933): 421–23.; Abram R. Brubacher, "A Formula for Citizenship," *The Social Studies* 29, no. 8 (1938): 339–342.

34. Ibid., 340.

3

Patriotism Revisited

Our Reliance is in the love of liberty . . . Our defense is in the spirit which
prizes liberty as the heritage of all men, in all lands everywhere.

ABRAHAM LINCOLN

Toward the end of the thirties isolationist sentiments began
to waver, and attitudes regarding patriotism experienced
similar change. In an article that appeared in a 1937 edition
of *Social Education* titled "Objectives in the Social Studies," Mio
Whittaker strongly advocated the direct teaching of patriotism by
asserting that "patriotism must be acquired unless our teaching is
to be judged unsuccessful."[1] Three years after Whittaker's article
first appeared, Seward Salisbury published an article in *Social Edu-*
cation titled "Positive Citizenship" where he emphasized that education must undergo some drastic changes in light of the world situation. He believed that, among other things, students must be
taught to vote, to understand the Constitution, to appreciate the
Declaration of Independence, and to salute the flag and sing patriotic songs.[2]

Chapter three appeared previously as part of: Putman, Errol. "The Changing
Tide of Professional Print Media and Teaching Patriotism: 1916–1956." *Theory*
and Research in Social Education 32 no. 2 (2004): 366–380. Copyright 2004 by
the College and University Faculty Assembly of National Council for the Social
Studies; reproduced with permission from the publisher.

1. Mio Whittaker, "Objectives in the Social Studies," *Social Education* 1, no. 9
(1937): 625.

2. Seward Salisbury, "Positive Leadership," *Social Education* 4, no. 8 (1941):
545–548.

By mid-summer of 1940, most of the world's major powers were embroiled in war, and for many Americans it appeared to be only a matter of time before the United States would be drawn into the conflict. Anticipating what appeared to be inevitable, many educators, including the leadership of the National Council of the Social Studies, began to reevaluate patriotism and how it was taught in America's schools. In his presidential address delivered on November 22, 1940, Howard Anderson, president of the National Council for the Social Studies, reflected this changing attitude when he advocated a restoration of patriotism to a level of meaningful emphasis in social studies education and urged the following objectives be taught:

1. To develop warm loyalties to the democratic way of life.
2. To impart the ideas of loyalty and sacrifice for the common good.
3. To convince students that democracy is the best system.
4. To emphasize that the democratic way of life should be maintained "whatever the cost."[3]

Perhaps thinking of the abuses perpetrated in the name of patriotism by totalitarian governments, Anderson was careful to caution that teachers who teach about democracy would do so in a manner requiring individuals to think for themselves.[4]

Just a few months before the Japanese bombed Pearl Harbor and the United States was drawn into World War II, Jegge Newton wrote "Democracy or Super-Patriotism" for *Frontiers of Democracy*. Reminiscent of Anderson's remarks the previous year, Newton suggested teachers exercise caution against advocating the kinds of extremism that had engulfed America's enemies and that teaching democracy should not degenerate into some form of super-patriotism. In addition to recommending that democracy be taught through the use of definitions and symbols with explanations, he offered four suggestions for effective instruction: (1) Help students understand the meaning of democracy through personal experiences obtained in the home, the school, and the community;

---

3. Howard Anderson, "The Social Studies, Patriotism, and Teaching Democracy," *Social Education* 5, no. 1 (1941): 14.
4. Ibid.

(2) Advocate loyalty to the values of democracy; (3) Study existing problems in light of the ideals and purposes of democracy; (4) Teach about democracy in a manner that requires individuals to think for themselves.[5]

WWII: The Need for Unity (1940–1945)

After December 7, 1941, the United States found itself drawn into a two-front war. Attitudes and passions experienced a marked change. Once again, the mood of America had reversed itself and most social studies journals began publishing articles that emphasized the need for schools to teach patriotism and to encourage their students to become involved in the war effort. Reflecting this renewed interest, journals like *Social Education* and *The Social Studies* endorsed patriotism with an affirmative degree of passion—the very passion they lacked during the thirties when they all but turned their backs on issues involving patriotism.

In early 1942, William Faherty, in probable reference to the publishing practices of social studies journals during the previous decade, published an article in *The Social Studies* titled "A Neglected Objective in the Teaching of History" that specifically identified the recognition "of ideals of patriotism" as a history objective.[6] The following year, in another *Social Studies* article titled "Schools and the War Program," Charles Coleman suggested that students could contribute more than just a belief in the basic tenets of patriotism. He recommended that students become involved in the war effort by setting "an example to the public through participation in school patrols, self-government, riding pools, letter writing . . . [and promoting] the war effort through involvement in salvage drives."[7]

---

5. Jegge H. Newton, "Democracy or Super Patriotism," *Frontiers of Democracy.* 16 April 1941, 208–211.

6. William B. Faherty, "A Neglected Objective in the Teaching of History," *The Social Studies* 33, no. 1 (1942): 27.

7. Charles Coleman, "The Schools and the War Program," *The Social Studies* 34, no. 6 (1943): 260–261.

Benjamin Brickman even went so far as to broach the subject of indoctrination. In his article titled "The Relationship between Indoctrination and the Teaching of Democracy," which also appeared in *The Social Studies*, he claimed that under certain circumstances teaching patriotism would not be considered indoctrination. To qualify for the exclusion, Brickman specified three criteria that must be met: (1) the student must receive complete and accurate information; (2) the information must be thoroughly discussed; and (3) the information must receive a thorough and critical evaluation.[8] Additional titles that appeared in social studies journals during the period included: "Teaching Citizenship for Defense and War," "Winning the War: A Job for The Schools," "Ration Stamps and Salvage: A Tenth Grade Project," and "Strengthening Our Morale."[9]

Articles highlighting the exploits of past and current American notables also began to appear in social studies journals, an effort apparently intended to remind Americans of the richness of their tradition of patriotic greatness or to inspire new heights of loyalty in the United States. Examples included "Thomas Jefferson: Crusader for Freedom," "Lieutenant General Omar N. Bradley," "Benjamin Franklin, the Patriot," and "General George C. Marshall," illustrating once again how much publishing practices had changed since the thirties. For the duration of the war, patriotism was a popular topic among editors and publishers of social studies journals and magazines.[10] Even Frederick Redefer, noted that "in total war we

---

8. Benjamin Brinkman, "The Relationship Between Indoctrination and the Teaching of Democracy," *The Social Studies* 35, no. 6 (1944): 248–252.

9. Enbert Lubbers, "Teaching Citizenship for Defense and War," *The Social Studies* 33, no. 6 (1942): 116–117.; Franklin A. Ross, "Winning the War: A Job for the Schools," *The Social Studies* 34, no. 2 (1943): 51–53.; Walter Ludwig, "Ration Stamps and Salvage: A Tenth Grade Project," *Social Education* 7, no. 5 (1943): 205–208.; Allen M. Pithenen, "Strengthening Our Morale," *The Social Studies* 35, no. 2 (1944): 57–59.

10. George H. Knoles, "Thomas Jefferson: Crusader for Freedom," *The Social Studies* 33, no. 7 (1942): 297–304.; John R. Craf, "Lieutenant General Omar N. Bradley," *The Social Studies* 35, no. 8 (1944): 341–344.; The National Franklin Committee, "Benjamin Franklin the Patriot," *The Social Studies* 35, no. 3 (1944): 124–126.; John R. Craf, "General George C. Marshall," *The Social Studies* 35, no. 1 (1944):13–15.

are together—together in sharing the sacrifices, together in our work, together in winning the war and peace.[11]

Considering the gravity of circumstances caused by America's entry into World War II, in a seemingly curious, and somewhat ironic move, the United States Supreme Court elected in 1943 to reverse its earlier *Minersville v. Gobitis* decision, decreeing that schools could not require students to recite the Pledge of Allegiance. In the 1943 court case, *West Virginia State Board of Education v. Barnett*, the High Court issued two particularly strong statements that would profoundly impact the teaching of patriotism for future generations. In the majority opinion, the court declared

1. If there is any fixed star in our constellation, it is that no official high or petty can prescribe what shall be orthodox in politics, nationalism or other matters of opinion . . . .[12]
2. To believe that patriotism will not flourish if patriotic ceremonies are voluntary . . . is to make an unflattering estimate of the appeal of our institutions to free minds.[13]

Journal and magazine articles that were intended to inspire patriotism and provide information on how students could best contribute to the war effort were not directed solely toward audiences of secondary teachers. Elementary educators were also encouraged to involve their students in patriotic activities and support of the war. Included on the list of ideas popular with children during the period were the sale of War Stamps, the collection of milkweed, and involvement in scrap metal drives. One teacher reported, for example, that a corner of her elementary classroom was converted to a post office run by students where War Stamps could be

---

11. Frederick Redefer, "The Schools Role in Winning the War and the Peace," *Progressive Education* 19, no. 6 (1942): 300.

12. Michael W. La Morte, *School Law: Cases and Concepts* (Boston: Allyn and Bacon, 1996), 106–108.

13. Harold. Chase, ed. *The Guide to American Law: Everyone's Legal Encyclopedia, Vol.5* (New York: West Publishing Company, 1985), 263.

purchased on a weekly basis, not only by students, but by members of the community as well.[14]

Young children were also involved in scrap drives for the express purpose of collecting tin cans. As one author noted, in addition to the obvious benefits of contributing to the war effort, collecting tin cans permitted total involvement by students. Regardless of their economic background, "every child could bring something, that he could bring it as often as he had it on hand, and that each contribution was considered worth while."[15] A final activity popular among children involved collecting milkweed pods to be used in manufacturing flotation devices and aviator jackets.[16] Although the war was ever present with its accompanying demands, education did not cease in the classroom. In addition to supporting natural inclinations toward teaching patriotism, teachers attempted to make each effort contributing to the defeat of the Axis Powers an educational experience whenever possible.

Along with encouraging cooperation, competition, and a sense of community among their students, teachers also provided instruction on a variety of relevant topics, depending on age and grade. High school students, for example, could receive instruction on such topics as responsibility in a democratic society, thrift in wartime, and the many ways individuals might contribute to the war effort. For elementary students, similar efforts evolved around keeping detailed and accurate records of War Stamps purchased, studying the milkweed as a science project, and researching and writing on the history of tin from a food container to a tank.[17]

Instructor magazine and *Grade Teacher,* two magazines that catered to the needs of elementary teachers, printed numerous articles in support of the war effort. In addition to the references previously cited, articles included titles such as "A Unit On Flag Day,"

---

14. R.L. Hallenbeck, "We Sold Stamps," *Grade Teacher* 60, no. 6 (1943): 29, 64.

15. M. Noel, "Getting the Scrap," *Instructor* 53, no. 3 (1944): 33

16. "Milkweed in the War," *Grade Teacher* 62, no. 1 (1944) 20–21, 89.

17. Ibid., see also M. Noel, "Getting the Scrap", L.J. Kisselbrack, What About War Stamps?," *Grade Teacher* 61, no. 7 (1944): 28, 60.; R.L. Hallenbeck, "We Sold Stamps," *Grade Teacher*, 29, 64.; M.I. Heckman, "War Stamps Sale Organization," *Grade Teacher* 60, no. 1 (1942) 20–21, 07.

"Helping the War Effort," "Seatwork on Washington and Lincoln," "Save Coal, Save American," "We Educate for Victory," "Your Flag and My Flag," "Mother Goose Helps Defense," and "Here's A Way To Help Your Country." In addition, *Instructor* magazine periodically printed a series of articles titled "They Made Our Country Great—Biographical Series" which featured stories of prominent Americans, past and current.[18]

As further evidence of widespread support for the war, the National Education Association ran ads for the *American Citizen Handbook* in its *NEA Bulletin*. Described in the advertisement as containing "all the information anyone could need on either the flag or the country that would be required in any patriotic service," the handbook left little doubt where its authors stood on issues concerning patriotism and support for the war.[19]

In addition to efforts by schools to instill patriotism among American youth through the acquisition of knowledge (studying the Bill of Rights) and the appeal to emotion through reading "O Captain, My Captain," there appeared a number of other creative proposals. One suggestion offered late in the war included plans for involving students directly in patriotic productions. This unique idea had the encouragement and support of the Writers War Board in the hope that plays would be used by young Americans to inspire support for the war effort. However, the war ended before much of anything was done, and the effort, like many at war's end, never achieved fruition.[20]

In 1944, shortly before the end of the war, appearing in the same edition of *The Social Studies*, two additional views on the sub-

---

18. Helen K. Evans, "A Unit on Flag Day," *Instructor* 50, no. 8 (1941):16.; G. Morris, "Helping the War Effort," *Grade Teacher* 61, no. 1 (1943): 20–21.; Mary Burke, "Seatwork on Washington and Lincoln," *Instructor* 51, no. 5 (1942): 24–25.; "Save Coal, Save America," *Grade Teacher* 62, no. 6 (1945): 52–53.; N. Frost, We Educate for Victory," *Grade Teacher* 59. no. 9 (1942): 42, 53.; Everett L. Thompson, "Your Flag and My Flag," *Instructor* 50, no. 8 (1941): 36–37.; V.W. Dalby, "Mother Goose helps Defense," *Grade Teacher* 59, no. 10 (1942): 26.; Selma A. Kerr, "Here's a Way to Help Your Country," *Instructor* 51, no. 6 (1942): 7.

19. "Educating for patriotism," *N.E.A. Bulletin* 31, no. 8 (1942): 255.

20. Harold S.Tuttle, "Drama for Democratic Citizenship," *N.E.A. Bulletin* 33, no. 1 (1944): 18.

ject of patriotism offered caution. On the one hand, Benjamin Brinkman suggested that teaching about patriotism should not be considered indoctrination if the information was complete and accurate, thoroughly discussed, and critically evaluated.[21] On the other hand, Franklin Ross noted that those who taught what America stood for should be happy and proud since its accomplishments have been the product of a wholesome and honest effort. After all, according to Ross, "American patriotism did not develop with the practice of the goose step."[22] Clearly, Brinkman and Ross were offering a reminder of the various objections to fascism that were so prevalent worldwide before and during World War II.

With the surrender of Japan on September 2, 1945, the war came to a close and for the first time since late 1941, Americans were not preoccupied with listening to news of the war on the radio and reading about it in newspapers. Topics closely associated with the war such as rationing, war bonds, and the draft evaporated with time. Nevertheless, Americans of all ages felt good about themselves; the unity they demonstrated during the war was without parallel and contributed significantly to the war's outcome.

Motivated by Fear: Patriotism in the Post War Years (1946–1954)

Due largely to several developments on the national and international fronts, teaching about patriotism did not experience an appreciable decline after World War II as it had after World War I. First and foremost, there existed the widespread belief that the Soviets were not to be trusted because of their continued occupation of Eastern Europe after the close of World War II. Additional causes of concern included the fall of China to the communists in 1949,

---

21. Benjamin Brinkman, "The Relationship Between Indoctrination and the Teaching of Democracy," *The Social Studies* 35, no. 6 (1944): 248–252.

22. A. F. Ross, "Has the War Taught American Teachers Anything," *The Social Studies* 35, no. 6 (1944): 241–244.

the conviction that a communist monolith would rule the world if unchecked, McCarthyism and the second "Red Scare," and the North Korean invasion of South Korea in 1950.[23]

Amidst this consternation A. Franklin Ross published in *The Social Studies* "Patriotism in an Upset World: Can It Survive?" He was adamant in his belief that even though other forces had failed in moral leadership, "the quiet influence of the teacher was still the means of sending forth patriots."[24] He explained that the best way for teachers to transmit the qualities of a good patriot is by conviction, and not by dogmatic teaching.[25] Writing in *Social Education,* John Roth expressed similar concerns regarding how patriotism could best be delivered to students. Emphasizing the need to accurately present the lessons of history, he noted that on several occasions the Nazis used (and abused) history through creating false interpretations as part of the effort to promote patriotism among German youth."[26]

Just a few years after World War II ended, Senator Joseph McCarthy stirred up a controversy about how to educate youth for democratic citizenship with "the public paranoia he helped to create."[27] As a result of the concern generated by McCarthy and the Cold War, an almost hysterical fear of communism engulfed the United States—a fear that directly impacted education. The National Education Association was one of the largest, and also one of the first, educational institutions to respond to the new threat. In 1952, the Educational Policies Commission of the NEA voiced the need to teach more "Americanism" by declaring that America's schools "must foster loyalty in both teachers and students,"[28] voic-

---

23. Harold H. Punke, "Loyalty and Patriotism as Social Necessity," *The Social Studies* 47, no. 2 (1956): 61–69.; Richard E. Gross, "Aims for American History in an Era of Crisis," *Social Education* 17, no. 6 (1953): 257–260.

24. Franklin A. Ross, "Patriotism in an Upset World: Can it Survive?," *The Social Studies* 40, no. 1 (1949): 4.

25. Ibid., 5.

26. John Roth, "History and Citizenship Training," *Social Education* 13, no. 7 (1949): 309–314.

27. Mary A. Hepburn, "Educating for Democracy in the United States," *Paper Presented at the Conference on the Development of Democracy after World War II. Federal Republic of Germany (September 24–30, 1989)*: 4.

28. Harold Punke, "Loyalty and Patriotism as Social Necessity," 61.

ing the need to help the youth of America "see the American patriots' dream of a nation with liberty and justice and opportunity for all."[29] As a direct result, there was a resurgence of articles in the professional media, perhaps more than during World War II, generally expressing an almost desperate appeal for national unity.

It is important to note, however, that there was at least one notable exception to the prevailing and popular sentiments reflected in much of the print media during the period. Concerned with the "newly militant conservatism" and the accompanying "general retreat to nationalism, militarism and defense of the status quo," *Progressive Education* confronted the issue directly.[30] Representative articles included "Do we Need a New Approach to Democracy," "Teachers and the Democratic Struggle," and "Some Current Projects in Citizenship Education."[31] In the Childs' article, for example, direct reference was made to the "militant patriotic groups" and their unexamined assumptions about national security, leading them to demand that "authoritarian political creeds be taught in the schools."[32] Childs proceeded to explain that such an environment is not conducive to sound educational practices and that teachers naturally lose their enthusiasm for their work when they no longer have feelings of security and freedom. Moreover, and perhaps most important, he suggested that such a frightening environment will drive the really good teachers from the profession.[33]

In addition to a profusion of articles that defined communism and described its evil features, articles written about patriotism expressed, perhaps even more than those produced during World War II, an almost desperate appeal for national unity. In 1953, Richard

---

29. National Education Associaltion, *Report of the Educational Policies Commission*, (1952): 105.

30. A. Bingham, "Are Our Rights Insecure?," *Progressive Education* 25, no. 5 (1948): 67.

31. E.C. Linderman, "Do We Need a New Approach to Democracy?," *Progressive Education* 25, no. 5 (1948): 80–81,; J.L. Childs, Teachers and the Democratic Struggle," *Progressive Education* 25, no. 6 (1950): 116–122.; and M. Lewenstein, "Some Current Projects in Citizenship Education", *Progressive Education* 29, no. 7 (1952): 249–252.

32. J.L. Childs, "Teachers and the Democratic Struggle," *Progressive Education* 25, no. 6 (1950): 117.

33. Ibid., 118.

Gross, in an article written for *Social Education* titled "Aims for American History in an Era of Crisis," reflected popular thinking when he demanded the educational structure be reshaped "and patriotism, pride, and devotion to our nation and way of life" be given priority.[34] Similarly, in an article written for *The Social Studies* titled "Loyalty and Patriotism as Social Necessity," Harold Punke added that "large group loyalty" was necessary to provide for the welfare of the whole.[35] He emphasized that "at a time when a menace to [our] continued national existence seems imminent . . . a high percentage of the group will patriotically support their government against external encroachment."[36] It is interesting to note, however, that even though the feelings of Gross and Punke reflected an ultra-patriotic mood, they both affirmed opposition to any system of indoctrination or forced loyalty.[37]

Largely as a result of the "Cold War" and America's ubiquitous friction with the "godless" Soviet communists (encouraged by the Knights of Columbus) Congress in 1954 enacted the second significant change in the Pledge Of Allegiance, adding "under God."

> *I pledge allegiance*
> *to the Flag*
> *of the United States*
> *of America*
> *and to the Republic*
> *for which it stands,*
> *one nation, under God,*
> *indivisible,*
> *with liberty*
> *and justice for all.*[38]

---

34. Richard E. Gross, "Aims for American History in an Era of Crisis," *Social Education* 17, no. 6 (1953): 258.

35. Harold H. Punke, "Loyalty and Patriotism as Social Necessity," 62.

36. Ibid., 62.

37. Richard E. Gross, "Aims for American History in an Era of Crisis," *Social Education* 258.; Harold H. Punke, "Loyalty and Patriotism as Social Necessity;" 62.

38. John W. Baer, The Pledge of Allegiance—A Short History, [online source] (last accessed 11 May 2004) http//history.vineyard.net/pledge.htm: Internet. Since Congress had adopted the Pledge of Allegiance in 1942 as the official pledge of the United States, it was within Congress' authority to enact such measures.

McCarthy, who had received a favorable rating in a Gallup Poll just one year before his fall from power, had caused confusion regarding the way patriotism should be taught.[39] Unfortunately, his high-handed methods produced less than desirable results, and those who subscribed to a liberal philosophy came to look on patriotism as "a cancer of the spirit."[40] As the hysteria of the second Red Scare and the antics of Senator Joseph McCarthy subsided, the attention granted patriotism by the professional print media subsided with it. Moreover, since the period had produced a substantial level of confusion concerning the manner in which patriotism should be defined and taught, many began to perceive patriotism as socially unhealthy and politically unacceptable. Even though the McCarthy Era and its accompanying hysteria eventually faded, it would be several years before social studies journals, especially journals intended for audiences of secondary social studies teachers, would again show significant interest in publishing topics relating to patriotism.

---

39. Mary A. Hepburn, "Educating for Democracy in the United States", Paper Presented at the Conference on the Development of Democracy after World War II. Federal Republic of Germany, September 24–30, 1989, p. 3.

40. Leonard Kreigel, "Boundaries of Memory: Liberals, Patriots, and Melting Pots," *The Virginia Quarterly Review* 71, no. 1 (1995): 28.

4

Teaching Patriotism Amid
Periods of Conflict

Freedom is never voluntarily given by the oppressor; it must be demanded by the oppressed.

MARTIN LUTHER KING JR.

The second half of the twentieth century witnessed several challenges to accepted practice in the arena of education—challenges that in many cases resulted in wholesale change. Among the areas impacted was social studies education, especially where patriotism was concerned. Although criticism of the manner in which patriotism was taught had occurred from time to time, the criticism was generally of short duration and had little lasting impact. It was not until the sixties that a major assault on traditional perspectives regarding patriotism and its proper place in the classroom began to take place. On several fronts, Americans of all persuasions, including educators, began to question traditional beliefs and values that had previously been among the accepted cornerstones of American pedagogy. Some even began to suggest that new definitions of patriotism would be in order, or at the very least, old definitions should be liberalized. The age of unquestioning subservience to time-honored belief systems rapidly drew to a close. The impact of the sixties, influenced in large measure by the Civil Rights and antiwar movements, took its toll. Teaching patriotism in the United States would never be the same.

Social Upheaval
(The Second Half of the 20TH Century)

The Civil Rights Movement that began in the fifties and the antiwar movement launched a few years later provided the necessary catalyst for change. Among the casualties were traditional definitions of patriotism. Black America, for example, was no longer willing to accept "prejudice, lynching, and segregation" in order to prove its patriotism and loyalty.[1] In addition, anti-war advocates, rallying in significant numbers, especially after the overwhelming passage of the Gulf of Tonkin resolution, rejected outright the traditional belief in "my county, right or wrong."[2] For the first time since the aftermath of the American Revolution, liberals seriously challenged conservatives to determine how patriotism would be defined in the years to come.

Antiwar activists advanced the view that although protests against the war were anti-government and anti-administration, they were very much pro-country. They also believed it was the responsibility of the individual to criticize one's country when convinced that it was wrong, and that the individual's own conscience and judgment could deny that "patriotism can be made the exclusive property of any class, group, or school of thought."[3] For many, this transition, really a return to the original definition, meant that Americans were free of a single-minded allegiance to the state; they had the right to freely exercise their personal brand of patriotism.

Furthermore, according to John Pullen, author of *Patriotism in America*, the differences between patriotism in a democracy and patriotism in a totalitarian system were unquestionably clear. In a democracy, individuals were loyal to several groups and idea systems. The ideas, ideals, and standards of the family, the school, the church, clubs, work organizations, sports teams, and other groups with whom they were in frequent contact were objects of their allegiance, and rewarded them by enriching their lives in one way or

---

1. Cecilia O'Leary, "Americans All," *History Today* 44, no.10 (1994): 21.
2. John J. Pullen, *Patriotism in America* (New York: American Heritage Press, 1971), 19.
3. Ibid., 21.

another. Somehow all these loyalties merged and combined into loyalty to the nation. In a totalitarian state, on the other hand, every attempt was made by the government to capture or destroy all intermediate loyalties so that the individual's loyalty was totally controlled by the state.[4]

Although the assault on traditional perceptions regarding patriotism was certainly significant, it was not colossal. While some sought to find answers to their questions through reading literature rooted in provocative patriotic themes, such as *All Quiet on the Western Front, It Can't Happen Here,* and *1984,* others found support for their respective views in the popular culture generated by the period. The endless and often conflicting array of patriotic themes and messages ranged from Hollywood productions that included "Patton," "Johnny Got His Gun," and "Born on the Fourth of July," to a music industry that produced "Masters of War," "Give Peace a Chance," and "The Fighting Side of Me." Collectively, they reflected all too well, at least where patriotism was concerned, the dichotomy of perceptions.

And, if matters were not muddled enough, there also existed an abundance of commercially produced posters, radio and television advertisements, bumper stickers, comic strips and clothing that conveyed a variety of conflicting messages. Typically, they ranged from the admiring "America You're Beautiful," and the threatening, "America—Love it or Leave it," to the reckless and irresponsible, "Burn Baby Burn," and "Tune in, Turn on, and Drop out."

This ideological conflict produced a variety of thoughts on the subject of patriotism. News columnists, talk show hosts, representatives from organizations such as the American Legion and the Veterans of Foreign Wars, politicians, and a host of others, including representatives of the Left who claimed to represent mainstream America, are just a few examples. Each group had its own perception of patriotism and rarely failed to make its views public.[5]

But the reality was that attitudes popularized during the period regarding patriotism, especially among America's youth, changed more than at any other time in the history of the United

---

4. Ibid., 30.
5. Gary B. Nash, "Reflection on the National History Standards," *National Forum* 77, no.3 (1997): 15–17.

States. And the changes were not necessarily positive. As a result, conservatives found themselves on the defensive, and, in the decades that followed they suffered significant setbacks. Nevertheless, regardless of how many reversals they suffered, they refused to capitulate and continued in their efforts through the remainder of the century. Persistent in the belief of "my country, right or wrong," they supported laws to ban flag burning and opposed court decisions that denied schools the right to require student recitation of the Pledge of Allegiance. The losses experienced by conservatives in the various flag cases and the Pledge of Allegiance cases were viewed as major defeats.

Two Supreme Court cases in particular that earned the wrath of conservative elements and also impacted the manner that patriotism was taught in American schools were *United States v. Eichman* in 1990, and *Sherman v. Community School District 21* in 1992. In *United States v. Eichman*, the court declared the Flag Protection Act of 1989 unconstitutional. In its 5 to 4 decision, the court held that "the government may not prohibit the expression of an idea simply because society finds the idea itself offensive or disagreeable."[6] In the second case, *Sherman v. Community School District 21*, the court reaffirmed its 1943 decision in *West Virginia State Board of Education v. Barnett*, that the state could not require a student to recite the Pledge of Allegiance.[7]

In providing a counterbalance to the changes rapidly sweeping the nation, there was also a resurgence of various extremist organizations. Divisive by design, and originating from the Right, they preached their own brand of patriotism. Although historically the Ku Klux Klan was the most notable, in the latter years of the twentieth century the militia movement was most successful in garnering the dramatic headlines. The KKK, militia, and other similar groups such as the neo-Nazis had much in common. Born in hatred and brandishing their self-righteous variety of patriotism, these groups decried everything they either did not understand or perceived as different.[8]

---

6. Michael W. La Morte, *School Law: Cases and Concepts* (Boston: Allyn and Bacon, 1996), 108.

7. Ibid., 106.

8. Patsy Sims, *The Klan* (New York: Stein and Day, 1978), 200.; Maurice Dees, *Gathering Storm* (New York: Harper Collins, Publishers, 1996), 64–65, 100.

The New Wave of Progressive Patriots (Beginning with the 60s)

The impact of the social upheaval wrought by the sixties revolution and advances in technology and communication was readily felt in educational circles; the result was an expanded description of the value of teaching patriotism. Traditional methods that emphasized patriotic songs, pledges, and the celebration of symbols were out; non-traditional approaches that involved students in investigation and analysis were in. Among the first to turn their backs on traditional methodologies, again, were the very professional organizations and professional journals which had previously provided direction on such issues. Unlike the past, where such sources provided integral direction and ideas for teaching patriotism, professional social studies organizations and journals, especially at the secondary level, suddenly either criticized openly or fell silent on issues involving traditional patriotism.

This change in emphasis must have been what *The New York Times* had in mind when it titled an advertisement for educational materials that appeared in *Social Education* in 1971 "What's Happened to Patriotism?" Accurately reflecting the change in attitudes among educators regarding patriotism and how it should be taught, the topics addressed in the educational package ranged from "the subtle shift of patriotic attitudes in this country," to "defining patriotism in terms of the many ways we serve our country."[9]

Teaching about patriotism raised a number of questions and presented unique problems for teachers. Where could the patriotically inclined professional find adequate resources to teach patriotism? Previously, they had only to look to their professional organizations and journals or other similar sources for assistance and/or direction. But for the most part, this option was no longer available. An examination of social studies instructional sources, especially methods textbooks and professional journals, reflected a sharp decline in providing direction for teaching about patriotism.

The content of high school social studies textbooks was similarly affected by prevailing social and political events. In the not too

---

9. "What's Happened to Patriotism?," *New York Times* advertisement, 1971,.*Social Education* 35, no. 6 (1971): 653.

distant past textbooks had been filled with numerous accounts of patriotic feats that helped shape America's greatness; teachers could easily find uncontested safe ground for teaching about patriotism simply by opening the pages of any standard high school social studies textbook. But this too had changed. Patriotic deeds seemed to be less valued in contemporary texts; textbook authors had seemingly come to be more influenced by historians who provided convincing arguments that many past actions of the United States were blatantly unpatriotic or, at best, highly questionable.

Even as late as 1995, for example, Howard Zinn's *A People's History of the United States* was still widely received. In this well documented and popular history, Zinn described many less than honorable actions committed by the United States during its history. The removal of Indians from their ancestral lands in the American southeast, the invasion of Mexico in 1845, and the imprisonment of thousands for daring to speak against American participation in World War I, are just a few of the examples.[10]

Reflecting the changing social philosophy, and at the same time attempting to accommodate the changing belief systems of American youth, numerous innovative approaches for teaching about patriotism were developed for secondary students during and after the turbulent sixties. An endless array of non-traditional strategies was devised to replace the ostensibly archaic traditional methods. In example after example, authorities in the field of social studies education emphasized the need to avoid methods that smacked of mindless xenophobia and chauvinism.

At least as early as 1968, Lawrence Metcalf and Maurice Hunt, highly regarded at the time, offered conscientious guidance for teaching patriotism. In their methods textbook titled *Teaching High School Social Studies,* they recommended that, regardless of the approach used, teachers needed to consider three questions before the study of patriotism was introduced. First, is it better to serve the government's wishes, right or wrong, in times of emergency, or is it best to engage in constructive criticism? Secondly, do patriotic ceremonies such as saluting the flag, pledging allegiance to

---

10. Howard Zinn, *A People's History of the United States* (New York: Harper Perennial, 1995), 133, 149, 359.

the flag, singing the national anthem, and holding memorial services for the war dead produce more patriotic citizens? Finally, if one of the purposes of historical research is to determine the relative amounts of truth and falsity incorporated in any nation's myth and legend, is it possible to teach about patriotism and at the same time teach that certain myths and legends are false?[11]

In subsequent years, several theories were proposed in an effort to resolve the issue of patriotism and identify its proper place in the school curriculum. Linda Chavez, for example, argued that since freedom appealed to students' sense of individuality and desire for liberty, they should be encouraged to understand the obligations freedom entailed and that patriotism be shown in private observance of the law.[12] James Shaver, on the other hand, suggested that educators should make a greater effort to involve students in the definition and shaping of the problems they are asked to consider. He believed such an approach helped students understand the connection between value conflicts in society and value conflicts in one's own personal life.[13] In contrast, Morris Janowitz, assuming that schools lacked the ability to properly mold civic consciousness, suggested a system of national service. Claiming that civic education and patriotism were intertwined, he believed that both should be taught in schools to better promote the moral enhancement of the nation and a more orderly world.[14] In addition, James Banks advocated reflective patriotism as a viable alternative for teaching. He reasoned that students, in order to improve the nation, must be made aware of the struggles and shortcomings of the United States, as well as its successes.[15]

---

11. Lawrence Metcalf and Maurice Hunt, *Teaching High School Social Studies* (New York: Harper and Row, 1968), 363–364.

12. Linda Chavez, "Citizenship Education: Recovering a Lost Dimension," in *A Blueprint for Education Reform* Ed. M. Conaught (Chicago, Illinois: Regney/Gateway, 1984), 131–140.

13. James P. Shaver, "Commitment to Values and the Study of Social Problems in Citizenship Education," *Social Education* 49, no.2 (1985):194–197.

14. Morris Janowitz, "Toward a New Patriotism: Educating for Civic Consciousness," *Curriculum Review* 24, no. 4 (1985): 14–18.

15. James A. Banks, *Teaching Strategies for the Social Studies* (White Planes, New York: Longman Inc., 1990), 282–283.

Almost 30 years after Muessig and Rogers' article first appeared in *Social Education*, the debate still continued.[16] In a paper presented before the annual meeting of the Comparative and International Education Society titled "Teaching Patriotism as a Moral Matter," Thomas Murray asserted that loyalty consisted of a person embracing and seeking to promote the values held by the object toward which loyalty was directed. He suggested that although most often the object of loyalty is accepted as the nation, it could be individuals, groups, institutions, ideals, or schools. He believed that teaching patriotism was a fundamental task that should be assigned to a nation's schools and that they should teach about patriotism as an exercise in analyzing moral issues. Murray based his beliefs on three propositions: (1) Patriotism is a moral matter; (2) Patriotism involves loyal dedication to values that serve as the nation's philosophical foundation; and (3) The key task of each nation's educational system is that of teaching values.[17]

There was little that escaped criticism; even the very foundations of traditional patriotism—patriotic symbols, songs, and pledges—came under attack. Among the practices that received criticism were the celebration of heroes, ceremonial rituals of patriotism that included patriotic songs, and the Pledge of Allegiance.[18] Hyman Kavett, for example, identified several reasons why it was pointless to require students to recite the Pledge of Allegiance. First of all, he noted that the issue resulted in several court battles, clearly illustrating that it was not worth continuing. Secondly, he calculated that requiring students to participate in "pledge" ceremonies for five days a week for a whole school year, multiplied by the number of years they are in school could only be considered overkill.

---

16. A detailed explanation of the views of Raymond Muessig and Vincent Rogers is provided in the Introduction to *Teaching New Patriotism in the 21ˢᵗ Century*.

17. Thomas R. Murray, *Teaching Patriotism as a Moral Matter*. Paper presented at the annual meeting of the Comparative and International Education Society, 1993, 2.

18. Linda Chavez, "Citizenship Education: Recovering a Lost Dimension," 131–140.; Frank J. Estvan, *Social Studies in a Changing World* (New York: Harcourt, Brace & World, Inc., 1968), 315.; Hymen Kavett, "How Do We Stand With the Pledge of Allegiance Today?," *Social Education* 43, no. 6 (1976): 135–140.

And finally, he observed that students rarely paid attention and that the whole charade" render[ed] the spirit of the pledge meaningless."[19] Besides, he asked, "What do you do with students who are actually opposed to patriotic ceremonies on religious or moral grounds?"[20]

Even the research of the period seemed to indicate that attitudes had changed, perhaps explaining in part why innovative ideas regarding the replacement of traditional perspectives for teaching patriotism continued to evolve. In 1987, for example, in an effort to assess what good citizenship meant to high school students, Thomas Dynneson conducted a study of four groups of seniors with diverse social and economic backgrounds from four geographical regions in the United States. They were asked to rate the qualities they thought characterized a good citizen. The results of Dynneson's research, published in *Social Education* in 1992, revealed that patriotism was rated as of moderately low importance as compared with current events and acceptance of authority of those in supervisory roles. In essence, evidence from the period following the Vietnam War seemed to suggest that teaching about patriotism was a difficult task for educators, at least at secondary levels.

However, the conclusions reached for secondary students did not necessarily apply to elementary students. In a survey conducted a few years previous to the Dynneson study, Lynell Johnson and Robert Hess, while assessing patriotic values among elementary children, reached conclusions that strongly contrasted with those in the Dynneson study. They discovered, for example, that when students in grades four through seven were asked which one of several patriotic or religious displays should be part of the school day, the Pledge of Allegiance won by a large margin, with a patriotic song coming in second place.[21]

Interestingly, the results of the Johnson and Hess survey seemed to agree with the apparent continued popularity of articles espousing a traditional approach to teaching patriotism appearing in popular educational journals and magazines targeting an audience of

---

19. Ibid., 136.
20. Ibid., 135.
21. Lynell Johnson and Robert Hess, "Kids and Citizenship: A National Survey" *Social Education 48*, no.7 (1984): 502–505.

elementary teachers. Activities centering around studies of the American flag, the Pledge of Allegiance, and notable Americans, found to be appealing before the Vietnam War, continued to be appealing after the Vietnam War. While published themes from the pre-Vietnam era included "A Study of the Flag", "What the Colors of the Flag Symbolized," and "My Country and My Flag . . . Their Story," similar themes appeared in journals and magazines from the post-Vietnam era such as "The Pledge of Allegiance and What it Meant," "Flag-Waving Fun," and "One Nation Indivisible . . ."[22]

The findings of the Dynneson and the Johnson and Hess studies, coupled with the contrasting tone of professional educators in secondary and elementary education, seemed to suggest that for the first time in American history, different approaches for teaching patriotism were required for elementary and secondary levels. Prior to this period, elementary and secondary students, for example, said the Pledge of Allegiance, saluted the flag, and were told by their teachers which events in history were patriotic and which events were not. Increasingly since the sixties, however, secondary educators had come to believe that issues surrounding patriotism were exceedingly complex and required, at least for their students, a complex solution, something far different than simply reciting patriotic pledges and songs.

Teaching Patriotism in The 20ᵗʰ Century (The Final Decade)

As the United States entered the last decade of the 20ᵗʰ century, aside from the continued popularity of Howard Zinn's *People's History of the United States*, evidence suggested a renewed interest in

---

22. Ova L. Coleman, "A Study of the Flag," *Grade Teacher* 75, no. 6 (1958): 92–94.; Maxwell Kushner, "The Birthday of Our Flag," *Grade Teacher* 77, no.10 (1960): 41–42.; M. D. Wilson, "My Country and My Flag . . . Their Story," Grade *Teacher* 79, no.10 (1962): 50–52.; Rosalie Minkow, "We Pledge Allegiance," *Instructor* 84, no. 6 (1975): 22–23.; Charles J. Walker, "Flag-Waving Fun," *Instructor* 92, no. 6 (1983): 44.; Sandy Zjawin, "One Nation Indivisible . . ." *Instructor* 92, no. 6 (1983): 30–31.

returning to more traditional views, including respect and rever-
ence for flag, heroes, and country. Although this return to more
traditional perspectives may be attributed to a variety of factors, certainly "Operation Desert Storm" and the widespread popularity of
Tom Brokaw's book, *The Greatest Generation*, had an impact. Once
again, change became the watchword. With few exceptions, the
movies, books, and music produced during the decade reflected
positive attitudes toward patriotism.

A similar renewal occurred among educators such as Jack
Zevin and Neil Postman. According to Zevin, in an article published in the *Social Science Record* titled "Clashing Conceptions of
Citizenship," while conservatives stressed a traditional brand of patriotism, liberals tended to emphasize the right of individuals to
think critically. Interestingly, he also believed that both views of
democratic citizenship, the patriotic and the critical should occupy
a place in the education of future citizens. Schools, according to
Zevin, must somehow accommodate conservatives and critics alike
and reconcile points of conflict in the curriculum. Finally, he directly challenged the educational system to create a curriculum that
"simultaneously promoted pride of country and critical participation in the political process."[23]

Even the liberal-thinking Neil Postman assumed a surprising
stance on the issue, suggesting in his popular *The End of Education*
that one of the responsibilities of schools was to educate students in
ways that instilled a sense of national pride. Believing that "students
deserve [it], and their parents expect it," Postman recommended a
general return to studying the great documents of American history, requiring students to memorize all, or parts of, great documents such as the Bill of Rights.[24] Postman further suggested that
memorization be followed by a thorough historical examination of
the implications of each document, including its current applica-
tion(s), in order to provide students with a truly inspiring educational experience.[25]

---

23. Jack Zevin, "Clashing Conceptions of Citizenship," *Social Science Record*
31, no.2 (1994): 23.
24. Neil Postman, *The End of Education* (New York: Vintage Books, 1995), 71.
25. Ibid., 133–135.

The ambivalence regarding the proper place of patriotism in student instruction was not anywhere better illustrated than through an examination of the *National Standards for Civics and Government* and the *National Standards for United States History.* Although one should be able to identify similarities in descriptions of patriotism in these publications identifying the unique aspects of American government and American history, this was not the case.

In the National Standards for Civics and Government, patriotism was identified as "one of the fundamental values of the United States" and defined as "loyalty to the values and principles underlying American constitutional democracy."[26] Conversely, the *National Standards for United States History* neglected to mention the term patriotism. Largely for this reason the document has been subjected to a great deal of criticism, mostly from conservative quarters. Included on the list of critics were Lynn Cheney, author and conservative critic, former presidential candidates Pat Buchanan and Bob Dole, Newt Gingrich, Speaker of the House of Representatives at the time, and Rush Limbaugh, talk show host.[27]

In an article written for *The Social Studies*, Gary Nash attempted to disarm much of the criticism by providing several, though not explicitly labeled, examples of patriotism that appeared in *The National History Standards.* Agreeing that studying national heroes and national symbols was an effective way of inculcating basic lessons in civics and national identity, Nash identified several examples from the early period of the United States worthy of study. Included on his list were references to George Washington, Thomas Jefferson, the Constitution, specific military leaders, military campaigns, the two-party system, and the anti-slavery movement. He claimed that each example offered students the opportunity to analyze, assess, compare and contrast, and explain various actions of American heroes. Although he emphasized a need to teach analytic skills and meet the students' thirst for historical knowledge that goes beyond celebration of "plaster saints," he conceded that "fathoming the purplish veneration of earlier generations is a lesson in itself. And

---

26. Center for Civic Education. *National Standards For Civics And Government.* (Calabasas, California: Center for Civic Education, 1994), 38.

27. Gary B. Nash, "The National History Standards and George Washington," *The Social Studies* 88, no. 4 (1997): 159–162.

there will always be a role for patriotic relics and shrines focused on larger-than-life individuals who sum up the emotions and ideals of an earlier age."[28]

By century's end, numerous arguments and suggestions regarding how, when, and under what circumstances patriotism should be taught were proposed, without any definitive answers provided. Teachers and non-teachers alike still had not reached agreement on precisely how patriotism should be defined and taught. Although the period ended without answering all the questions raised, one thing was certain: most educators agreed that a form of patriotism, as long as it did not rely exclusively on songs, pledges, and symbols, was preferable. As a result, a plethora of new approaches for teaching patriotism with a non-traditional emphasis was advanced. No longer was it fashionable for teachers, especially those at secondary levels of education, to teach patriotism solely by using traditional approaches.

---

28. Ibid., 161.

5

Teaching New Patriotism: Enjoining Traditional and Non-Traditional Concepts

The events of September 11, 2001, form a crucible out of which an even stronger nation can be forged.

HILLARY RODHAM CLINTON

B eginning with the display of yellow ribbons and the parades held for veterans returning from Desert Storm, and encouraged by Tom Brokaw's *The Greatest Generation*,[1] beliefs and attitudes regarding patriotism began to change again during the nineteen-nineties. The widespread antipathy toward patriotism that originated during the Vietnam era and continued through the Civil Rights movement had softened considerably, yet it was still not fashionable for one to publicly profess his patriotism. Suddenly, on September 11, 2001, all of this changed. Although Americans were aware of betrayal in their history—the Zimmerman Note, the attack on Pearl Harbor, and the construction of Soviet missile bases in Cuba—somehow this was different. Americans of all ages and from all walks of life witnessed the horror firsthand, and the fear, and the anger, and finally the rage engulfed them, together.

---

1. Tom Brokaw, *The Greatest Generation*, (New York: Random House, 1998).

51

After September 11, 2001

Enjoying near overwhelming support from Congress and across America, the United States government, in just a few short weeks, retaliated swiftly, attacking Taliban controlled Afghanistan on October 7, 2001. Named "Operation Enduring Freedom," the action was initiated for the purpose of destroying al-Qaeda, their Taliban protectors, and killing or capturing Osama bin Laden, the suspected leader of the attack on the United States.

The events of September 11, 2001 altered dramatically, perhaps for all time, life in the United States. Deaths of brave young men and women fighting to stem terrorist efforts, long lines and cumbersome security at airports, and higher insurance rates became realities. But that was just the beginning. Who would have thought that backpacks, purses, and camera cases would no longer be permitted past the gates leading to national monuments including the USS Missouri and the Pearl Harbor Memorial? Or that diaper bags, purses, and camera cases would be searched prior to entry into Florida's Walt Disney World?

Changes wrought by September 11 were not entirely negative, however; all across the political and social spectrum, Americans came together in ways rarely seen. The patriotic changes included widespread flag flying, people reaching out to help others, and individuals professing levels of patriotism unheard of since World War II. Posters and paper flags with slogans such as "United We Stand," "Standing Strong Together," and "These Colors Don't Run," became the rule and not the exception. While "God Bless the USA," "Riding With Private Malone," and "Where the Stars & Stripes and the Eagles Fly," were popularized by country-western radio stations, pop music fans rocked to "Freedom," and the hip-hop generation responded positively to "Raise Up (USA Flag Remix)."[2] The movie "Blackhawk Down" enjoyed near instant popularity, and the 2002 Super Bowl adopted a patriotic theme of "Heroes, Hope, and

---

2. Brian Mansfield, "Patriotism Revs 'Private Malone' into High Gear," *USA Today*, 2 October 2001, p. 10.

Homeland,"[3] amid media speculation that the 2002 winter Olympics would be heavily laden with patriotic expression.[4]

The sense of unity that swept the United States reached levels that were seldom realized. Labels such as Irish-Americans, Italian-Americans, Arab-Americans, African-Americans, and Jewish-Americans no longer applied. First and foremost, we were *all* Americans. It was that simple. As but one example of the prevailing sense of unity, the African-American syndicated columnist Julianne Malveaux, who by her own admission normally did not consider herself patriotic, noted that she had "many reasons to be thankful as a citizen of this country."[5]

A series of interviews conducted among "Generation Xers," identified as those born between 1964 and 1981, produced some interesting findings. Long considered silent, or even apathetic, they claimed that for them "patriotism has become more meaningful."[6] In particular, they were quick to point out that they have always respected the country's founders and veterans for their strengths and sacrifices and the events of September 11 have helped them rediscover the meaning behind patriotic emblems and songs learned in childhood.[7]

For many Americans, perhaps, the heightened level of patriotism that occurred after September 11 was best explained by "Doonesbury." In the comic strip released on November 4, 2001, the liberal-minded Mark, while displaying the American flag in his office, is seen commenting on the way conservatives "hijacked" the flag during the Cold War, especially the Vietnam era, turning it into an example of "unquestioning jingoistic nationalism." In a later

---

3. Michael Hiestand, "Patriotic Super Bowl," *USA Today*, 10 January 2001, 1(C).

4. Patrick O'Driscoll, "Patriotic Could Become Name of These Games," *USA Today*, 22 January 2002, p. 2.

5. Julianne Malveaux, "Give Thanks With Some Exceptions," *USA Weekend*, November 23 2001, 13(A).

6. Robin L. Flanigan, "Generation X Hears, Heeds its First Call to Patriotism," *Rochester (New York) Democrat and Chronicle*, 21 September 2001, 10(A).

7. Ibid.

frame, Mark explains that "the flag is back to being a symbol of patriotism and love of country, not a particular agenda."[8]

Despite the massive outpouring of support for the United States government induced by the terrorist attacks, there was no immediate evidence to suggest that concern for civil liberties diminished as a result. Fortunately, there still existed substantial belief that the very ideals on which the United States was founded must be maintained, that freedom and liberty, emphasized in innumerable documents and speeches throughout American history, was still held in high regard. The message was clear: if we turned our backs on freedom and liberty, or in some way de-emphasized the importance of civil rights, it would mean that the terrorists had won.

In the days following the attacks, concerns regarding liberty and justice were voiced on several fronts. In an editorial titled "The Return of Teach-Ins," *The New York Times* cautioned that colleges and universities must ensure that campus debate is not "constrained or censured."[9] The article emphasized how important it was that Americans in a free society hear dissenting views as well as the views of the majority. To do otherwise, "academic institutions betray their core principles if they stifle intellectual inquiry and robust debate."[10] Clarence Paige, a syndicated columnist, agreed in principle with the *New York Times* editorial. While voicing concerns regarding the prospects of thought police that would attempt to quell opposition to the war, he pointed out that one "can be a patriot and still disagree with actions or policies that a particular administration has embraced." He also emphasized that, "in a democracy, dissent is often the sincerest form of patriotic flattery."[11]

The issue attracting the most widespread notice centered on the unpopular lone vote cast in opposition to military action in Afghanistan by California's Representative Barbara Lee. But, as she explained, "I feel that a true patriot stands up and says what needs to

---

8. Gary Trudeau, "Doonesbury," (Sunday Comics) *Rochester (New York) Democrat and Chronicle*, 4 November 2001.

9. "The Return of Teach-Ins," *The New York Times*, 21 October 2001, p. 14.

10. Ibid.

11. Clarence Page, "Here Comes the Patriotic Police," *Rochester (New York) Democrat and Chronicle*, 21 December 2001, 22(A).

be said."[12] Marco della Cava, who interviewed Lee, was also quick to emphasize that "Liberty has long roots in American soil. It gave rise to the USA's very existence and finds support in the First Amendment."[13] In a broader sense, commenting on the same issue, Cokie and Steven Roberts pointed out that, "patriotism and courage take many forms. The cops and firefighters who died saving others are heroes. But it also takes courage to criticize [popular] national policy you think is wrong. Representative Barbara Lee . . . was no less a patriot than the lawmakers who backed the president."[14]

Several aspects of the federal government's national security plan to fight terrorism, invited, and even encouraged, criticism. One particular element of the plan that incurred wrath from both liberals and conservatives was the prospect of using military courts to try suspected terrorists. Although liberals fumed and scowled, the most poignant attack came from the conservative columnist, William Safire. In a *New York Times* article titled "Terror tribunals a dictatorial abuse of power," Safire referred to President George W. Bush's effort as "the replacement of the American rule of law with military kangaroo courts."[15] With this ruling, according to Safire, Bush effectively stripped the accused of even the limited rights provided by courts martial. Noting that simply by citing national security concerns, the "kangaroo courts" can make up their own rules and find a defendant guilty, even if one-third of the officers disagree, and can execute him without any hope of review by a civilian court, an action inconsistent with American beliefs.[16]

A *New York Times*/CBS news poll conducted in early December 2001 showed that while 90% of the American public supported George W. Bush's campaign against terrorism, 65% of those surveyed were either very concerned or somewhat concerned with losing some civil rights. In addition, 50% (as opposed to 40%) favored

---

12. Marco R. della Cava, "All They Are Saying is Give Peace a Chance," *USA Today*, 2 October 2001, 1(D)

13. Ibid., 1(D), 2(D).

14. Cokie Roberts, and Steven V. Roberts, "Souls of Steel," *USA Weekend*, 12–14 October 2001, p. 7.

15. William Safire, "Terror Tribunals a Dictatorial Abuse of Power," *Charlotte Observer*, 21 November 2001, 15(A).

16. Ibid.

using criminal courts over military courts to try suspected terrorists; and 45% feared government would enact laws that would restrict civil rights, while 43% feared that any laws enacted would not
be strong enough.[17]

Citing evidence of a close connection between al-Qaeda, Saddam Hussein, and Iraqi possession of weapons of mass destruction
(WMD), the United States invaded Iraq in a preemptive strike on
March 20, 2003. Dubbed "Iraqi Freedom," and initiated before all
objectives were achieved in Afghanistan, the war never enjoyed the
level of support extended to the effort in Afghanistan. This failure
can be attributed to three factors: failure to find weapons of mass
destruction, disclosure of prisoner mistreatment at Abu Ghraib
prison, and the conclusion reached by a special bipartisan commission that there was no evidence of a connection between Saddam
Hussein and al-Qaeda.[18]

As support for the war in Iraq declined, concern over civil
rights increased. One law in particular that received extensive criticism from both liberals and conservatives, was the Uniting and
Strengthening America by Providing Appropriate Tools Required
to Intercept and Obstruct Terrorism. This sweeping law passed late
in 2001 after the 9/11 attacks, generally known as the USA Patriot
Act, expanded considerably the government's powers by, among
other things, the following:

1. Enlarging the government's powers to conduct electronic surveillance or obtain personal records not only in terrorism cases but
   also in other criminal investigations.
2. Permitting surveillance of domestic organizations, even as the Patriot Act made it easier for the CIA to share information with the
   FBI or other domestic law enforcement agencies.
3. Incarcerating 660 "enemy combatants," captured in Afghanistan
   at Guantanamo Naval Base in Cuba without charges, access to

---

17. Robin Toner and Janet Elder, "Public is Wary but Supportive on Rights
Curbs," *The New York Times,* December 12 2001, sec. A1 and sec. B9.

18. Bill Powell and Aparisim Ghosh, "Paul Bremer's Rough Ride," *Time,* 28
June 2004, 44–51.

lawyers or any form of judicial review, while the government plans military trials.[19]

The extent of the controversy involving the Patriotic Act carried over into the Congress. By a solid bipartisan majority, on July 22, 2003 the House of Representatives voted 309–118 to bar funding for one of the act's provisions to conduct so-called "sneak and peek" searches with delayed notification to the subjects of the investigation.[20] As C.L. Otter, the Republican Representative from Idaho remarked, "this is the first of a whole group of assaults we are going to launch on the Patriot Act."[21]

Interestingly, however, on June 21, 2004, *Newsweek* reported that "defense officials recently slipped a provision into a bill before Congress that could vastly expand the Pentagon's ability to gather intelligence inside the United States, including recruiting citizens as informants."[22] Apparently disregarding concerns over the Patriot Act, in closed session the Senate Intelligence Committee approved the new law which would permit intelligence agencies, such as the Defense Intelligence Agency, to approach and collect personal information from potential sources without informing them that they work for the government. In effect, the law would extend to the Pentagon the same exemption enjoyed by the CIA, although the CIA is prohibited from applying the law inside the United States.[23] Consequently, the issue regarding civil rights is still very much alive.

Two additional perspectives that have serious implications for social studies teachers are that of Jessica Stern and Fareed Zakaria. Stern, a Harvard lecturer, and author of *Terror in the Name of God: Why Religious Militants Kill*, identified two fundamental errors in American thinking. The first is the belief that the war can be won entirely on the battlefield. Stern cites the evidence provided by the Rand Corporation that for the two years prior to September 11,

---

19. Kenneth Jost, "Civil Liberties Debates," The CQ Researcher Online 13, no. 37 (24 October, 2003): 893–916. http://library-cqpress.com/cqresearcher.

20. Ibid.

21. Ibid.

22. "The Pentagon: Spying in America," *Newsweek*, 21 June 2004, 6.

23. Ibid.

2001, there were 2,303 terrorist attacks, while for the two years after September 11, there were 4,422 terrorist attacks.[24] The second
is the belief that God is on our side and we are beyond "the reach of
normal moral inquiry and law, [especially] in regard to detaining
and interrogating supposed terrorists." According to Stern, this
thinking has caused the Bush administration "to make a serious
moral error—one not that different from the error made by the terrorists themselves," an error that has made us more vulnerable to
terrorism.[25]

Although Stern concedes that to win today's battles, mini-
mally visible and carefully planned and implemented military action
may be necessary, she noted that to win the war will require a
"Manhattan Project-type effort—involving the best and the bright-
est from all over the world—to develop an effective strategy."[26] Included on Stern's list of tools required to forge weapons of human
dignity are schools, hospitals, respect for human rights, and an understanding that "the law applies to everyone—including those
who believe that God is on their side."[27]

Fareed Zakaria, a noted authority on the Middle East, also
concluded that the United States must drastically overhaul its policy
in the Middle East if it ever hopes to recover its lost diplomatic
edge, especially since revelations of in-mate mistreatment at Abu
Ghraib prison. Shocked by the images, Zakaria noted that the general perception among most Middle Easterners is that "America is
hypocritical."[28] He also reported that the unilateralism, arrogance,
single-minded blind support for Israel, and a general lack of understanding of the people in the region had cost the United States
dearly and that "anti-Americanism is morphing from a purely anti-
Bush phenomenon into a much broader cultural attitude."[29]

---

24. Ibid.

25. Jessica Stern, "Terrorists' Own Words Can Help Us Stop Them," *USA Today,* 24 June 2004, 13A.

26. Ibid.

27. Ibid.

28. Fareed Zakaria, "The Good, the Bad, the Ugly," *Newsweek,* 31 May 2004,
33.

29. Ibid.

Looking to the Future:
Implications for the Social Studies Classroom

One of the challenges confronting social studies teachers in the 21st century is to teach an enlightened patriotism that blends song, pledge, and symbol with an in-depth analysis of the historical foundations that helped the United States advance its potential for greatness. In addition to learning the Pledge of Allegiance, patriotic songs, and the meaning of America's symbols, students need to have an understanding of the principles of democracy, a respect for civil liberties (including the right to dissent), and an appreciation of diversity. This is important for three reasons. First, because of advances in technology, the government has enormous potential, as in the Washington based "Command Center," to closely monitor the activities of its citizens.[30] Second, it is too easy for a government, motivated by fear, urgency, or other reasons, to pass laws that may jeopardize the liberties of its citizens. Finally, the existence of an ever widening chasm of understanding between diverse groups inside the United States and world-wide is evidenced by protests, terrorist attacks, and the dramatic increase of racist, xenophobic, and anti-Semitic propaganda appearing on the Internet.[31]

Referred to as the *New* Patriotism, this renaissance is intended to renew emphasis on the core values of the United States, incorporating the interests and concerns of *all* Americans, regardless of age, race, wealth, gender, or social status. Though it was previously believed that traditional and non-traditional approaches for teaching patriotism were too philosophically different to teach in combination, the events that occurred after September 11 suggested otherwise. Collectively, the response to the catastrophes sent a clear message: patriotism is still a fundamental value held by most Americans. While symbols and songs provide a necessary cohesion, patriotism does not rely solely on overt demonstration. As related issues, often

---

30. Kathleen Parker, "Yet Another Spy Center Opens in Washington," Rochester (New York) *Democrat and Chronicle*, 12 June 2004, 12A.

31. According to this *Associated Press* article, International experts identify the increased use of the Internet for such purposes as a major factor in the rise of hate crimes world-wide.; "Hatred's just a click away," Rochester (New York) *Democrat and Chronicle*, 17 June 2004.

controversial, developed it became increasingly clear that to protect America's core values, Americans should be well schooled in the historical background that laid the foundations of their beliefs.

In response to the reaction to September 11, New York University's Diane Ravitch remarked that "we've seen the overwhelming response of the American people who say they do believe in something larger than our own well-being as individuals." Ravitch also observed that, "this is absolutely going to have an effect on schools."[32]

Although support exists for Ravitch's conclusions regarding the teaching of patriotism, there still persist substantial concerns rooted in the not too distant past. John Marciano, author of *Civil Illiteracy*, for example, noted that "love of country is important, but the problem with patriotism is that it often blinds us to the negative side of American history . . . we need to stand up when our country is wrong."[33] In addition, according to Margaret Branson, Associate Director of the Center for Civic Education, "what we're after with kids is not just being patriotic in a flag-waving sense, but understanding why they are being patriotic, why they should be committed to basic principles of democracy."[34] In effect, leading educators opened the door to teaching some form of patriotism, as long as it does not rely too heavily on traditional approaches.

This need to implement an enlightened patriotism in America's schools is particularly important since the end of terrorism may be a long way off. Shortly after the events surrounding the World Trade Center, Pentagon, and Flight 93, Vincent Cannistraro, a former CIA anti-terrorism chief, claimed that information contained in materials left in Afghanistan by fleeing al-Qaeda helped foil more major attacks by terrorists after the United States began bombing in October, 2001. He also claimed that investigators have begun to assemble an analysis of al-Qaeda that is larger and more widespread, and less dependent on Osama bin Laden than previously thought.[35]

---

32. Kathleen Kennedy Manzo, "Education Experts Expect Resurgence of Patriotism in Nation's Classrooms," *Education Week*, 26 September 2001, 10.

33. Ibid.

34. Ibid.

35. Fred Bayles and Kevin Johnson, "U.S.: Shoe Suspect Linked to al Quaeda," *USA Today*, 17 January 2002, 3(A).

In addition, Secretary of Defense Donald Rumsfeld, aware of FBI and CIA discoveries that al-Qaeda may have studied water supply systems and American dams or possessed diagrams of nuclear devices, said the U.S. must be prepared for surprise attacks "vastly more deadly" than the September 11 attacks.[36] Almost three years later, in an article titled "Tackle the Nuke Threat," Fareed Zakaria, concerned with the availability of bomb-grade uranium, recommended that the United States oppose terrorist potential by spending more money to "thwart the most likely method of delivery—a suitcase bomb."[37]

There always exists the need to be aware of possibilities that appointed or elected officials, from the lowliest department head up through the presidency of the United States, may attempt to take advantage of, or at the very least embellish, political realities for political gain. Under such circumstances, it is incumbent on the individual to make his views known. There is never an instance of injustice anywhere that is either too big to be feared or too small to be ignored. For this reason, if for no other, it is essential that citizens of all ages be educated to be watchdogs against misuse of power. The United States must be prepared to rebuff any threats to our freedoms and national well-being, regardless of whether the threats come from forces originating outside our borders or from within. The loyalty to patriotic values, traditional and non-traditional, needs to be continuous, not just a knee-jerk single dimension reaction each time a threat occurs.

In order to be effective in the classroom teachers must have access to the truth; hence, the importance of free speech, and a free press that is not influenced by political concerns. Unfortunately, according to Paul Krugman writing in the *International Herald Tribune*, this was not the case regarding the administration of George W. Bush in the two years following September 11, 2001, particularly in reference to the war in Iraq. He noted that "poorly documented claims of a dire threat received prominent, uncritical cover-

---

36. Robert Burns, "Rumsfeld: U.S. Must Prepare for More Attacks," [online source] (Associated Press, CBS News Online, last accessed 27 April 2002), http://www.cbsnews.com/stories/2002/02/20/attack/main501779.shtml; Internet.

37. Ibid.

age."[38] In explaining this lack of critical judgement on the part of news organizations, Krugman points to "intimidation," and refusal to believe that "the President of the United States was being dishonest about such grave matters," a "misplaced patriotism."[39]

The reference that Krugman makes to misplaced patriotism is noteworthy. First, misplaced patriotism is not uncommon among those who adhere too rigidly to traditional thoughts on patriotism. Secondly, the implications of such narrow interpretations show the need for a newer more encompassing definition of patriotism. Archaic interpretations of patriotism can only lead to archaic decision-making, a course of action that too often leads to mistakes and errors in judgement.

The interests and concerns of the many political, social, and education critics are valid. And therein rests the question: when, where, and how do we begin to teach the new patriotism? Since America's national awareness has matured considerably, and her global interests have grown enormously, it is time to rethink the way we define patriotism. And since the definition of patriotism and how it is taught has changed throughout its history, with the last significant change occurring after the Civil War, perhaps the time for re-thinking is long overdue. A belief system founded on understandings that are almost 150 years old can hardly be appropriate in all respects for the 21st century.

As a symbolic first step to implement change, it would be appropriate to begin with the Pledge of Allegiance, one of the strongest symbols of patriotism. First written in 1892, the pledge was changed in 1924 and again in 1954, in an effort to accommodate changing perspective. Perhaps it is time to again rewrite the Pledge of Allegiance. After all, most Americans realize, from a historical perspective, that the United States neither now nor ever has had "liberty and justice for all." The history of American slavery, the theft of Indian lands, and the internment of Japanese-Americans during World War II, to name but a few examples, provide ample evidence. For more recent examples, one need only look at the disproportionate number of minorities awaiting their fate on death row, or to note the significant numbers of inadequately de-

---

38. Paul Krugman, "America's press has been too soft on Bush," *International Herald Tribune*, 29–30 October 2004, 7.

39. Ibid.

fended prison inmates released in recent years, exonerated only as a result of DNA testing.

Teaching New Patriotism in the 21ˢᵗ Century endorses adoption of the Pledge of Allegiance first proposed over 30 years ago by the (then) U.S. Commissioner of Education, James E. Allen. Reflecting the political mood of the period, *Look* magazine, in 1970, printed an article by Leonard Stevens titled "Do We Need A New Pledge of Allegiance?" Although the article was devoted to a description of various court cases concerning patriotic issues, the writer also questioned the value of patriotically inspired public recitations and perfunctory salutes as a means of inculcating patriotism in American youth. Furthermore, he suggested that "true patriotism was most likely to develop from school programs that explained the meaning of our great Constitution."[40]

At the invitation of the editor of *Look* magazine, Allen rewrote the Pledge of Allegiance in an effort to alleviate concerns of parents and students regarding the lack of reality in the pledge. Allen's changes added only three significant words to the existing text: dedicate, principle, and truth, but altered dramatically the meaning of the Pledge of Allegiance.

> *I pledge allegiance*
> *of the United States*
> *of America*
> *and dedicate myself*
> *to the principle*
> *that the Republic*
> *for which it stands*
> *shall be in truth*
> *One Nation, under God,*
> *indivisible,*
> *dedicated to liberty*
> *and justice for all.*[41]

---

40. Leonard Stevens, "Do We Need a New Pledge of Allegiance?," *Look* 34, no. 24 (1970): 20. At the time the *Look* article was written, the U.S Commissioner of Education was the highest education officer in the United States. The United States Department of Education and the elevation of the Secretary of Education to a cabinet level position did not occur until 1980.

41. Ibid.

If the Pledge of Allegiance were changed to accommodate evolving perspectives of society, views that include promoting freedom and justice—and not hypocrisy—as ultimate goals, the United States could truly stand before its citizens, and the world, as a symbol of hope for a more positive tomorrow. Moreover, such a sincere forthright effort toward encompassing reality may prove to be an important step toward gaining the confidence of disenchanted American youth.

In addition, the opportunities for youth to make positive change are limitless. One example is the "Pledge Across America" endorsed by Rod Paige, President George W. Bush's Secretary of Education. Initiated ten years ago by Paula Burton, a retired schoolteacher, the Pledge Across America, an effort to encourage student participation in reciting the pledge all across the United States, has been held annually, albeit with little support. In 2001, however, the support was overwhelming.[42] It is important that our youth be taught to share a commitment to a more giving and understanding America, and world; a revised pledge would be a good place to start.

Another idea that has merit is the "Make a Difference Day." Initiated by *USA Weekend* 10 years ago, an idea that mushroomed thanks to the generosity of small children and large charities, "Make a Difference Day" is currently the country's most active day of volunteering. Probably due in large measure to the events of September 11, over 2.6 million people participated on October 27, the designated "Make a Difference Day" for 2001.[43] According to *USA Weekend*, reaching out to those who are in need is an essential element of our national character. "This is the most basic way Americans demonstrate their basic belief that *all* citizens deserve an equal chance at life, liberty, and happiness."[44] But why restrict the effort to one day a year? Students should be taught to work toward wholesome efforts on behalf of others throughout the year.

American students can make a contribution on the international front as well. President George W. Bush confirmed this when

---

42. Kevin Hicks, and the Associated Press, "Pledge Unites Nation's Schools," *Rochester (New York) Democrat and Chronicle*, 13 October 2001, 8(A).

43. Marcia Bullard, "Change the World," *USA Weekend*, 19–21 October 2001, 6.

44. Ibid., 7.

he called upon American school children to earn a single dollar and send it to the White House to help the children of Afghanistan, and children throughout the United States responded in overwhelming numbers. Within six months from the President's initial appeal, youth from all over the United States sent $4.5 million to the White House. Noting the success of the appeal, President Bush asserted that "American children have been extremely generous in helping the children of Afghanistan."[45] Much of the money, according to President Bush, was used to buy pencils, notebooks, crayons, and soccer balls. In fact, since the war in Afghanistan began, the United States has sent more than 4 million textbooks to Afghanistan.[46]

The need to develop in America's youth a powerful social conscience is especially important to reverse current trends which show a lessening of concern for others. According to a 2004 Harvard University study, baby boomers "read and vote less . . . are less likely to join groups, and they don't volunteer as often."[47] According to Susan Moses, deputy director of the Center for Health Communications at Harvard School of Public Health, this change in civic mindedness could have a significant impact in areas that are supported by volunteering, such as museums, hospitals, and charities. Moses concluded that, "in the future, in some communities, without volunteers some services won't be offered."[48]

As difficult as this is to accept, it is entirely possible that the nature of the next generation of wars may well involve clandestine groups, such as terrorists, in armed struggles against established nations. Throughout man's history, conflict has taken many forms. Originating with battles between families and clans, man has progressed in the last century to involving massive armies engaged in huge conflagrations fought on several continents. Now we are in a new age. If the enemy to fear is terrorism, and not other nations, we need to be prepared on several fronts; one of the fronts should be in

45. Associated Press, "Bush Praises U.S. Children's Generosity of Afghan Youth," *The Buffalo News*, 17 March 2002, 10(A).

46. Ibid.

47. Doug Guthrie, "Boomers to Redefine Retirement," *The Detroit News and Free Press*, 4 July 2004, 8(A).

48. Ibid.

classrooms and in the arena of an enlightened patriotism. Such a proactive approach is necessary if the analyses of Jessica Stern and Fareed Zakaria are anywhere near the truth. As Jared Diamond explained in a *New York Times* article, new forms of terrorism are most effective when the targeted society is unprepared psychologically as well as physically. And the essence of terrorism is to kill or injure opponents in ways specifically intended to cause fear and disorganization far out of proportion to the number of victims.[49]

What social studies teachers do in the classroom—encouraging students to walk the walk and not just talk the talk—may well prove to be the integral part of the greater whole. If teachers are successful in the classroom, they may help lay the foundation for a more positive future. When they encourage young people to respect, accept, and reach out and give assistance to others, they help their students to become part of the solution rather than part of the problem. If social studies classrooms send a serious and forceful enough message, future leaders throughout the world might heed the wisdom in the message and make a greater effort to resolve existing differences to better promote a safer world.

---

49. Jared Diamond, "Keeping Panic at Bay," *The New York Times*, 21 October 2001, 15.

6

Easy-to-Use Ideas for Teaching *New* Patriotism in Primary Classrooms

∼

. . . But these things don't matter at all, because once you are Real you can't be ugly, except to people who don't understand.

THE VELVETEEN RABBIT

By the end of their elementary years, students should have a firm grasp on the basic definitions of patriotism and good citizenship, and should be able to describe the characteristics of patriots and good citizens. Teaching these concepts early lays the foundation for more in-depth discussions in later years. Elementary lessons should focus on providing examples, forming definitions, and especially providing opportunities for expressing patriotism and citizenship.

The ideas assembled here combine traditional and nontraditional ways of teaching patriotism, including concepts such as tolerance and respect. The ultimate goal common to all the lesson outlines is to shape participating, patriotic, caring, respectful community members. It is important that students experience first hand what it is like to care about others, share with others, appreciate others and develop tolerance and respect for all people. With that in mind, it seems clear that the best way to teach patriotism and citizenship is through direct involvement. The following activities, selected specifically for students in primary grades, are designed for this purpose, and can be modified and/or adapted to meet individual needs. Included here are ideas, methods of instruction, explanations and resources, as well as lesson plan ideas. Depending on the maturity level of the Primary students, additional ideas can also be found in chapter seven.

TITLE: *Let Freedom Ring!*

DESCRIPTION: In this lesson, students learn the song *My Country 'tis of Thee*, verse one. When coming to the words, liberty, pride, and freedom, explain these words, and encourage the students to make up motions that they can associate with these words. The students must also sing these words louder than the rest of the song. This helps them focus on what our country stands for: liberty, freedom, and pride. Additionally, have students learn and sing the song *This Land is Your Land,* and, accurately place markers on a map in relation to locations mentioned (e.g. New York island, California). As a result, the students will have a visual reference of the places referred to in the song, creating a better understanding of the song and places in the United States.[1]

TITLE: *We are all alike. We are all different. And that's okay.*

DESCRIPTION: In this lesson, students will explore the ways in which they are alike and different from one another. They will express these similarities and differences through speaking, writing, and drawing. Using prompts to guide their thinking, have students brainstorm ways in which they are alike and different. Examples of guiding questions are "What color is your hair, skin, and eyes?" "What is your family like?" "Where do you live?" "What do/don't you like to eat?" "What do you like to do?" Present the students' responses in a class book, on a bulletin board, in a play, on a web page, in a mural, or in a song. Students should begin to understand that it is okay to be different, and that in many ways we are alike.[2]

---

1. Addie Gaines, *Proud to Be Americans* [online source] (Seneca Missouri, geocities.com, 1997, last accessed 6 May 2002), http://www.geocities.com/Athens/Aegean/2221/america.html; Internet.

2. Cheltenham Elementary School Kindergartners, *We are all alike . . . We are all different.* Photographs—Laura Dwight. (Scholastic Inc: USA., 1991).; M. Fox, *Whoever you are* (Scholastic Inc: USA., 1997).

TITLE: *Goofy Glasses*

DESCRIPTION: Students should partner up with a friend in class. Each student is to list positive traits of the person (what he/she likes about the other). Then each student should make a pair of "goofy glasses" out of colored cellophane and construction paper. Explain to students that no color is better than another. Ask students to look at their friend through the glasses and ask: What changes do you see in your friend? Have your feelings for him or her changed because he or she no longer has the same color skin? This lesson emphasizes the fact that outer appearances should not be used to judge people.[3]

TITLE: *Serving Soup*

DESCRIPTION: Direct a class discussion of what students think it means to be a good citizen or a good person, guiding them to focus on how they feel when they help someone or someone helps them. Have the students make soup for the local soup kitchen and then take a field trip to the soup kitchen and serve it for lunch. Read the book *Stone Soup* written by Ann McGovern and then make soup with the ingredients discussed in the book and/or student ideas for what to put in the soup. As closure, ask the students how it felt to volunteer their time by helping someone else. Ask the students to interview a parent/guardian on what kind of volunteer activities they have done in their lifetime and to write down ideas of other ways to help the local community. Allow time to show these ideas with the class.

SUGGESTED BOOK: *Stone Soup* by Ann McGovern

TITLE: *A Celebration of Diversity: Immigration and Citizenship*

DESCRIPTION: Discuss the concept of cultural diversity and why it is important to Americans. Read *The Great Ancestor Hunt: The Fun of Finding Out Who You Are,* by Erika Weihs to introduce students to the concept of a family tree. Have the students interview their family members to find out about their ancestry and to create their own personal family tree. Students can use push pins in a world map to identify the countries represented in the class. Attach small strips of

---

3. ProTeacher [online source] (1998–2002, last accessed 6 May 2002), no other publication information present, http://www.proteacher.com; Internet.

paper or little flags with the students' names on them to indicate the country of origin of each student's ancestors. Further valuable and engaging activities may be found on the source website.[4]

TITLE: *The Ingredients of Our Flag*

DESCRIPTION: In this lesson, students explore what the colors and symbols on the flag of the United States mean to them. Students use construction paper, felt, glitter, etc. to mix into a large bowl, "making" the flag. For example, a student might say "the blue stands for the beautiful water in our country," and then puts something blue into the "mixture." Once all of the students have added something to the mix, pull the flag out of the bowl. Then, discuss how all of these things that we mixed together are also mixed into the American flag.

TITLE: *Facts About Our Flag*

DESCRIPTION: In this lesson the students will be investigating facts about the American flag and discovering the symbolism of the flag. Have students brainstorm and share their feelings about the American flag. Two books that can be read in conjunction with this lesson are *The Flag We Love* by Pamela Munoz Ryan and *Betsy Ross* by Alexandra Wallner. Follow with a discussion about the new facts learned from the books. Students can continue their research of the American flag by using the Internet, encyclopedias, and other books on the topic. As a culminating activity, students can create a class flag based on the symbols, colors, and design of the American flag.[5]

TITLE: *America the Beautiful*

DESCRIPTION: While singing America the Beautiful, have students create motions to act out what they are singing. For example, students could raise and extend arms when singing "Spacious Skies", or sway back and forth when singing "Amber Waves of Grain". Students

---

4. Krysia Braun and Jennifer Link, *Collaborative Thematic Unit: A Celebration of Diversity: Immigration and* Citizenship [online source] (Columbia: University of South Carolina, 1997–1999, last accessed May 6 2002), http://www.libsci.sc.edu/miller/diversity.htm; Internet.

5. ProTeacher [online source] (1998–2002, last accessed 6 May 2002), no other publication information present, http://www.proteacher.com/090019.shtml; Internet.

could also interpret the song lyrics through pictures and display each picture as the verses are sung. Students may also choose more modern songs such as Born in the USA or Proud to be an American.[6]

TITLE: *Patriotism through Music*

DESCRIPTION: After having taught students the lyrics to "America the Beautiful," and the "Star Spangled Banner," engage them in a discussion about how these songs describe the ways Americans feel about their country. Follow up by having the students note at least 2 similarities and 2 differences between the songs. Using these songs as a basis, brainstorm a list of words and phrases that can be used to describe the United States. As a class, use entries from the list to create a new patriotic song saluting our country.

TITLE: *Doing My Part*

DESCRIPTION: In this lesson, which focuses on cooperation, sharing common goals, needs, and traditions, students will learn what it means to be a good citizen and part of a community, how people respect one another's rights, take responsibility for their actions, and live peacefully with each other. Begin with a discussion of books such as *The Patchwork Quilt* by Valerie Flournoy, *Wednesday Surprise* by Eve Bunting, that focus on contribution and success in the communities. Have the students brainstorm a list of people in their community and why they are important. From this the class can develop a book about the community in which they live.[7]

TITLE: *Helping Others*

DESCRIPTION: The purpose of this activity is to provide students with the feeling of helping others. After showing students the video *All Dogs Go to Heaven*, engage them in a discussion on the merits of helping others. Involve students in conducting food drives, especially during holiday seasons such as Thanksgiving and Christmas. Arrange for students to visit an area nursing home to plant flowers, read to the residents, or pen pal letters to the people living at the

---

6. Milton Polsky, "America the Dramatic." *Instructor* 92, no.6 (1985): 33.

7. This site was not accessible on 6 May 2002, however, the above abstract was an adaptation of information from: http://ideanet.doe.state.in.us/publications/pdf_citizenship/ctzgrade01.pdf; Internet.

nursing home. It is important for the children to see that they can contribute to and make a difference in the world.

TITLE: *Following the Rules*

DESCRIPTION: At the beginning of this lesson, have students discuss their ideas about the statement: Teamwork means following the same rules. As a class, develop rules for the classroom, and discuss the importance of following the rules. Point out that when everyone follows the rules, everyone has pride in the classroom. Students should be proud to be a part of a classroom that follows the rules.

TITLE: *What Symbol Makes You Think of America?*

DESCRIPTION: Brainstorm a list of symbols of America and discuss why these symbols represent our country. In small groups, students will research different symbols of our nation (e.g., the Statue of Liberty, Liberty Bell, flag, Great Seal of the United States), and create a poster that includes a picture of the symbol, the significance of their symbol, and any other information they feel is important. Groups will display their posters and share what they found with the class.

TITLE: *From the Ground Up*

DESCRIPTION: The class will use the Railroad sign, (RXR) to represent Responsibility and Respect. Using the symbol as a reminder, students are expected to: respect themselves and others, accept and appreciate diversity, to take responsibility for their actions, to tolerate opposing viewpoints, and to contribute to the school community. Display the symbol all over the school in as many places as possible by making bumper stickers, buttons, posters, and other visuals to remind students on a daily basis to be responsible and respectful of others.[8]

TITLE: *The Citizenship Tree*

DESCRIPTION: Using the theme of citizenship, create a class citizenship tree. Begin the lesson by writing the words "citizenship" and "services to others" on the board and then define these terms. Read a story that expresses a strong message of service to others, and discuss

---

8. *Starting Small* (Teaching Tolerance, A Project of the Southern Poverty Law Center, 1997) 55–71.

how the main characters in the story exhibited citizenship behaviors. Then, have a large cutout of a tree on a bulletin board entitled "Our Classroom Citizenship Tree." Students can brainstorm actions to help others and then make leaves for the tree by completing the prompt "I can help others by _____." Ideas might include helping a peer with homework, recycling, picking up trash on the playground, donating non-perishable food to a church/shelter, talking to a friend when they are upset or angry, setting the dinner table or drawing a get well card for a sick neighbor. Explain to the students that citizenship deeds are similar to giving a gift to someone else. Encourage students to perform their deeds as many times as possible for one week. At the end of the week, the students will share the way in which they performed their good citizenship deeds. Students can be encouraged to continue with their citizenship deeds or choose new ones from the tree to continue the project throughout the unit or school year.[9]

TITLE: *Responding to Special Needs*

DESCRIPTION: This lesson provides some excellent ideas for teaching tolerance and respect for individuals with disabilities. First, provide toys, books posters and other materials that show individuals with disabilities living lives similar to their own. Next, invite guests with disabilities to speak to the class and participate in everyday activities. Ask the speaker to focus on traits other than his/her disability at first (family life, job, hobbies and interests), to show students that there is much more to the individual than the disability and that despite the disability, the individual leads a "normal" life. Hopefully, this will provide a relaxed atmosphere in which students feel comfortable asking about the individual's life. Be sure to provide students with the proper terminology (wheelchair, brace, etc.). Before the speaker comes, the teacher may want to provide a brief activity on the human body and show that not all bodies work the same way. If possible, include the speaker as a part of an entirely different unit, so that students can separate the individual from the disability.[10]

---

9. S. Berenstain, and J. Berenstain, *The Berenstain Bears to the Rescue* (NY: Random House, Inc., 1983).; P. Cohen, *The Content of Their Character*, ASCD Curriculum Update (Spring, 1995).

10. *Starting Small* (Teaching Tolerance, A Project of the Southern Poverty Law Center, 1997) 133–135.

TITLE: *Liberty and Justice for All*
DESCRIPTION: Have students recite the Pledge of Allegiance, paying special attention to the last few lines. . . ." one nation, under God, indivisible, with liberty and justice for all." Teach the students how to "say" the Pledge in American Sign Language. Reciting the Pledge in this manner will help the teacher reach two important goals: giving meaning to the pledge through symbols and teaching students tolerance of those who may communicate in other ways than speaking. An American Sign Language Dictionary may be found on the Internet.

TITLE: *The Kindness Chain*
DESCRIPTION: As a class, have students brainstorm acts of kindness that they can carry out in their communities, including things such as picking up litter in a public park, visiting the elderly in a nursing home, raking leaves or shoveling snow for a neighbor in need, etc. Direct students to choose one of these tasks as feasible, and then describe the act of kindness and how it made them feel, on 8X2 strips of paper. Students should then glue the two ends of the strip together around another student's "act of kindness" link in order to create a chain. This is a project that can be continued throughout the school year, with the goal of making the chain as long as possible.

TITLE: *How Communities are Different*
DESCRIPTION: This lesson begins with the teacher reading a book titled *The Folks Who Lived in Backward Town* (a book with a similar theme can be substituted). Engage the class in a discussion about where the story took place, what characteristics the community in the story had, what type of community it was and how it was different from or similar to their own community. After the discussion, provide groups of students with a photograph or postcard depicting a community different from their own. Students should make a list of characteristics that describe the community in the picture. After students have listed about ten characteristics they can share their lists with the rest of the class. After each group has shared its list, place an oversized Venn diagram on the board. One section should be labeled "My/Our Community" and the other section is titled "Other Communities." After

completing the Venn diagram the teacher should lead a discussion about the differences/similarities between communities.[11]

TITLE: *Fireworks and Flags*

DESCRIPTION: Begin the lesson by discussing what students think of when they think about fireworks. Brainstorm a list of what the students know about the Fourth of July. Read selections of the book, *Fireworks, Picnics, and Flags*, by James Cross Giblin, to show how the Fourth of July came to be a holiday that Americans celebrate. After the discussion, have students create pages for a "Big Book about the Fourth of July."

TITLE: *Patriotic and Historical Plays for Young People*

DESCRIPTION: Involve students in seasonal pageants that commemorate historical events such as the first Thanksgiving, the making of the first flag, etc. A good source for patriotic plays that focus exclusively on the events of the American Revolution is *Patriotic & Historical Plays for Young People* edited by Sylvia E. Kamerman. Boston: Plays Inc.

TITLE: *Participating in a Democratic Society*

DESCRIPTION: It is important in the beginning of the year to establish a democratic atmosphere with the students. A good way to do this would be by writing a constitution or bill of rights, which would represent what is traditionally known as "Classroom Rules" or a "Class Constitution." Since our society is not a dictatorship, students should participate in rule making. This will allow students to have a better idea of what it means to take part in a democratic society.

TITLE: *Appreciating American Veterans*

DESCRIPTION: Celebrate national holidays by asking students to express patriotism in the form of an activity. For example, while some students may create and perform a skit or play which exemplifies the meaning of patriotism, other students can write a poem or a song,

---

11. Lesson Plans Page.Com, *How Communities are Different* [online source] (EdScope,L.L.C., 1996–2002, last accessed 6 May 2002), http://www.lesson planspage.com/SSCommunityDifferencesVenn3.htm; Internet.

create a drawing, or poster that expresses patriotism. Alternatively, on holidays such as Memorial Day or Veteran's Day, invite war veterans to visit the classroom to discuss what patriotism means to them.[12]

TITLE: *Symbolism in the Statue of Liberty*
DESCRIPTION: One way to instill a sense of pride and patriotism in students is to ask why so many immigrants desired to live in America. One incentive was to experience freedom and liberty, which is why so many immigrants were moved when they first saw the Statue of Liberty upon arrival in New York Harbor. Use the Internet to locate websites on the Statue of Liberty. Ask students to examine the symbols inherent in the Statue if Liberty. As an extension activity, allow students an opportunity to create their own art or poem or story which captures what living in America means to them.

TITLE: *Important Symbolism in the Statue of Liberty*
DESCRIPTION: Students will explore the symbolism behind the components of the Statue of Liberty by examining pictures and listening to or reading text explaining the symbolism. Lead students in a group discussion where they will begin to discover symbolism that is important to the United States as well as to the immigrants who arrived here in the 1900's. After learning about the symbolism behind the important parts of the Statue, students should use the themes or symbols and create their own "Statue of Liberty." Students may come up with their own statue or may use the Statue of Liberty itself and add new symbols to it.[13]

TITLE: *A Million Visions of Peace*
DESCRIPTION: This lesson is based on the book *A Million Visions of Peace: Wisdom from the Friends of Old Turtle* by Jennifer Garrison and Andrew Tubesing, a book that expresses visions of peace com-

---

12. Lynn Quinn, *My County 'Tis of* Thee [online source] (Boston: Massachusetts, Boston Teachnet.org, last accessed May 6 2002), http://www.boston.teachnet.org/quinn/quinn.htm; Internet.

13. *National Monument and Ellis Island: Symbols of Liberty* [online source] (National Park Service Education Specialist, last modified January 1, 2001, last accessed 7 May 2002), http://www.nps.gov/stli/teachercorner/page8.html; Internet.

piled from people of all ages across our the US based on the Old Turtle Peace Project. The main ideas include a worldwide community, the importance of taking care of our earth, violence prevention, finding inner peace, and coming up with answers to the question "How do we find peace?" Read sections of the book over a period to time, to expose students to multiple perspectives and ideas of peace. Students can then create their own page that reflects his or her own vision of peace. Combine the student's pages to form a class book.[14]

TITLE: *The First Patriots*

DESCRIPTION: Create a "Patriots Hall of Fame" in which students research the lives of the leaders of the American Independence Movement. Students may draw a picture of their patriot and post the drawings and the biographies around the room. Have students observe each others' work and then, as a class, have a discussion that centers around the following questions: What characteristics do these individuals possess which make them "patriots?" In what ways did the actions of the individuals demonstrate patriotism? Why should we remember these patriots? How can you follow their example? Whom do you consider to be a patriot in your own society and why?

TITLE: *Facing Prejudice*

DESCRIPTION: This lesson provides several suggestions for dealing with prejudice in the classroom. Teachers are encouraged to provide opportunities for cross cultural, cross-racial and cross-gender interactions, providing they reflect both cultural diversity and commonalities. Teachers are also cautioned not to single out a student based on color or culture. *Starting Small* also recommends that teachers take an active role in preventing prejudice by addressing and discussing hurtful situations when they come up in the classroom. This will help children overcome stereotypes and help them understand that their words can hurt others.[15]

---

14. J. Garrison and A. Tubesing, *A Million Visions of Peace: Wisdom from the Friends of Old Turtle* (New York: Pfeifer-Hamilton: Scholastic Inc., 1996).

15. *Starting Small* (Teaching Tolerance, A Project of the Southern Poverty Law Center, 1997) 103–104.

TITLE: *Proud to be a Citizen*

DESCRIPTION: To begin this lesson, ask students to brainstorm things for which they are proud. Explain that sometimes an entire community can be proud of the same thing. Show students pictures of fireworks, the American flag, and a map of the United States of America. Ask the students what these pictures represent and record student's responses on the board. Explain how people in their community show their pride in being a citizen of the United States by flying flags, watching fireworks, and celebrating such holidays as the Fourth of July. Discuss the fact that citizens of the community are also proud of their freedom. Next, pass out the words to *This Land is Your Land* by Woodie Guthrie. Sing the song and discuss why this song is important. Wrap up with a discussion of how pride in ones community is similar to having pride in the United States of America.

TITLE: *Important Memorials, Monuments and Statues*

DESCRIPTION: This lesson focuses on significant monuments and memorials throughout the United States and the reasons they were erected. To start, the students will brainstorm a list of possible monuments to study, including, for example, the Statue of Liberty, the Washington Monument, the Viet Nam Veteran's Memorial wall, the Pearl Harbor Monument, and the World War II Monument. The students should research in small groups to learn about the structural details of the memorial, reasons why it was built, and why the structure is significant to our country. Groups can then present their findings to the class.

7

Easy-to-Use Ideas for Teaching *New* Patriotism in Intermediate Classrooms

A hundred children, a hundred individuals who are people—not people-to-be, not people of tomorrow, but people now, right now—today.

JANUSZ KORCZAK

By the end of their elementary years, students should have a firm grasp on the basic definitions of patriotism and good citizenship, and should be able to describe the characteristics of patriots and good citizens. Teaching these concepts early lays the foundation for more in-depth discussions in later years. Elementary lessons should focus on providing examples, forming definitions, and especially providing opportunities for expressing patriotism and citizenship.

The ideas assembled here combine traditional and non-traditional ways of teaching patriotism, including concepts such as tolerance and respect. The ultimate goal common to all the lesson outlines is to shape participating, patriotic, caring, respectful community members. It is important that students experience first hand what it is like to care about others, share with others, appreciate others and develop tolerance and respect for all people. With that in mind, it seems clear that the best way to teach patriotism and citizenship is through direct involvement. The following activities, selected specifically for students in the Intermediate grades, are designed for this purpose, and can be modified and/or adapted to meet individual needs. Included here are ideas, methods of instruction, explanations and resources, as well as additional lesson plan ideas. Depending on the maturity level of the Intermediate students, additional ideas can also be found in chapter six.

TITLE: *Veteran's Day*

DESCRIPTION: Engage students in a discussion about Veteran's Day. Discuss with them why it is important and what the word "veteran" means. Share with the students a story about a notable veteran, Private Watson. Private Watson was on board a ship hit by Japanese bombers off the coast of New Guinea on 8 March 1943. When the ship had to be abandoned, instead of seeking to save himself, he stayed in the water for a long time, courageously helping other soldiers who could not swim reach the life rafts. Weakened by his exertions, he was eventually dragged down by the sinking ship and drowned. Private Watson was the first black solider to receive the Distinguished Service Cross during World War II. He was 28 years old, had been drafted into the Army and was assigned to the 29th Quartermaster Regiment. Adjust the story to meet the developmental level of the students. The students would then imagine that they are away at war and write a fictional letter home, telling friends and family what it is like. They can also write a page in an imaginary diary about their war experiences. If possible, invite a local veteran to speak to the class.[1]

TITLE: *Flag of Promises*

DESCRIPTION: "Ask not what your country can do for you, but what you can do for your country"—John F. Kennedy. In teaching the concept of patriotism, introduce the students to the Pledge of Allegiance. Explain to the students the meaning behind the symbolism of the flag and the pledge. In learning the pledge, students will discover how the pledge is a promise to our country, and how as citizens, we say the pledge to demonstrate our love of country. Ask

---

1. Beth Lewis, Elementary Educators: Veterans Day 2001 [online source] (About Inc. 2002, last accessed 6 May 2002), http://k-6educators.about.com/library/weekly/aa110101a.htm; Internet.; The Quartermaster Museum, Private George Watson Medal of Honor, World War II, [online source] (last accessed 6 May 2002), http://www.qmfound.com/watson.htm; Internet.

students to share promises they have made to people, and discuss their feelings and thoughts about those promises. Ask the students what promises they can make to their country, such as doing things at home or community service. Teach the students that their small actions of demonstrating patriotism are an important addition to our country's patriotic beliefs. As a class, begin a "Chart of Patriotism." Provide a large sheet of paper resembling a flag, and explain to the students that they will receive a red, white or blue foil star for each patriotic action they carry out. Place the stars on the flag chart to "color" the flag, which will remain in the classroom for the entire school year as an incentive to keep on carrying out patriotic measures.

TITLE: *What Makes a Good Citizen?*

DESCRIPTION: For this lesson on citizenship, begin by asking "What makes a good citizen?" and record student responses. Explain to the students that they will be broken up into groups of four in order to read books that portray good citizens. Use a handout to help guide them in some of the aspects they should be looking for in a good citizen so they can apply these criteria to one of the book's characters. Ask the students to choose one group member to participate in the "interview program" about the characters that they have chosen and why they believe that character is a model of a good citizen. Students not role-playing will be audience members who ask questions. After the activity, redirect the students' attention to the chalkboard and their brainstormed list in order to see if there are any more characteristics of good citizens they would like to add.[2]

SUGGESTED BOOKS:

Just a Dream by Chris Van Allsburg
Washing the Willow Tree Loon by Jacqueline Briggs Martin
A Day's Work by Eve Bunting
The Story of Ruby Bridges by Robert Coles
Teammates by Peter Golenbock
Just Like Martin by Ossie Davis

---

2. Laurel R. Singleton, *What makes a Good Citizen?: Models in Literature* [online source] (Boulder, Co: SSEC Publications, 1999, last accessed 6 May 2002), http://www.ssecinc.org/less/Pg_ls_what.htm; Internet.

TITLE: *Citizenship is a Special Status*

DESCRIPTION: Invite two or three people who have recently immigrated to the United States to speak to the class about their experience in becoming a US citizen and what that means to them. Ask speakers to discuss such topics as why they chose to move here, how they got here, and what they needed to do to become citizens.[3]

TITLE: *Diversity Quilt*

DESCRITION: Students will focus on their ethnic backgrounds to determine the countries of origin of their ancestors: Where are their families from? Were their grandparents immigrants? Great-Grandparents? Great-Great-Grandparents? Students will ask their parents, grandparents, or other family members a list of questions developed by the class. After the data are gathered, the class will construct pie charts to provide visual representations of student ancestral origins. Each student will then make one quilt square and the teacher will connect the pieces together to make a classroom quilt to represent their collective ancestral backgrounds. A square could include the colors of the national flag of their ancestors, their last names, a favorite food from their ancestral country, a famous person from their country or origin, etc.

TITLE: *City Poetry*

DESCRIPTION: Part of a great American tradition is writers celebrating or constructively criticizing their hometowns in poetry or song. Some examples include Carl Sandburg's *Chicago*, Langston Hughes's *Harlem*, and Frank Sinatra's *New York, New York*. After hearing and/or reading some examples, students can write poems about their hometown. The poem can tell a story or describe scenes. Or a student's rhyme could be put to music, etc. To help students generate ideas for this project, take a walk or field trip around the town or city. The teacher should stress the process of observation through all five senses. Primary source documents (i.e., newspaper article, diaries of local historical figures, or letters) would also be helpful for generating ideas and will provide students with the experience of working with

---

3. This site address has been changed due to site updating at ERIC, the abstract was adapted from information taken from: http://www.askeric.org/virtual/lessons/social_studies/Civics/CIV0004.html

primary sources. Students may then publish their works on a webpage or a classroom journal/newspaper.

TITLE: *Teamwork is Working Together*
DESCRIPTION: Begin this lesson by asking students to explain why civic responsibility is important within a community. After students have brainstormed ideas, discuss how members of the community work together, much like a team. Introduce the books *Teamwork* and *Work* by Ann Morris. Take the class outside and hand each person a piece of paper with a list of items that they must find in three minutes. After the three minutes, regroup and discuss the difficulties and successes the students had. Now, allow the students to work in teams in order to find everything on the list. After the second hunt, regroup and discuss how working in a team was more efficient than working individually. Follow up with a discussion of how teamwork in a community can make things work more smoothly and efficiently.

TITLE: *Music, Music, Music*
DESCRIPTION: Use a variety of songs to introduce students to character education. After listening to the songs with the students, discuss what the lyrics mean to them and how they can include these qualities in their daily lives. Students should be encouraged to discuss how they feel when they see people being disrespectful or intolerant, etc. Use songs such as:

We're Just Like Crayons, Melody House (Tolerance)
I'm Just a Little Person, Multi-S Music (Compassion)
The Greatest Love of All, Whitney Houston (Self-Discipline)
Would You Like to Swing On a Star? Maria Muldaur (Responsibility)
Hero, Mariah Carey (Perseverance)
Shalom, Jerry's Girls (Tolerance)
Peace I Ask of Thee O River, Camp Song (Compassion)
What a Wonderful World, Louis Armstrong (Respect)
The Rose, Bette Midler (Self-Discipline)
Blowin' In The Wind, Peter Paul and Mary (Compassion)[4]

---

4. "Music, Music, Music," *Teaching Pre K–8*, (February 2002): p. 42–44.

TITLE: *What is Citizenship*

DESCRIPTION: Students will learn about the concept of citizenship, and what they can do to be responsible citizens. Begin with a discussion of what the students think it means to be a citizen of the United States of America. Follow up by reading the book *A Very Important Day*, by Maggie Rugg Herold, a story about becoming, and what it means to become, a naturalized citizen of the United States. Follow with a discussion focusing on how the life of a citizen differs from that of a non-citizen. Students should then brainstorm some actions that exemplify responsible citizens in their communities. After the lesson, each student will decide on one specific action he or she could practice to be a good citizen, create a journal entry describing that action, and then carry it out before the end of the unit. For example, a student might want to help an elderly neighbor do some chores around the house.

TITLE: *Pledge Allegiance to the Flag*

DESCRIPTION: Start the lesson with the question "why do we say the pledge every morning?" Give groups of students a copy of the pledge with unfamiliar words highlighted. Provide students with the opportunity to go to fifth grade classrooms to interview the students and their teachers about the meanings of those words. Encourage students to take notes during the interviews. As groups, they will rewrite the Pledge of Allegiance by replacing the harder words with the easier words they received from the interviews. Back in the classroom, discuss why we say the pledge to the flag. Ask a member of the community, such as a Veteran, to visit the classroom to talk to the students about the American Flag, its display, and use. Students will practice the traditional method of folding of the American Flag, under the visitor's guidance. After the lesson, students will write a journal entry about the Pledge of Allegiance and the American Flag, highlighting why it is important for citizens to have this knowledge.

TITLE: *A Community Controversy*

DESCRIPTION: In order to help students understand what happens when citizens of a community have a conflict over rules, rights, and responsibilities, give them the following scenario:

The townspeople are given $1000 to spend any way they see fit. Half of the people want to spend the money on a new playground and the others want to spend the money on a new swimming pool. As citizens, how can they solve this problem?

Divide the class into two groups, one in favor of the playground, and one in favor of the swimming pool. Choose two students to be neutral leaders of the town debate. Groups should brainstorm ways they could deal with this issue as responsible citizens, and role-play the process of resolving the conflict. When the students are satisfied that the issue has been solved, they should discuss how difficult it can be to come to a decision when there is a conflict about rules, rights, and responsibilities in the community.

TITLE: *You're a Grand Old Flag*
DESCRIPTION: March around the room, holding a flag, passing out smaller ones to each student, and singing *You're a Grand Old Flag.* Begin a class discussion with three questions: What is a flag? Why do we have a flag? What does our flag represent? Write the three questions on the board to invoke thinking about the flag. Students will have ten minutes in groups of four to brainstorm and come up with ideas to share. Write the ideas on an easel board as a web organizer. Direct students to search the Internet to try to answer the question: Has our flag always looked the way we see it today? Groups of students will then choose different flags from our past and research them. What significance does the appearance have? At what point in time was this flag used? Is there a geographical reference to the flag? What kinds of events were happening in our country at the time? Groups will create replicas of their flags to present to the class and hang around the classroom.

TITLE: *The Constitution: The Founders Make History*
DESCRIPTION: This play gives students an opportunity to be a part of the Philadelphia Constitutional Convention of 1787. Students role-play characters such as George Washington, Alexander Hamilton, James Madison and Benjamin Franklin. Additionally, students debate the representation issues the founding fathers faced and discuss solutions such as the New Jersey Plan and the Virginia Plan. Eventu-

ally, students begin to understand the process which the founding fathers went though in agreeing to the Three-Fifths Compromise and the Great Compromise. This is a very useful play to begin a discussion on the Constitution.[5]

TITLE: *Talking Walls*
DESCRIPTION: This is a character-development lesson based on the book, *Talking Walls* by Margy Burns Knight. The lesson revolves around the question: "What are the walls that unite and divide us?" Have students write a poem in which they complete lines such as:

> *I am*
> *I wonder*
> *I hear*
> *I see*
> *I want*
> *I am*
> *I pretend*
> *I feel*

based on what they have read in the book. Then have students get into groups and share their poems. Students must then create a skit where the plot revolves around an individual being left out. After the skit, have the students brainstorm ideas to promote tolerance and respect for all people.[6]

TITLE: *Old Glory Grows Up: The History of Our Nation's Flag*
DESCRIPTION: This play re-enacts historic events in the life of the American flag. From its birth in the hands of Betsy Ross to it's glorification by Francis Scott Key in the *Star-Spangled Banner*, students learn the powerful symbolism inherent in the American flag. Students role-play historical figures such as George Washington, and

---

5. Sylvia E. Kamerman, *Patriotic & Historical Plays for Young* (Plays Incorporated, 1975), 174–181.

6. Rosa Furumoto, Luis Gamarra, Juith Iguina, Ignacio Reyes-Saldana, Adriana Rubalacva, and Phyllis Scadron, *Teaching Steps to Tolerance* [online source] (Sharp Avenue, California, Museum of Tolerance, last accessed May 6 2002), http://tst.wiesenthal.com/resources/talkinghands.html: Internet.

bring the fictional character "Uncle Sam" to life. Give students plenty of opportunities to sing and salute the flag. The play allows for incorporating other themes at teacher's discretion, such as tolerance and citizenship.[7]

TITLE: *The Right to Vote*
DESCRIPTION: To introduce this topic, show students pictures of people voting and political campaign signs. As a follow up, discuss what the people are doing in the pictures and why people vote. Generate a list of reasons why people vote then introduce the word "patriotism," a person's love of their country, and associate it with voting. With the new understanding that voting is one way to show your patriotism, students can practice voting in their classroom. Students could be encouraged to vote on classroom issues such as snacks, free time, field trips and other classroom activities. Tie the students' votes in the classroom to the importance of the adult vote in United States elections.

TITLE: *International Foods Day*
DESCRIPTION: This lesson begins with each student learning about the country of his or her ancestry and sharing that information with the class. This information should focus on the native language, clothes, costumes, and artifacts from their culture, and foods and customs native to their country of ancestry. If possible, invite parents into the classroom to speak about their cultural backgrounds. Students may choose to present the information they have gathered in the form of a poster, travel brochure, or PowerPoint presentation. A nice follow up to this study is "International Foods Day," in which each family prepares a dish from their culture and brings it in for a class feast.

TITLE: *How Does our Government Work?*
DESCRIPTION: Have students investigate other forms of government and identify the roles they play in the lives of the citizens. Spend one day demonstrating each of the governments in class. To illustrate a dictatorship, randomly choose one student to be the dictator and let him or her choose the activity for the day. This would be in-

---

7. Ibid., 196–203.

formative for the students and help them to remember the different governments and how they are run. The ballot box could be used as part of the lesson in that some students may be randomly denied the right to vote. The teacher may ask: "How did it make you feel that others made decisions for you without your input?" Teacher could use this as a springboard for discussion on people in U.S. history who were denied the right to vote and why it is important in a democracy that all have this right.[8]

TITLE: *The World Around Us Multicultural Fair*
DESCRIPTION: Students will select different countries they would like to research. After they have made their selections, students will make a poster that includes the flag and map of their country, information such as the current population, the type of food the country is known for, and what the people and culture are like. Display posters on the walls around the classroom. Finally, students will be responsible for preparing a native food from the country they researched. In conclusion, lead students in a discussion so that they begin to realize that many of the countries presented have people living in the United States today.

TITLE: *Posters & Presidents*
DESCRIPTION: Students will research the lives of United States presidents, and choose five influential presidents for their project. Students should then prepare an illustrated poster showing a map of the places where the particular president lived and traveled, and construct a timeline of major events during the lives and terms of these presidents. Along with these documents, students should prepare short reports that include important aspects of their lives and their contributions to our country. Students must include primary source materials such as photographs, charts and graphs when appropriate. Students should then present their projects to the class.

TITLE: *One Nation, Indivisible . . . and Individual*
DESCRIPTION: In this lesson, students will learn about the differences in the individual states within the US as well as the common features

---

8. The information from this site is downloadable at the address http://teacher. scholastic.com/lessonrepro/lessonplans/profbooks/patriotismactivities.pdf, when last accessed May 7 2002 unable to open the file.

of every state that help keep the United States, a country that spans a large geographic area, united. Use a large outline of the United States and cut-outs of individual states to make puzzle-piece flash-cards so that students can practice visualizing and naming all 50 states; as students name the states, place them on the large U.S. map. Next, have students choose an individual state (or states) to study. Students can search for information about population, size, geo-graphic features and climate, products produced, natural resources, nicknames of states, state flowers, trees, flags and birds, etc. Engage students in a discussion to compare the features of the states. Ques-tions for discussion include the following: What common features do states share? What common beliefs so people hold which help unite them? What language is spoken? What religion is practiced? How did it happen that the United States was divided during the Civil War? What differences between states may have contributed to that division?[9]

TITLE: *Pursuit of Patriotism*

DESCRIPTION: Use the Internet to go on a "treasure hunt for patrio-tism." Using primary source documents found, students will exam-ine key historical documents such as "The Gettysburg Address" and the "Pledge of Allegiance" in order to answer higher order questions about the documents. After completing the exercise, students must define what patriotism means to them in the form of a poem, speech, song or piece of art.[10]

TITLE: *Who are the "NACIREMA"?*

DESCRIPTION: Use the classic essay "Body Ritual among the Nacirema" by Horace Miner to demonstrate the concept of ethno-centrism. Begin the lesson by asking students to identify a few of their own religious or cultural customs or practices. Next, begin reading the essay as it describes Nacirema body rituals such as lacer-ating the face, putting a hogs hair brush into ones mouth to cleanse

---

9. Sandy Zjawin, abstract adapted from "One Nation Indivisible . . . ," *Instruc-tor* 92, no.6 (1983): 30–31.

10. Chathy Schulof, *pursuit of Patriotism: an Internet Treasure Hunt on Patrio-tism* [online source] (Filamentality, Pacific Bell, 1996–2002, last accessed May 6 2002), http://www.richmond.edu/academics/a&s/education/projects/hunts/patriotism; Internet.

the mouth, etc. Allow students to freely comment, "That's so gross!" or "I can't believe they do that!" When finished reading the essay ask students what they think of the Nacirema. Then reveal that Nacirema is really "American" spelled backward and introduce the term "ethnocentrism".

TITLE: *National Monument Web-Quest*
DESCRIPTION: Start the lesson by explaining the meaning of the word "monument." Create a list on the board of monuments (local, state or national), that students have visited and discuss what or who was being remembered at each monument visited. Assign students to find different national monuments on the Internet and to identify who or what is being remembered. As a culminating activity, you may wish to plan a trip to one or more of these monuments.

TITLE: *Pride in Flags*
DESCRIPTION: After showing students pictures, slides, and real flags of many states and/or nations, discuss the similarities and differences found in the flags. Direct students in a discussion of the symbolism inherent in the flag that focuses on national/local pride, various aspects of our culture, and feelings of patriotism. As a follow up, group students into new "countries," and have them create a name for their country, describe its climate and location on a globe. They should design a flag that represents their country and be able to explain its significance to the class.[11]

TITLE: *Diversity of Cultures in America*
DESCRIPTION: Begin this lesson by asking your students what the saying "America is a melting pot" means to them. In this discussion, include family origins and history as well as holidays and traditions they celebrate. In small groups, have the students name different cultures in America that they think make up the "melting pot" and then research those cultures by collecting newspaper clippings, articles, pictures, etc. Brainstorm a list of the ways these Americans deal with issues like a new language, new jobs, new school, new holidays/traditions, a new way of living, and how can we help them to

---

11. Sandy Kemsley, *ABC Teach Network* [online source] (ABC Teach Network, 2001, last accessed May 6 2002), www.abcteach.com; Internet.

adjust to our culture. Extensions to this lesson might include having immigrants come in and speak about their transition to life in this country, and investigating what you have to know and do to become an American citizen.

TITLE: *Acrostic Poem on Citizenship in a Multicultural Sense*
DESCRIPTION: Have students research their family heritage and the country of their ancestry. Write the word CITIZENSHIP down the left side of a piece of paper, then using each letter individually, the students should choose a word or phrase that represents citizenship in the ancestral country. Display acrostic poems to illustrate the diversity of the citizens of the United States.

TITLE: *Activities for Patriotism and Multiculturalism*
DESCRIPTION: This activity is designed for students to explore what it means to be an Arab American. The intent of the lesson is to defuse stereotypes and barriers that might exist in the class. Lead the class in a discussion to find out what they know about Arab Americans and how they feel towards Arab Americans. Follow-up activities might include having students research famous Arabs to see how they have contributed to the United States, learn about the Arabic language, see when immigrants from Arab nations immigrated to their city, investigate Arab nations to determine where they live, how they live, what industries they have, etc. This will help students develop a deeper understanding of and appreciation for the Arab culture and Arab Americans in general.[12]

TITLE: *The Melting Pot*
DESCRIPTION: This lesson helps students think about how America changes immigrants and how immigrants change America. To help students understand how America changes immigrants, they can interview an immigrant family. To help them understand how immigrants change America, they can survey members of their community. Follow up these interviews with a discussion centering on the fact that our country was once thought of as "the great melting pot" wherein

---

12. Jennifer R. Halladay, *Who are the Arab Americans?* [online source] (A web project of the Southern Poverty Law Center, last accessed May 6 2002), http://www.tolerance.org/teach/expand/act/activity.jsp?cid=155; Internet.

people from all different lands would blend into a single American identity, but that idea really is not popular anymore. Many new immigrant groups work hard to maintain a connection with their cultural identities, and enrich the culture of the United States.[13]

TITLE: *Learning about Patriotism through Song*
DESCRIPTION: This lesson engages students in understanding the meaning of patriotism through patriotic songs found in America's history. The students should first read the words of the national anthem together. As a class, discuss the lyrics and the reason why the song was written. The students should describe how they feel when singing the song and how it illustrates the pride they have in the United States. Next have students examine other patriotic songs that have been popular throughout history, including the *Battle Hymn of the Republic, America, My Country 'Tis of Thee*, and *You're a Grand Old Flag*. Break the students into groups to discuss the lyrics of these songs and how they illustrate patriotism. Students should then be encouraged to work together in groups to create their own patriotic song lyrics using some of the themes that they have studied.[14]

TITLE: *Teacher and Student Partnerships*
DESCRIPTION: Using classroom meetings at the elementary level are useful for showing students how they can participate in classroom management, a form of government. From the beginning, it is important to describe how students will have the opportunity to enjoy privileges, but must also accept responsibilities. After this has been explained, students should be provided with opportunities to learn the relationship between privileges and responsibilities. For example, they may be given several options for completing a reading or writing assignment, in order to learn how to make reasonable and responsible decisions. As time passes, and students mature, the teacher may increase the amount of responsibility offered to students. In this manner, students will learn to appreciate their new role as a partici-

---

13. Jordan Brown and James Ciment, *learning Adventures in Citizenship: The Melting Pot* [online source] (pbskids.org, 2002, last accessed May 7 2002), http://www.pbs.org/wnet/newyork/laic/lessons/e4_t4–lp.html; Internet.

14. http://www.lessonplanspage.com/SSLAMusicCivilWarUnitC-patrioticSongs 46.htm

pant in the management process in the classroom. In time, each student can be encouraged to participate in and contribute to a "safe, dynamic, and healthy classroom community."[15]

TITLE: *Responsibility Collage/Bulletin Board*
DESCRIPTION: Developing a bulletin board or collage around the concept of RESPONSIBILITY, the class defines responsibility to self, school, and community in a visual representation. In this activity, students should cut out newspaper articles and magazine ads, collect or take pictures of their own community action, write poems, or come up with other visual representations to illustrate responsibility. Through this activity, students develop a sense of what responsibilities are, as well as where they themselves fit into the larger community.

TITLE: *Keep the Beat*
DESCRIPTION: Understanding the meaning behind the music is the rationale for this article. "Keep the Beat" encourages teachers to use music when teaching patriotism, but to take the music one step further. Begin by having students look up the meaning of the word "march." Then have students choose a march, patriotic song, or composer such as John Philip Sousa and research the meaning behind the music. Students may use a research log to gather historical information on the song and/or composer. Librarians and music teachers could also assist in planning and implementing this lesson. Once the students have completed their research, collect their reports to keep in a binder so they are available for current and future students to use.[16]

TITLE: *Literature in the Upper and Middle Grades*
DESCRIPTION: There are several trade books on the market that nicely supplement the curriculum of any teacher concerned with imparting to their students the necessary "knowledge, skills, and attitudes required to be an informed citizen." The last book, for example, offers information about the United States government, and other related

---

15. Devon Metzger, "Young Citizens: Partners in Classroom Management," *Social Studies & the Young Learner* 12, no. 4. (2000): 21–22.

16. Elizabeth Swarts, "Keep the Beat." *Teaching K–8* 32, no. 6 (2002): 62.

information. High on the list is a preamble to a High School Constitution, the Bill of Rights, and additional information that could add
to the Social Studies curriculum. Additionally, this book contains the
email addresses of members of Congress and the President.[17]

Some examples of children's literature that may be used include:

Gay W. Allen, ed., *American Poetry* (New York: Harper and Row,
1965)

Ellen Levin, *A Fence Away from Freedom* (New York: G.P. Putnan's
Sons, 1995)

Ken Mochizuki, *Heroes* (New York: Lee & Low Books, 1995)

Ann Rinaldi, *The Secret of Sarah Revere* (San Diego: Harcourt Brace
& Company, 1995)

Graham Salisbury, *Under the Blood-Red Sun* (New York: Scholastic,
1995)

Zilpha Keatley Snyder, *Cat Running* (New York: Dell Yearling,
1966)

Alan Schroeder, *Minty* (New York: Dial, 1966)

Stanley Jemy, *Big Annie of calumet: A True Story of the Industrial
Revolution* (New York: Crown Publishers, 1966)

Michael O. Tunnell, and George. W. Chilcoat, *The Children of Topza*
(New York: Holiday House, 1966)

Daniel Weizman, Take a Stand: Everything You Wanted to Know
About Government (Los Angeles: Price, Stern Sloan, 1966)

TITLE: *World Celebration: A UN Unit Kick-off*

DESCRIPTION: This lesson centers on the United Nations and culmi-
nates with a "Global Celebration" for UN Day, on or around October 24. Begin by having students locate the website for the United
Nations International School in Manhattan. In groups of two or
three, students choose one of four available school newsletters to pe-
ruse, and select articles to read and present to the rest of the class.
Assign students to move from the school website to the UN site, at
www.un.org. Here the students will expand their knowledge base

---

17. Alexa L. Sanderman and John F. Ahern, "More Children's Literature to
Promote Citizenship in the Upper and Middle Grades," *Social Studies & the Young
Learner* 10, no 2 (1997): 25–28.

and create a banner timeline of the UN from inception to current. This banner may be displayed in a public area of the school for all students to see. In addition to the banner, students can create a world map that highlights the UN nations and the dates in which they joined the UN.[18]

TITLE: *One People, One Nation; Exploring Unity through Flag Symbolism*
DESCRIPTION: This is a project where students have the opportunity to discuss the significance of the American flag, and then show their understanding by producing a flag of their own. To begin, engage students in a discussion about the American flag, including the history of the flag, and the reasons for the changes it has been through. Discuss the legends that have grown around the meaning of the colors of the flag. Show the class a flag from another country and relate its history to the class, being sure to mention any changes that have come about and the legends surrounding it. Be sure to note the commonalties in the flags and that the ideas and values the flags represent are universal. Have the students use a Venn diagram to illustrate the similarities and differences they have discovered through the discussion. These may include physical differences and similarities as well as the meanings behind the symbols and colors of each flag. Finally, discuss the values that Americans hold. After brainstorming some ideas, allow each student to draw a flag of their own design, with a caption explaining the significance of the designs on the flag.

TITLE: *Places Where I See the Flag*
DESCRIPTION: In this lesson, students will create a class book about the American Flag. Students should take photographs of Americans flags displayed in different ways and in different locations around town. Everyone in the class will contribute at least one page of the book they have completed either on their own or with someone else. Students should look for flags displayed at the town hall, local homes,

---

18. *United Nations International School* [online source] (Contact information: United Nations International School, 24–50 FDR Drive New York, NY 10010, last accessed May 7 2002), http://www.unis.org; Internet.; United Nations [online source] (New York: United Nations, 2000–2002 all rights reserved, last accessed May 7 2002), www.un.org.;Internet.

car bumper stickers, clothing, etc. Students may also ask people why they display the flag, and how they decided on the way they display it. At the end of the project, have students reflect on the completed book. How do the ways in which Americans display the flag reflect patriotism?

TITLE: *Citizenship Test*
DESCRIPTION: To teach students about citizenship, obtain a copy of the INS test for citizenship in the US. Explain that the person who takes this test needs to know certain information to show they will be loyal to their country. Have the students take the test and re-search the questions they didn't know; discuss why this is informa-tion every citizen should know. Follow up with discussion about why people from other countries want to live in the United States. Stu-dents can search the Internet, library, human resources, etc. to learn about the process of becoming a U.S. citizen and to determine what it means to be a citizen. A sample INS written test for citizen-ship may be obtained from the INS website at: http://citizenship.insexperts.com/instests.htm#civicstest.htm

TITLE: *Learning Citizenship through Rights and Responsibilities*
DESCRIPTION: Instruct students to define the words "rights" and "re-sponsibilities." Using a Venn diagram, have students brainstorm at least 8 rights and responsibilities that they have in school and place them in the appropriate place on the diagram. In a short essay, have them define these rights and responsibilities and discuss how they correlate with one another. As an extension of this assignment, have the students interview an adult to find out what their rights and re-sponsibilities are where they work. Students can create Venn dia-grams detailing workplace rights and responsibilities, or an American citizen's rights and responsibilities and explain how they are similar.

TITLE: *The Renewed Glory of Old Glory*
DESRIPTION: Students will investigate how the increase of patriotism as a reaction to national crisis can serve as both a uniting and a dividing force. Students will also discuss their views on the issue, and inter-view adults representing different generations to gauge their histori-cal perspectives. First, students will read *Flag Fever: The Paradox of Patriotism* by Blaine Harden, as a class. They will then discuss how

the events in this book pertain to what happened in the United States on September 11, 2001. As a class, students will then compile a list of interview questions they will use to interview adults from different eras. After the interviews are completed, students will discuss then compile their findings and creatively display them about the classroom.[19]

TITLE: *International Chat Sessions on Democracy*
DESCRIPTION: In order to familiarize students with democracy as not only a form of government, but as a creative and constructive process of active local and global community involvement, organize international "chat sessions" between students and teachers and students from other countries. Students can perform online surveys/discussions using, for example, the website for the "Global School Warehouse," to directly ask questions concerning government policies and the opinions of other children like themselves living under differing systems of government.[20]

TITLE: *Mock Trials: Truth, Justice, and the American Way*
DESCRIPTION: Holding "mock trials" based on issues of fairness and justice in a democratic community, students make judgments about appropriate social behavior, and are exposed to the difficulty of making decisions about what is right and wrong. This activity encourages children to explore their own values, while at the same time taking a look at the community at large. When performing the "mock trials," students play the roles of judge, jury, prosecution, and the accused. In this simulation the students act out the cases following a prepared script. Following each case, have a debriefing session in which students make the judgment and discuss the social issues brought up in the case.

---

19. The New York Times on the WEB Learning Network, *New York Times Daily Lesson Plan Page* [online source] (New York: The New York Times, 2002, last accessed May 7 2002), http://www.nytimes.com/learning/teachers/lessons/archive.html; Internet.

20. Elizabeth Anne Yeager, and Diane Yendol Silva, "Activities for Strengthening the Meaning for Democracy for Elementary Children," *The Social Studies* 93, no. 10 (2002) p. 18.

TITLE: Experiencing Prejudice

DESCRIPTION: This lesson is a good lead-in to a discussion of the difficult topic of *prejudice*. It could be used during Black History Month to introduce a discussion of Civil Rights, Rosa Parks' bus ride, slavery and the Underground Railroad. The lesson also could be used as an introductory lesson to a discussion of the Holocaust, Japanese internment camps, and many other topics of historical importance.

Before the Lesson

Prepare two sets of ribbons; each set should be a different color. Provide one ribbon—equally divided between two colors—to each student.

The Activity

As each student enters the class, pin one colored ribbon to his or her shirt. (Ask permission before pinning. Students who prefer to not wear the ribbon can display it in some other way.) When students have settled down, ask them if they would like to take part in an experiment.

Proceed by setting up a spelling bee, with students forming teams based on the color of their ribbons. The catch is that all students wearing one color ribbon will be given very easy words to spell; students with the other color ribbon will be given very difficult words.

As the spelling bee progresses, you might award a simple prize, such as a lollipop or pencil, to each student who correctly spells a word. (If you do that, however, you should be prepared to give all students the same reward at the end of the activity.)

Very quickly, students should notice what is going on. When they do, give them an opportunity to tell you how it makes them feel. Ask students who were on the team given difficult words how they felt knowing they would get a difficult word because they were wearing a certain color ribbon. Ask the others how they felt.

When the introductory activity is complete, you might begin a discussion of an historical event in which people were singled out for unfair treatment.[21]

---

21. Pauline Finlay, [online source] (Holy Trinity Elementary School, Torbay, Newfoundland (Canada), last accessed June 5 2004), http://www. education-world.com/a_tsl/archives/04–1/lesson006.shtml; internet.

8

Construct-Your-Own Elementary Social Studies Unit from a Potpourri of Lesson Plans

The principle goal of education is to create men who are capable of doing new things, not simply of repeating what other generations have done.

JEAN PIAGET

The importance of unit planning cannot be underestimated when discussing issues surrounding patriotism and its relationship to good citizenship in the elementary social studies classroom. Individual lessons focusing on concepts such as respect, tolerance, and acceptance have an important role in the daily curriculum. By allowing time to investigate and reflect on ideas in depth, teachers can help students broaden accompanying concepts so they can take them beyond the walls of the classroom and into the larger community and ultimately make a difference.

This chapter contains a wide variety of lesson plan outlines that may be grouped together, modified for grade level, and/or supplemented to form a cohesive unit with a focus on concepts of patriotism and its relationship to good citizenship. It is also suggested that teachers consult the abstracts in Chapters six and seven for additional ideas on socio-economic, educational, cultural, and racial diversity in order to develop a complete unit reflecting the philosophy inherent with *Teaching New Patriotism in the 21st Century.*

It is especially important that teachers make an effort to explain the meaning of patriotism at the beginning of the unit, regardless of which combination of lesson plans is selected. A good place to start is with a discussion of the original definition that first appeared in 1676, and was simply explained as "love for your country." Students should be encouraged to think in terms of patriotism in a broad context that includes all those things that could in some way prove beneficial to a stronger, safer, and accepting United States for everyone. Discussion of this relationship with each lesson should help students achieve a deeper understanding of patriotism and its relationship to citizenship, and should help them learn to apply these ideals in their daily lives.

Making Classroom Rules

Through this lesson, students will learn the importance of having laws in the classroom, community, state and nation. They will also learn about what may happen when no laws exist. Keeping in mind themes of citizenship, students will create their own rules for the classroom.

Learning Outcomes: As a result of having completed this lesson, students will be able to understand the importance of having laws in a society, to explain consequences of not having laws and rules, and to write their own rules for the classroom, using principles from themes of citizenship.

Begin by asking students what life at home/school/society might be like without rules. At first, students may think it would be great, but encourage them to think about chaos. Remind students that even though they would not have to follow rules, neither would anyone else, and that could cause trouble.

From that discussion, ask students why we need to have rules at home, in school, and in our society. "Do you think that our classroom should have rules?" "Do you think that you should have a say in the rules since you are the ones who will be following them?" "Do you think that I should have a say in the rules since I will be following them, too?"

Next, ask students to think about different themes of citizenship and brainstorm a list of rules. Examine the recorded list, and determine which rules are best for the classroom. Once the rules are written on a large sheet of paper, each student will come to the front of the room and sign his/her name saying that they are in agreement with the rules and will do their best to obey them.

Finally, discuss the new set of classroom rules. "Are the rules fair for everyone?" "Are there any other rules you think should be added/deleted?" "What are some ways that you can follow the rules and encourage others to do the same?" "What are some rules that you have or should have in your home?"

Interpreting the Pledge of Allegiance

This lesson requires students to take an analytical approach toward the Pledge of Allegiance. After discussing its vocabulary, students will interpret the pledge and rewrite it in their own words.

Learning Outcomes: As a result of having completed this lesson, students will be able to make patriotic connections to the pledge that reflect civic values, past and present.

- Place students into groups and distribute to each group a copy of the Pledge of Allegiance.
- Assign each group of students to identify vocabulary and/or ideas in the Pledge of Allegiance that they either do not understand or that need clarification.
- Provide students with an opportunity to research the origins of the pledge to find the answers to their questions. As they discover the answers, they should record them in their notebooks.
- Bring the class back together as a whole and make a master list of the vocabulary and ideas outlined by the students. Lead a discussion to assure that each student has the correct answers.

In conclusion, assign students to rewrite the pledge in terms that they understand, being careful not to lose the essential meaning of the Pledge of Allegiance. In addition, assign students to interpret or explain the meaning of the values contained in the Pledge of Allegiance.

An Introduction to Understanding Poverty and Hunger

In this lesson, students will experience an unequal distribution of food and share their feelings. Students will participate in a discussion on the global hunger issue and then have the opportunity to raise money for UNICEF if they so choose.

Learning Outcomes: As a result of having completed this lesson, students will develop an awareness of poverty and hunger and be able to define hunger (a condition in which a person of any age does not get enough food to provide nutrition for a healthy and happy life). Students will thus gain tolerance and acceptance of socio-economic diversity.

Contact UNICEF and obtain enough cardboard collection boxes for each child. Before class begins, unequally distribute M&Ms into the empty boxes. Some boxes should have just a few or no M&Ms while others contain twenty or more (quantities should widely vary).

- Hand out boxes, directing children not to open them yet.
- Have all students at the same time open their boxes to see what's inside. Notice the range of emotions. Allow students to reveal to their classmates how many M&Ms they have received.
- Once students have discovered the unequal distribution, ask questions such as:
  1. How did it feel to see your friends have more candy than you?
  2. For those who had a lot of M&Ms, did any of you think you should share your snack with fellow classmates with few or none?
- Remind students how important it is to help others less fortunate if able. Discuss food and clothing drives. Compare the importance of food, clothing and shelter to toys and entertainment. Students may be unaware of hunger locally or that children are often innocently affected by poverty.
- Remember the sensitivity of this subject; some students may have experienced hunger firsthand.

Encourage students to raise money for UNICEF with the boxes they have received. Students could also research nations with large impoverished populations and brainstorm ways they can help. Remind them that they can make a difference in a global effort to defeat poverty and hunger.

Understanding a Map of the United States

In this lesson, students will look at a map of the United States. Together, we will locate New York, (or the state of your choice) and talk about how there are fifty states, and discuss borders.

Learning Outcomes: As a result of having completed this lesson, students will know that the United States is made up of fifty states, be able to name and locate New York on a map, understand that there are borders between states and countries, and to identify states that border New York, Canada, and Mexico. (Change the state of interest to match the state in which the students live.)

- Provide each individual student with a world map to consult along with the larger map in the front of the classroom. Begin by reviewing a world map, and discussing the location of the United States, Canada, Mexico, and the world's oceans.
- Next, focus the students' attention to the map of the United States. Ask the students if they know the name of the state in which they live. Have someone come up to the map and point it out to the rest of the class. Direct each student to point out the state on his or her individual map.
- Call students' attention to the lines that separate each state (borders). Ask students to identify the states that border their state, the states that border Mexico, and those that border Canada.
- Divide the students into small groups and have them complete a puzzle map that is divided into regions.

As students work on the puzzles, ask comprehension questions such as "What are the parts of the United States called?" "How many states are there?" "What are the lines called that divide the states and countries?"

What It Means to be a Good Citizen

As part of the effort to explain what a citizen is, students will first be shown on the overhead projector the definition of a citizen from a standard dictionary. For example: A native or naturalized member of a state or nation, or, an inhabitant of a city or town. From this beginning point, discussion will extend to describing a good citizen.

Learning Outcomes: As a result of having completed this lesson, students will be able to define what it means to be a citizen.

- Students should first brainstorm with a partner the attributes of a good citizen and record their ideas in their notebooks. Guide the students to share the attributes of citizenship they have identified and record the list.
- After the list is complete, ask students to circle the attributes that best describe them. They should then write a paragraph explaining why they believe that they are good citizens.

As a culminating activity, assign students to create their own "Good Citizen Award." Each award should include a picture and one or more paragraphs justifying the award. Students should be encouraged to use books, newspapers, and the Internet as research tools.

Differences and Similarities

This lesson will enable students to explore the distinctions and connections between themselves and other people. After meeting and creating lists in partners, the class will create a list to examine their results.

Learning Outcomes: As a result of this lesson, students will discover how they have more in common with others than they may have thought, while also celebrating their unique differences.

- Place students into partners and provide a copy of a blank Venn diagram.
- Instruct the students to choose a circle and place their name above the circle.
- Encourage the students to write down in the separate parts of the circle the things that make them different from each other and in the portion of the diagram where the circles overlap to write what makes them similar. Promote positive brainstorming and encourage students to make a balanced diagram with at least as many similarities as differences.
- Bring the class back together to discuss each group's findings. Make two columns on a large piece of paper and have the students present their results. Discuss how differences make people special, and unique, while similarities tie them together. Note that even though the class has many differences, there are just as many similarities.

In conclusion, have the students choose what they think their partner's most interesting difference or similarity is and create a card celebrating this attribute.

Creating a Citizenship Tree

This lesson engages students in a discussion of citizenship, culminating in the creation of a "Classroom Citizenship Tree." Students will decorate the tree with ideas for helping others.

Learning Outcomes: As a result of having completed this lesson, students will be able to describe the ways in which they, as good citizens, are able to help others in their community.

- Begin by asking students to identify the kinds of things they do to help members of their families.
- Next, write the terms, "citizenship" and "service to others" on the board. Discuss and define each term, using the dictionary as needed.

- Provide students with the prompt (written on a "leaf") "I can help others by _____." Then discuss several ways students may help others. Students will then complete the prompt by choosing a way in which they can reasonably help others.

Ask students to present their ideas to the class. Lead a brief discussion with students on how they can best implement the ideas contained in their sentences. Finally, display the "leaves" on top of the trunk of the Citizenship Tree.

Independence Day

The purpose of this lesson is for students to learn how to read and find dates on a calendar.

Learning Outcomes: As a result of having completed this lesson, students will develop an understanding about holidays, in particular, Independence Day and its meaning.

- Hand out small calendars to each student and ask what calendars are and why we use them. Call students' attention to a holiday and ask them what holidays they know that we celebrate. After reviewing their list, ask them when we celebrate each of these holidays and have them write them on their calendars.
- If it does not come up in the initial discussion, ask if anyone knows when and why we celebrate Independence Day on the Fourth of July.
- Explain to students that Independence Day is our country's birthday. For many years, the United States belonged to another country called England, which is on the continent of Europe.
- Explain that on July 4th, in the year 1776, our country declared its independence from England. After that, it didn't belong to England anymore.
- Ask students how we usually celebrate the Fourth of July. Play *America the Beautiful* and ask students to listen the first time and sing the second time.

Finally, have students brainstorm a list of other additional national holidays that we celebrate that are unique to America. Point them to Martin Luther King Day, President's Day, Memorial Day, Labor Day, Columbus Day, Veteran's Day and Thanksgiving. (This last activity may be used to provide the basis for a whole sequence of additional Lessons. See the lesson titled *The First Thanksgiving* or the lesson titled *Holidays in Our Country* for additional lesson plan ideas.)

Understanding State Maps

In this lesson, students will learn to read a map of New York State. They will also learn how to read a map key, observing the symbols for cities and state capitals.

Learning Outcomes: As a result of having completed this lesson, students will understand how to use map keys to identify symbols on a map, understand that map keys contain symbols that stand for real things and places, and to understand that cities are located in states. (Change the state of interest to match to match the state in which the students live.)

- Begin by discussing some of the characteristics of the states—such as which state is the smallest state and which is the largest.
- Provide each student with a map of the United States. Ask the following questions: "What state do we live in? What country is it a part of?" "Which is bigger: Our state or the United States?" Describe the area of the country in which the state is located (e.g. northeast, southwest).
- Direct students' attention to the map legend, and discuss what a legend is and what the different symbols mean. Point out the symbol for a city and ask students to name some cities in their state. Be sure they understand that not all cities are listed on the map.
- Ask students to use the key and find the capital of their state and several others. Also have them look for rivers on the map, and try to determine the number of rivers in their state.

As a follow up activity, make a map of the classroom, using a legend.

Coming to America

Throughout history, America has been seen as a land of freedom and opportunity. This lesson will explore the history of why and how people came to America.

Learning Outcomes: As a result of having completed this lesson, students will be able to interpret the meaning of America as a "melting pot," to trace the movement of immigrants into America and to list the nationality of their ancestors.

- Using a map of the United States, tell the students that a long, long time ago no one, not even Native Americans, lived in America. Ask them how they think people got here, and record their responses on the board. Re-read the student-generated list to the class to recall all of the possible ways people could have come to America. Tell the class that we will be reading a book that answers the question: How did people come to America?
- Show the cover of *Coming to America* by Betsy Maestro. Point to the picture of the Statue of Liberty. Ask if anyone knows what the statue is called (the Statue of Liberty) and what *liberty* means (freedom).
- Read *Coming to America*. While reading, pause for understanding of the words *immigrants*—people who come to a new land to make their home; *melting pot*—many cultures or ways of life from all of the different immigrants have blended together to make our country. Explain that America is called the melting pot because all of these people from different countries and cultures have come here and blended together as Americans.
- Ask if anyone has made Rice Krispie Treats before. Discuss what happens when you put the marshmallows and butter in the pan together and put the pan on the burner. Make Rice Krispie Treats according to the recipe on the cereal box. Allow children to help prepare the recipe as you see fit.

- Emphasize the "melting pot" idea when the marshmallows and butter have blended together. Show the students the new mixture. See if students can use the metaphor that the Rice Krispie Treats are like people in that they become "fused" together and take on a new shape and a new flavor. By themselves, the butter, cereal, and marshmallows taste different. The mixture is like a community where all kinds of people come together.
- With the help of the class, retell the story using the World Map to show the movements of the immigrants. Relate the following while at the same time showing the movement on the map with your finger or a pointer: Thousands of years ago the Native Americans' ancestors came from Asia, across a land bridge into what is now Alaska. Ask students: What are *ancestors*? The ancestors of the Native Americans traveled all around and settled in both North and South America.
- Later people came from Europe to America. Some people were brought here from Africa. Later more and more people came. They landed in New York, Boston and Philadelphia. Later, people moved west and settled. People started coming from Asia.
- The students should ask parents or other relatives their ancestry to find out where their ancestors may have traveled from to get to America. Allow the students, with teacher's guidance, to mark the map with pushpins in the locations from which their ancestors came. Some students will require more than one pushpin. Share your own ancestry with the class.

Allow time for everyone to examine the diversity, or lack of diversity, in the countries of origin of the students ancestors. If there is not much diversity, discuss possible reasons why so many of one nationality settled in the same area.

Responsibilities of Citizenship

Americans have responsibilities as citizens as well as rights. It is important for children to learn about these responsibilities at an early age. Students will be able to get along better in their classroom, neighborhood, and community if they do their duty as good citizens.

Learning Outcomes: As a result of having completed this lesson, students will be able to define the term *responsible* and to list duties and responsibilities of American citizens.

- Begin by writing the words "respond" and "able" on the board and ask for definitions. Explain that you are able to respond, you are responsible. Discuss students' responsibilities at home and list responses on the board. As family members, we all have duties or responsibilities.
- Review our rights as American citizens. Along with those rights we have something else: responsibilities or duties. Americans have to be able to respond to the duties of being an American citizen.
- Have students brainstorm a list of possible citizen duties and record their responses. Probe for responses that include obeying laws, respecting the rights and property of others, helping police, serving on a jury, paying taxes, voting, staying informed, and conserving America's natural resources.
- Explain that a country or community is held together because citizens do their duties. Ask students what it would be like if people did not do these duties and record responses. Tell the class that they are going to make a community chain. Chains are made of links. When the links are attached to each other, they make a chain that is strong and hard to break. Pass out three or four strips of construction paper to each student. Ask them to write one duty of a citizen on each strip, then link them together to make a chain.

Describe the way in which everyone worked together to make the chain very long. If students had made their chains individually, it would have taken a longer time to make it the same length. Display the community chain in the classroom.

Resources Found in the United States

In this lesson, students will learn about the many resources of the United States. They will also learn the difference between natural, man-made, renewable, and nonrenewable resources.

Learning Outcomes: As a result of having completed this lesson, students will know that the United States has many kinds of resources, be able to name several resources found in the US, be able to distinguish between natural and man-made resources, and be able to distinguish between renewable and nonrenewable resources.

- Show students several pictures of resources and ask them to name the objects. As they name the resources, list them on the board in two columns, one for natural resources and one for man-made resources.
- Discuss what resources are: items that provide materials to make things, provide food, or provide power, for example, water, coal, and trees. Discuss the difference between the items on the two lists, focusing on the distinction between natural and manmade resources. Have the students add to the list and indicate the appropriate column in which to list their resources.
- Further divide the list by categorizing resources as renewable and non-renewable. Discuss the advantages of using renewable resources.

Divide the students into groups and provide them with magazines from which to cut out pictures of resources. Have them glue their pictures onto construction paper pages labeled "Natural" and "Manmade." Students should also indicate which resources are renewable and which are not.

The Bill of Rights

The Bill of Rights ensures that all Americans are afforded certain rights. Immigrants who wanted to become American citizens came to our country to be able to enjoy these rights.

Learning Outcomes: As a result of having completed this lesson, students will begin to develop an understanding of the Bill of Rights and the concepts of voting and trial by jury.

- Note: This portion of the lesson is written with the assumption that all of the children in class are American citizens. If this is not the case, you may acknowledge that there are differences, but these are the rights of Americans.
- Begin with a brief discussion of our nationality. Reinforce the idea that even if we went to Australia, for example, and someone asked our nationality, we would say "American."
- Ask the class: What is a citizen? Many immigrants came here to become citizens because American citizens have certain rights. Many of the countries they came from did not have these rights.
- Have students fold a piece of construction paper in half, in half again, and in half again so that the paper is divided into eight sections, with four rows horizontally. Have each student write on the top of the page *MY RIGHTS,* and, explain that they will be illustrating the boxes with eight of their rights as US citizens.

Guide students through the following rights, providing an appropriate explanation, and encouraging them to sketch a picture for each: freedom of religion, freedom of speech, the right to live where you want to and the right to own things, the right to meet when and where you want to, the right to go to a good school, the right to vote, the right to have a trial by jury, and the right to keep people from searching your home without a search warrant. Discuss the rights we have in the classroom, school, and neighborhood.

Preserving America's Resources

Protecting and preserving our natural resources is one of the responsibilities of an American citizen. In this lesson, this idea is presented in a way that children can relate it to their own lives.

Learning Outcomes: As a result of having completed this lesson, students will be able to define *natural resources* and give examples of natural resources, and to generate ideas of ways to conserve, preserve, and protect our natural resources.

- Name three or four natural resources (water, coal, trees, copper) and ask what they have in common. Read the book *Our Planet:*

Earth by Lisa Feder-Feitel (Scholastic Books: New York, 1993) pausing at page 24. Ask what the words "natural resources" mean by considering each word in turn. Remind students that it is everyone's responsibility to take care of our resources.

- Continue reading the book, pausing at pages 30—31 and ask, "What can you do to help?" Brainstorm and record students' responses. Discuss what we get from trees and what we could do to save them and how we use water and ways to conserve it.

Pass out "Conservation Journals" to the students and have them write and illustrate their conservation ideas. They should label the natural resources that they are addressing on the page before writing their helpful idea, for example, "Water is a natural resource. Don't let the water run when you brush your teeth."

Courage

This lesson is designed to teach students about courage in a way that they may never have thought before. Students will learn how courage contributes to the themes of citizenship, and how they can make a difference by being courageous. They will also learn the importance of historical figures showing courage and how they changed society.

Learning Outcomes: As a result of having completed this lesson, students will be able to understand the meaning of the word 'courage' as it applies to the themes of citizenship and why it is an important characteristic; to give examples of famous historical figures who showed courage; and to give examples of themselves showing courage.

- Begin the lesson by asking students what courage means. Tell them that there are many different kinds of courage and many ways to show it, but prompt for responses that include standing up for what you believe is right.
- Read the book *Happy Birthday, Martin Luther King*, by Jean Marzollo and ask students to check for similarities with their initial ideas on courage. Now ask "Did Dr. King show courage? How?"

"Is his example of courage different from someone who sticks up for a kid who's being bullied on the playground? How?"

- Guide students to understand how much courage it took for Dr. King to stand up for what he believed in, and that not many people agreed with him at that time. Brainstorm a list of some characteristics of courageous people.
- Now, divide students into small groups and have each group choose one additional person in history who showed courage. They will do a small amount of research on this person, and give a brief presentation to the class about why this person was courageous and how he/she affected society.
- Engage students in a discussion of the presentations. "How did these people show courage?" "Why was it important that they took courageous steps toward change?" "How might our country be different if we didn't have courageous leaders?" "How are these leaders similar? How are their causes similar?" Make a connection between courage and the other five themes of citizenship.

As closure, have the students write in their journals, stating their own definitions of courage. They should write about the person they researched and how he/she showed courage, giving an example of when they themselves showed courage.

I Know My Rights!

Students will learn about the rules, rights, and responsibilities that they have at home, in the classroom, and as Americans, and how understanding those rules, rights and responsibilities is part of being a citizen.

Learning Outcomes: As a result of having completed this lesson, students will learn that part of being a citizen is having an awareness of the rules, rights, and responsibilities of their community and country as well as those at their home and school.

- Read: Sommer, Carl. (2000). *Mayor For A Day*. Houston: Advance Publishing, Inc.

- Discuss what would happen if we had no rules and no responsibilities. What would we do? Would this be good, or would we have problems? Discuss some possible problems (e.g. someone took your brand new set of markers) and what we would do in light of those problems. Remember that if no one has any responsibilities, there would also be nothing the teacher could do.
- Without rules, we also have no rights. Brainstorm what rights are and record student responses. Read the book *Mayor For A Day*, by Carl Sommer. Encourage students to be thinking about important rules, rights, and responsibilities as they listen.
- Lead students in a discussion about rules, rights, and responsibilities in the classroom community. Have students work in small groups to answer the question "In school, what are some of our responsibilities?" A representative from each group should record these on the board under the heading *Classroom Responsibilities*.
- Next, have students decide in groups what rules are important to follow, and have a representative to the board to write the rules under the heading *Classroom Rules*.
- Students should now use the responsibilities they developed to determine the rights they have as citizens of the classroom. For example, if they said that a responsibility is to respect others, then they have the *right* to *be* respected by other people. Record these in a third column under the heading *Classroom Rights*.
- In conclusion, have the students vote on what they perceive to be the most important responsibilities, rules, and rights, and use them to create a Classroom Constitution using the headings *We Have the Right To . . .* and *Our Responsibilities Include . . .* which is ultimately *Signed By . . .* the entire class and teacher.

As closure, review why it is important that we have rules, responsibilities, and rights and consequences when a person goes against another person's rights.

Oh Say Can You See

Students will learn about the history of the national anthem, *The Star-Spangled Banner*, and other patriotic songs as symbols of the United States.

Learning Outcomes: As a result of having completed this lesson, students will be able to identify the "Star-Spangled Banner" as the national anthem of the United States of America, to appreciate that part of being a citizen is being able to recognize and recite the national anthem, as well as other patriotic songs that represent the United States, and to understand the symbolism behind the national anthem and the use of songs as a symbol for the United States.

- Begin the lesson by asking for examples of the symbols of our country.
- Next, play the Start Spangled Banner, and ask questions to guide students' thinking. "How many of you have ever been to a baseball or football game, or watched one on TV?" "What is the first thing that everyone does right before the game starts?" If necessary, tell students that everyone in the stadium stands up and takes off their hats. "What do they do then?" "Does anyone know what that song is called?" "Why do you think we sing that song instead of something else, such as *Take Me Out to the Ballgame*?"
- Ask if students know another way to refer to the *Star-Spangled Banner*, and explain that our national anthem is just as much a symbol of our country as our flag, the Statue of Liberty, the American Bald Eagle, and the Liberty Bell. Ask for an explanation of what it means to be a symbol of our country.
- Now, show students a reproduction of the original sheet music of the *Star Spangled Banner,* and provide them with the following basic historical information. Francis Scott Key originally wrote the *Star-Spangled Banner* as a poem (show picture of flag of 1812). In 1916, President Woodrow Wilson proclaimed it as the national anthem, and in 1931, Congress made it our official national anthem.
- Remind students there are other songs that we sing that are symbols of our country. Ask for suggestions, prompting toward *My Country Tis of Thee* and *America the Beautiful*, and play each of these songs for the class.

As closure, have students brainstorm ways in which these songs are all similar and the ways in which they are different. Have them record their ideas on a Venn diagram.

Following Laws

After students learn the importance of having laws, they will conduct an experiment to see the importance of following laws, by observing the reactions of cars to pedestrians at a busy crosswalk. Students will actually see the effects of laws in action.

Learning Outcomes: As a result of having completed this lesson, students will understand the importance of following laws in the classroom and community.

- Begin by asking students the importance of obeying laws of the classroom and society. Ask what would happen if no one obeyed the laws.
- Now divide students into groups. Tell them that they will be conducting an experiment to see how many cars yield to pedestrians at a popular crosswalk. Each group will observe a different crosswalk.
- As a group, students will make a prediction about how many cars will yield to pedestrians, and then decide how they will collect and record data. Groups may assign individual roles to students.
- With the help of parent volunteers or other adults, students may collect and record their data. Once this is done, students will return to the classroom to interpret the data by first graphing their results on a chart of their choice. They should calculate the percentages of cars that did and did not yield to pedestrians. Then students will then give a short presentation to the class explaining their methodology and data interpretation.
- After each group has had the opportunity to present their results, lead the students in a discussion of the importance of traffic safety laws, and some hypothetical consequences of people not following laws. Encourage students to make a connection between the experiment and following rules in the classroom. Finally, students will discuss how following laws relates to different themes of citizenship.

As a follow up, students could write a brief entry into their journals about how they are going to make themselves more aware of the laws in school and society, and the consequences that result from not following these laws.

Responsibility

This lesson will teach students about responsibility by using the example of Marty's character in the book and movie *Shiloh*. Students will learn the importance of being responsible for yourself and the things you care about, as well as taking responsibility for your actions. They will also see the benefits of responsibility.

Learning Outcomes: As a result of having completed this lesson, students will be able to understand the meaning of the word responsibility and provide an example, to understand why responsibility is an important characteristic, and how it ties in with the other themes of citizenship, and to describe one way in which they show responsibility.

- Ask students about the word responsibility—what does it mean? How can we find out? Have a student read the dictionary definition, and ask students to put the definition into their own words.
- Now show students a video clip from the movie *Shiloh*, and ask them to note the ways in which Marty demonstrates responsibility. Afterwards, make a list of student ideas on the board.
- Discuss responsibility and its applications to our own lives, by asking questions such as "Why is it important to be responsible and demonstrate that quality to others?" "How is it beneficial to you and others?" "In what instances would you want others to show responsibility to you?" "Can you think of an example where you or someone you know has shown responsibility?" "Adults have a lot of responsibility. Do you think that kids have a lot, too?" "How does taking responsibility for your actions tie in with honesty?" "With compassion?" "With respect?"

As closure, ask students to give definitions of responsibility in their own words. Tell them to think about how important it is to prove to themselves and others that they are responsible, and the benefits of such actions. Students should be encouraged to take every opportunity to prove to others that they are responsible.

Other Symbols of the United States

In this lesson, students will begin to learn about the United States. They will learn the importance of our country's symbols such as the Presidential Seal, Liberty Bell, American Bald Eagle and the Statue of Liberty. For a separate lesson on the American flag, see the lesson plan *You're a Grand Old Flag.*

Learning Outcomes: As a result of having completed this lesson, students will be able to identify our country as the United States, to define the word "symbol," to identify and name selected symbols of the United States.

- Display pictures of everyday symbols such as the "No" sign (e.g. "No parking"), a traffic light, male and female restroom signs, etc. After telling the class that each of these pictures is a symbol and that a symbol is a picture or object that reminds us of something else, ask the students to identify these symbols and name other symbols that they see frequently.

Discuss that we live in a country called the United States, and that our flag is a symbol of our country. Review with students the symbolism of the flag (e.g. What the stars stand for. What the stripes stand for.)

Ask students if they can think of other symbols of the United States and record the list for the class to see.

Next, show pictures of the Statue of Liberty, the Liberty Bell, American Bald Eagle, and the Presidential Seal.

Probe toward understanding of the meaning of each such as the Liberty Bell and the Statue of Liberty. For example, ask what *liberty* means.

Ask students why they think it is important for a country such as the United States to have symbols, and why it is important that we learn the meaning of American symbols.

Wrap up by asking students if they can think of any symbols that represent their school or community and record their responses. Have school and community symbols available and discuss their meaning.

Quilting Kindness

Through the reading of Jeff Brumbeau's *The Quiltmaker's Gift*, students will learn how to turn the advantages they have been given in life into ways to help others.

Learning Outcomes: As a result of having completed this lesson, students will discover the joy of giving to others in need, see that they can make a difference in others' lives, and be inspired to continue giving to those in need.

- Read to the students *The Quiltmaker's Gift* by Jeff Brumbeau.
- Initiate a group discussion after reading the book. Ask questions such as, "Why do you think the quiltmaker would only give to those who did not have much?" "Why do you think the king did not want to give his things away at first?" "What do you think made the king so happy after he started to give his things away?" "What are some things we could do to help others?"
- Hand out square pieces of paper with markers and crayons and have every child write one thing that they could do for someone in need.

In conclusion, after each student has completed the objective on his/her paper, have each child stick their "patch" onto the wall, creating a class "quilt of kindness" to be seen and admired by everyone.

The First Thanksgiving

Students will learn about the holidays and the symbols associated with those holidays that are unique to America, and how an understanding of those holidays is part of being a citizen.

Learning Outcomes: As a result of having completed this lesson, students will be able to understand that part of being a citizen is having an awareness of the holidays, celebrations, and symbols that represent America; to show an appreciation of knowing that America is a unique country with unique holidays, celebrations, and symbols; to understand how Thanksgiving celebrations have changed since 1621; to appreciate the reasons for celebrating Thanksgiving; and to identify types of food eaten at the first Thanksgiving.

- Begin the lesson by talking about important holidays that fall during the school year, focusing on Thanksgiving. Tell students that although we get several days off to celebrate Thanksgiving, students in other countries do not get days off at that time. Because Thanksgiving is an American holiday, it is important for all citizens of America to know what Thanksgiving is and why we celebrate it.
- Ask students to think about the name "Thanksgiving," and give ideas of why we celebrate it. Brainstorm and list the images that the word "Thanksgiving" brings to mind.
- Next, read a letter written by Edward Winslow, one of the Pilgrims, describing some of the foods that they ate at the first Thanksgiving. Read the letter once while students listen, then read it a second time, having them write down the names of the foods mentioned.

Have students compile a list of the foods they eat at Thanksgiving dinner. Discuss the ways in which these foods are similar to or different from those eaten in 1621. Note too, any images that are similar to those they mentioned earlier. (See lesson on *National Holidays* for additional lesson plan ideas.)

Your Role as a Citizen

This lesson will make students aware of their roles and responsibilities as citizens of the United States, and of the importance of those roles and responsibilities. Students will also learn what they can do to be better citizens.

Learning Outcomes: As a result of having completed this lesson, students will understand the many roles, rights, and responsibilities they have as citizens and family members, understand why it is important to fulfill their roles, rights, and responsibilities, be able to list two things they are doing now and two things they could be doing in order to be a good citizen. Also, they will be able to explain how their roles as citizens tie in with themes of citizenship.

Use the following questions to guide students' thinking about being a citizen in the U.S. "What does it mean to be a citizen?" "What kind of privileges do we have?" "What kind of responsibilities to our country do we have?"

- Next, read a short passage about citizenship in our country, having students read along silently. Discuss some of the roles that we have in our community. Prompt students to think of their roles as a family member, or a member of the community, and discuss why it is important for citizens to have responsibilities.
- "Think about what might happen if nobody ever took responsibility for anything." "How would people do their jobs?"
- Discuss how life would be if law enforcement officials, teachers, or doctors were irresponsible toward their jobs. Ask students what their jobs are, such as paper routes, babysitting, or being a good student, and what they must do in order to work responsibly.
- Now, discuss the difference between rights and responsibilities. Be certain that students understand the difference by handing out a chart that gives some examples. Ask students if they can add anything in either category. Have students discuss in groups some of the rights and responsibilities that they have at home and at school.

As closure, ask students how themes of citizenship help people become better citizens. They may then write in their journals about their roles in the community, answering the following questions: "What are two things that you do now that contribute to your community?" "What are two things that you could be doing to be a good citizen?"

Fostering Tolerance and Acceptance of the Handicapped

In this lesson, students will experience physical limitations that impair their ability to complete a jigsaw puzzle. By working with another student who has a different "disability" (blindfolded, unable to use arms, etc.), students will cooperatively perform the task by helping one another and appropriately adapting. Conclude with a class discussion of the many ways in which a handicap affects one's life.

Learning Outcomes: As a result of having completed this lesson, students will develop tolerance and acceptance of individuals with disabilities by experiencing some of the difficulties and limitations associated with various handicaps. By cooperating with their partners, students will recognize the value of both reliance on and patience with people of varying abilities.

- Provide each set of partners with a jigsaw puzzle (difficulty level should be relatively low). Instruct students to complete the puzzles together, noticing the ease of the task.
- One partner will then be blindfolded (similar to blindness) while the other is limited to the use of only his/her eyesight and speech (similar to paralysis).
- Next, ask the students to complete their puzzle again, this time while trying to adapt to their new "disability". The blindfolded students will have to listen closely as their partners direct their actions to complete the puzzle.
- Call students' attention to any emotions they are feeling as they perform the task that was much easier just moments earlier. Ask the students: How important is it to be patient while working with your partner? What difficulties are you encountering?
- Reverse roles if time allows.

Once students have completed the puzzles, ask comprehension questions such as: What does it mean to be handicapped? How do you think people get disabilities? Address both mental and physical handicaps and also those disabilities that may not be visible. Can you catch a disability? How do handicapped people adapt and adjust to their environments (ex: sign language, wheelchairs, seeing-eye dogs)? Use students' answers to emphasize the importance of tolerance and acceptance.

A worthwhile follow-up activity could include researching well-known individuals with disabilities, such as Helen Keller or Christopher Reeves.

American Heroes and Heroines

In this lesson students will learn about American heroes and heroines and the qualities that help define individuals as heroes and heroines.

Learning Outcomes: As a result of having completed this lesson, students will be able to identify selected American heroes and heroines and to identify the qualities that help define individuals as heroes and heroines.

- Begin by asking students to identify their personal heroes or heroines.
- Ask students to explain why they identified each as a personal hero or heroine. Make a list of the qualities.
- Ask students to compile a list of heroes and heroines in American history. The list might include: George Washington, Betsy Ross, Martin Luther King Jr., Cesar Chavez, Rosa Parks, Molly Pitcher, Davy Crockett, Sacagawea, etc.
- After a complete list has been drawn, divide the names among groups of students and ask that they start a KWL chart on each personality, filling in what students know about each and what they would like to know about each.
- Next, ask groups of students to research their assigned personality, completing the "L" portion of their chart, asking that they focus on the qualities that identify their assigned personality as a hero or heroine. Have groups discuss their findings as a class.

As a concluding activity, have students compare qualities they felt helped to identify their assigned personality as a hero or heroine with the qualities they believed their personal heroes and heroines possessed.

You're a Grand Old Flag

In this lesson, students learn various facts about the flag of the United States of America, including its history.

Learning Outcomes: As a result of having completed this lesson, students will be able to recognize the flag in various familiar places. Students will also learn and recite the song: "You're a Grand Old Flag."

- Begin by discussing everyday symbols that the students would recognize such as traffic lights and Pokemon balls. Ask students what they think of when they see these things and what they represent.
- Ask students if anyone knows how many stars are on the American Flag and what the stars stand for. Also, ask how many stripes there are and what the stripes stand for. Discuss the symbolism of the flag and show pictures of the flag at various times in our country's history.
- Now put the students into groups of four or five and hand out a flag packet to each group, asking the students to identify as many flags as they can. Have students circle the American flag.
- Ask the students where they have seen the flag displayed (classrooms, schools, office building, naval vessel, the White House, the Capitol, parades, etc.). Discuss what the flag stands for.
- Provide each group with pictures of the American flag at various times in history and have them make inferences on the flags based on the number of Stars and Stripes. Explain some of the history of these different American flags.

Gather students in a circle and hand out copies of *You're a Grand Old Flag*. Recite the song to students and engage students in a discussion of what each stanza means. Finally, sing *You're a Grand Old Flag* together as a class.

Holidays and Celebrations

The purpose of this lesson is for students to learn about the numerous holidays and celebrations recognized in the United States by its diverse population.

Learning Outcomes: As a result of having completed this lesson, students will develop an understanding of the variety of holidays and celebrations recognized by the many different citizens who live in the United States.

- Ask students to name their favorite holiday or celebration. Next, ask them to explain why the holiday or celebration they named is their favorite. Finally, brainstorm with students and compile a list of the holidays and celebrations they participate in with their family and/or neighbors.
- Hand out small calendars to each student and ask what a calendar is and why we use them. Call students' attention to selected holidays that appear in the calendar that are also on the list developed in class. After reviewing their list, ask students when and how we celebrate each of these holidays. Ask them to write in their calendars any additional holidays not mentioned.
- This is an excellent opportunity to recognize the diversity that exists in the United States by noting a variety of additional holidays and celebrations not normally celebrated by most of your students such as the Chinese New Year, Cinco de Mayo, Rammadon, Kwanzaa, Yom Kippur, and Nickommoh, to name but a few.
- Divide students into groups and have them research the additional holidays that they are not familiar with by assigning each group one responsibility. Have groups report their findings to the rest of the class.

This is an excellent opportunity to incorporate diversity in the classroom by acquainting students with the extensive variety and rich traditions of Americans of all color and ethnicity. For additional information, consult *Celebrations!* (A book about festivals, carnivals, and feast days from around the world.) by Bar Barnabas and Anabel Kindersley.

We Are All Alike, We Are All Different

This book relates a story about what would happen if zebras lost all their stripes—the net effect being zebras that were either black or white. The question is then posed: would the loss of stripes make the zebras become two separate groups, incapable of being friends.

Learning Outcomes: As a result of having completed this lesson based on acceptance, friendship, and love, students will accept and appreciate the differences we all possess and understand that differences cannot and should not hinder friendship.

MATERIALS:
What if the Zebras Lost Their Stripes? By John Reitano
two drinking glasses, one spoon
water
food coloring
blackboard
two strips of paper for each student
markers
stapler

Take out two empty glasses. Fill both glasses with water. Ask students to identify what was poured into the glasses. Next, add food coloring to one of the glasses and stir until the water has completely changed color. Ask students in what way the two glasses are different (guide students toward identifying color). Ask students if the colored liquid is still water. Help students to realize that the color does not make it different—it's still water (it looks the same, it feels the same, and tastes the same).

- Introduce the story, *What if the Zebras Lost Their Stripes?* by John Reitano. Ask students:
  - What is happening to the Zebras on the cover?
  - What might the other animals be thinking
- Read the story to the students, pausing as the story progresses to allow for predictions. Ask students:
  - What will the Zebras look like if they lost their black stripes? White stripes?
  - Do you think the Zebras will fight?

Note to teachers: The word "God" which appears in the text may be substituted with the word "nature".

- After reading the story, each student will take turns to identify one trait that makes him or her all the same (i.e. they all have a heart-

beat, smile, or they all can count to ten, etc.) Record the responses
on the board.

- Discuss characteristics that make each of the students special, (i.e.,
  I like to dance, I have a sister, etc). Record the responses on the
  board.
- Provide each student with two strips of paper. Have them illustrate
  or write one characteristic that makes them different than others
  on one strip and on the other write or illustrate a characteristic that
  makes them the same as others.

In closing, emphasize that we all have differences and similarities, which make us special and important members of the classroom community. State that both our similarities and differences
connect us and help us to be friends. Illustrate this statement by
connecting each of the strips made by the students into a chain.
Hang the chain in the room.[1]

---

1. Errol Putman, ed., *Teach the Lessons, Make a Difference.* (Houston: Holocaust
Museum Houston, 2000), p. 18–20. For additional titles on sharing, caring, tolerance and acceptance, consult the museum website at www.hmh.org.

9

Easy-To-Use Ideas for Teaching *New* Patriotism in Middle School Classrooms

⌒

Liberty without learning is always in peril and learning without liberty is always in vain.

JOHN F. KENNEDY

Teaching patriotism in middle school classrooms need not be limited to the study of traditional definitions of patriotism. Patriotism should also include citizenship and character education. It is important that students experience first hand what it is like to care about, share with, and appreciate others. Often the best way for students to learn such qualities is either by direct community involvement or through association with those who have been previously involved. The closer people feel to their communities, the better they are able to interact positively with others and to offer assistance where needed.

The following collection of ideas for lesson plans provides a starting point for promoting patriotism through solid citizenship in the classroom. The activities may be used as originally designed, or modified to create a variety of additional activities. Depending on the maturity of the students, teachers may also find activities appropriate for middle school in chapter ten.

TITLE: *The "Getting to Know Each Other" Picnic*
DESCRIPTION: Hold "Getting to Know Each Other" picnics regularly at a local park. The picnic should encourage a multi-ethnic group of

community members to come together. The sharing of ethnic foods and customs in a local setting is one way to appreciate other cultures and to emphasize the fact that all participants are from the same community. Students and adults can volunteer to introduce themselves and talk about their likes, dislikes, concerns, and suggestions for improving the community as a whole, together. This is a great way for students and adults to develop new friendships.[1]

TITLE: *Emblems of the Land I Love*

DESCRIPTION: Beginning with the era of the Revolutionary War, the meaning of patriotism has at one time or another experienced change, modification, and intermittent surges. Once again, in large measure a result of September 11th, 2001 and the terrorist attacks, America is experiencing a patriotic surge. The purpose of this lesson is to explore and learn from the different patriotic surges that have occurred. Beginning with the Revolutionary War, groups of students are assigned to find 8 to 10 primary sources (paintings, songs, speeches), each from a different era, depicting patriotism. For each piece, groups are required to explain its significance by describing when it was produced and what it referred to. Once the groups have completed their research/analysis, they will come together and identify at least one recurring theme that is present in each of their sources. If no theme is identified, they should explain how patriotism has changed through the years. Students should then take their collection of sources and display then chronologically, along with supporting information, on a timeline. Finally, each student should create a branch off the timeline. On this branch, students will identify what it is that patriotism means to them.[2]

---

1. Betty Greathouse and Barbara Goldman Young,"'Roots' A Stimulus for Community Involvement," *The Social Studies* 70, no. 2 (1979): 75–80.

2. Alison Zimbalist and Javaid Khan, "Emblems of the Land I Love: Exploring the History and Impact of Patriotic Images," The New York Times on the WEB Learning Network, New York Times Daily Lesson Plan Page in collaboration with the Bank Street College of Education in NYC [online source] (New York: The New York Times, Monday 29 October 2001, last accessed 13 May 2002), http://www.nytimes.com/learning/teachers/lessons/20011029monday.html?searchpv=learning_lessons#standards; Internet.

TITLE: *Exploring Nostalgic Occupations*

DESCRIPTION: In this activity a "Today and Yesterday" career fair is held at the school encouraging local individuals of varied career fields to demonstrate their trades. Farriers, tailors, mechanics, computer engineers, doctors, teachers, and merchants could share the history of their occupations in the local area. This both encourages students to look at possible career fields and gives them a broader sense of their community's makeup and development over time.[3]

TITLE: *Learn by Example*

DESCRIPTION: On a daily basis, the concept and importance of citizenship can be demonstrated by turning the classroom into a mini lesson on citizenship. Classroom management can be run in a democratic style where majority rules, but with respect for the minority. Students can run for class offices and they can even create and sign a constitution outlining the rules and rights for the class. Citizenship can be illustrated in the minor details of the classroom as well. For example, students need to raise their hands to speak and they have to show respect for others in the room. This exercise will teach the fundamental principles behind citizenship, and it will also allow the students to practice their rights and responsibilities as citizens.

TITLE: *The Renewed Glory of Old Glory: Examining Patriotism as a Response to National Crisis in Recent History*

DESCRIPTION: Here students investigate how increased patriotism, as a reaction to national crisis, can serve as both a uniting and a dividing force. First, the students will read *Flag Fever: the Paradox of Patriotism* by Blaine Harden, and as a class discuss how this relates to the incidents of September 11, 2001. As a class, the students will compile a list of interview questions to serve as an interview guide. The students will interview adults of a variety of ages, gather their findings and display them in posters or collages. Display the projects.[4]

---

3. Betty Greathouse and Barbara Goldman Young, "'Roots' A Stimulus for Community Involvement," The Social Studies 70, no. 2 (1979): 75–80.

4. The New York Times on the WEB Learning Network, New York Times Daily Lesson Plan Page [online source] (New York: The New York Times, 2002, last accessed 13 May 2002), http://www.nytimes.com/learning/teachers/lessons/archive.html; Internet.

TITLE: *Analyzing Patriotism through Song*

DESCRIPTION: Begin this lesson by reviewing the history of the Star-Spangled Banner. Group students into four groups, so each can analyze a different portion of the song. Following the group work, bring the class together so each group can report its analysis, explaining their interpretations of the lyrics. Discuss when and where the song is usually played and explain how it influences patriotic emotions, especially when it is sung. Brainstorm other prevalent displays of patriotism, such as fireworks. Follow this discussion by having students develop their own verses illustrating their own views of patriotism.

TITLE: *The American Quilt*

DESCRIPTION: This lesson is designed to teach the literal meaning of the word patriotism, and to also personalize the definition by associating it with the interpretations of individual students. Assign students to create a one-foot by one-foot square illustrating what patriotism means to them personally. These squares can contain things such as a picture of the student's family, a drawing of the flag, a collage of images, an essay on patriotism, illustrations of a national hero or role model, or a ballot symbolizing our freedom to vote. Attach all of the squares together to make an "AMERICAN QUILT." This is a tangible artifact that reflects the diversity of the class, yet at the same time unifies all the students in one concept. Discuss the ways in which the quilt symbolizes the motto of our country, *E Pluribus Unum,* 'from many, one.' The quilt can be displayed in the classroom, and may be enlarged by subsequent classes.

TITLE: *Personal Bill of Rights*

DESCRIPTION: Have students make a list of things they appreciate about the United States or that make them proud of our country. Next, introduce the idea that part of supporting our country includes questioning the actions and laws of our nation. Divide students into groups and have them collectively discuss and draw up an original Bill of Rights, including the principles they determine to be of primary importance for personal freedoms. Each group should present their new Bill of Rights to the class, and explain why they included the provisions they did. At this point, involve students in a discussion comparing their lists to the actual Bill of Rights—and dis-

cuss how these rights are preserved. Not all students will demonstrate absolute support for every aspect of life in the United States.
However, through thinking about what they appreciate, and the
rights that are guaranteed to everyone, they will gain appreciation
that we have the right to analyze such issues, and work for change
when necessary.

TITLE: *The Pledge of Allegiance*
DESCRIPTION: The purpose of this lesson is to have students explore
the different editions of the Pledge of Allegiance and participate in
an open dialogue about what the Pledge of Allegiance means to
them. The first part of the lesson addresses the time period that the
Pledge of Allegiance was written and focuses on the following questions: Why was the Pledge of Allegiance written? Who wrote it?
What was taking place in the country at the time that may have motivated its creation? Has the Pledge of Allegiance ever been changed
or altered, and if so, why? Students should explore each line of the
pledge and provide their own interpretations, and in a sense, rewrite
the Pledge of Allegiance. Discuss why the United States government
feels that it is important that the Pledge of Allegiance be recited at
the beginning of the school day. Students should also be encouraged
to debate the idea of refusing to say the Pledge of Allegiance as a
form of free speech protected in the Bill of Rights.

TITLE: *Ellis Island Reenactment*
DESCRIPTION: For this activity, ask students to research the history of
some of their family members. Following completion of their family
histories and after presenting their findings to classmates, students
will take part in a simulated activity depicting the path of their family
member(s) to the United States through Ellis Island. Students
should choose a family member(s) who immigrated to the United
States and experienced firsthand their processing at Ellis Island. This
experience will help students realize that our ancestral beginnings
varied, neither occurring at the same time or originating from the
same country for the majority of Americans.

TITLE: *Celebrating Ethnic Diversity in the Classroom*
DESCRIPTION: The goal of this lesson is to have students realize that
communities are made up of many different people, each group cul-

turally different from the next, but coexisting with each other creating the American "melting pot." Set up stations in your classroom (Brazil, Russia, Japan, Mexico, Ireland, Greece, Iran, India, etc.) representing the diversity that exists throughout the world and in many communities. Each station should include information about the music, clothing, food and language from that country or culture. Students will "travel" throughout the world in the classroom and experience the different cultures that make up communities across America. Students could conclude this focused study by writing a report about the importance of multiculturalism in their community.[5]

TITLE: *Rewriting the Declaration of Independence*

DESCRIPTION: Students should first understand the three main parts of the Declaration of Independence: The Declaration of Independence, the Reasons for Independence, and a List of Grievances against King George III of England. Students should be divided into groups of 4–5 to create their own Declaration of Independence by rewriting it in their own words. The purpose of this activity is to have students understand the significance of the document, what it meant in 1776 when Thomas Jefferson wrote it, and what it means today. Be sure to stress the concepts of patriotism, natural rights, and the freedom that the Founders were demanding.

TITLE: *Different ways to Incorporate Patriotism Throughout the School Year*

DESCRIPTION: Because America is built upon and has a strong history of democracy, freedom, and patriotism, these ideas cannot be properly addressed in one or two class periods. In order to encourage and explain patriotism, identify important figures, and spur critical questioning, first, pick a topic and spend ten minutes on it everyday for a week. Find short stories or clips from books on that topic for students to read or act out. In order to help bring history to the students through primary sources, provide examples of newspaper articles from WWI or WWII when people came together for the col-

---

5. Edwin Fenton, ed., A New History of the United States, Carnegie-Mellon Social Studies Curriculum (New York: Holt, Rinehart and Winston, Inc. 1975), 45.

lective good. These lessons should help the students learn what patriotism is, and what it means to them.[6]

TITLE: *Helping Others in Need*

DESCRIPTION: In his State of the Union Address President George W. Bush outlined a community service program that would require Americans to commit to work for two years of service to the community. In the spirit of this request, one idea would be for students to plan, design, and participate in a community service project. Students should brainstorm ideas to arrive at projects designed to give back to the community. This should be carried out over a long enough period of time to allow for planning all the activities necessary. This project gives students a sense of responsibility and professionalism, and at the same time builds teamwork and cooperation. At the end of the project the students should evaluate their service in terms of how well they reached the community and helped people in need. One goal of having completed this project is that student involvement in the community will continue after the assignment is done.

TITLE: *Perspectives on Patriotism*

DESCRIPTION: Students should first define what they believe patriotism means. Next, students should conduct two interviews, either individually or as a group. The first one should be with a person who has served in the military at some point in his or her life, preferably having been in the service during an armed conflict and/or war. The second interview should be conducted with a person of about the same age as the other interviewee, but who has not had any experience in the armed services. During these interviews the students should ask each individual to describe what patriotism means. After the interviews, students should compare and contrast their own description of patriotism with those of the people they interviewed. This comparison can be written or can be represented as a collage. If

---

6. Chathy Schulof, Pursuit of Patriotism: an Internet Treasure Hunt on Patriotism [online source] (Filamentality, Pacific Bell, 1996–2002, last accessed 13 May 2002), http://www.richmond.edu/academics/a&s/education/projects/hunts/patriotism; Internet.

students prefer, they may copy a photograph of their interviewees. If students make a collage they should also include a description that explains why this picture demonstrates patriotism to themselves and their interview subjects. A collage format should also include a drawing, photo, or written description that combines the three separate ideas of what Patriotism means, as a synthesis of the varying viewpoints.

TITLE: *Letters to Heroes and Families*
DESCRIPTION: Call for student volunteers to write letters to American Armed Force members abroad, stating appreciation for their efforts in preserving democracy in America and around the world. Additionally, students could write letters to soldiers' families stating their appreciation for the efforts of their relatives. It is difficult to sacrifice time with loved ones for the preservation of national freedoms. Seeing that students empathize with families as well as with the soldiers demonstrates community involvement and empathy for families. If a military base or facility is located near the school, students may be able to take a field trip to the base, which would give them a better understanding of how the Armed Forces operate.

TITLE: *The Stars and Stripes*
DESCRIPTION: Incorporating patriotism into a lesson can be as simple as a discussion about the flag. This lesson begins by talking about the stars and stripes, what they literally represent and how their numbers have changed throughout history. The next step involves showing photographs of the flag at various moments in American History. Two suggestions are the flag over the World Trade Center and the flag raised by the Marines at Iwo Jima in World War II. Complete the lesson with discussion of the increased emphasis on the flag in times of national peril and turmoil, and the patriotic feelings that the flag can evoke in such times.

TITLE: *Donating to the Community*
DESCRIPTION: One idea for teaching students the concepts of citizenship and community is to have students donate blankets, food, or money to organizations such as the United Way, Red Cross, local hospitals, soup kitchens or food pantries. The idea here is to help students recognize that there are many needy people in the world

and that many of them live in their local communities. Use this activity as an incentive for students to identify ways they can begin to help within their own community. In doing this, students will understand their responsibilities as citizens, one of which is to help those who are less fortunate.

TITLE: *Social Studies and Citizenship, a Perfect Match*

DESCRIPTION: Citizenship education is vital to the social studies curriculum. Social studies concepts have many ties to other curricular areas. Work with math, science, and English teachers to integrate the concept of citizenship into their curricula. For example, math teachers could have students research national or state or school budgets and present their findings to the class. In science, students can address environmental issues such as pollution and oil drilling. English classes could read and discuss the political implications of writings such as *1984,* by George Orwell. Citizenship is important enough to be interdisciplinary, and should be incorporated across the curriculum as much as possible.[7]

TITLE: *Understanding the American Flag*

DESCRIPTION: Students will explore the history, meanings, and etiquette of the American flag by investigating where the American Flag came from and what it stands for. Over the history of this country our flag has changed many times. Students should first explore the origins of the first Stars and Stripes. Who made it and how did it become the symbol of our country? Was it valued then in the same way it is today? Throughout this lesson students should also discuss the meanings behind the Stars and Stripes. One way to accomplish this is to have students make reproductions of all our different flags and compare them throughout American history. Lastly, students should identify the rituals and etiquette behind the flag. Why is our flag folded into a triangle? Why are the stars always to be flown in the upper left corner? If possible, a member of the American Legion or the Veterans of Foreign Wars should be invited to come into the class and answer questions and describe the way old tattered flags are dis-

---

7. S. G. Grant, and Bruce A. Vansledright, "The Dubious Connection: Citizenship Education and the Social Studies," The Social Studies 87, no. 2 (1996): 56–69.

posed of. In addition, students could discuss why people who wave the flag proudly in honor of America also have the right to burn the flag in an act of protest.

TITLE: *A History of Local Indians*

DESCRIPTION: In order to understand American culture more completely, including the foundation of many communities, students should explore the role of Native Americans and their contributions. They can start by researching individuals or groups of Indians. Have students explore historical maps showing the areas where Native Americans lived and where they reside today. Students can gather information about Indian tribes who were in their local area before Europeans. Students should begin to understand that Native Americans have been a very influential group in American culture. In conclusion, have students gather all the information and connect the historical aspects of Native Americans and their contributions to the communities that they live in today.[8]

TITLE: *Helping Your Neighbor*

DESCRIPTION: Being an effective citizen incorporates several ideas and elements. One component is the responsibility one has to help those who are in need. Too often people equate citizenship solely with protecting one's rights. Although this is certainly a vital part of citizenship, there is much more to be considered. Individuals should also be encouraged to reach out to help their neighbors when they are incapable of doing so for themselves. The March of Dimes provides one opportunity with their annual "March" to help thousands who might not survive much past birth. Encourage students to participate in events such as these so they realize the importance of their involvement and the effect their community service has on other people, some of whom they may never meet. Students must also learn that giving should be colorblind and without prejudice. Students should research various service organizations and learn how they can contact them if they wish to participate. They should learn that the goal is not to receive recognition or personal benefit from

---

8. Edwin Fenton, ed., A New History of the United States, 23.

their service, and that a sacrifice of time, money, and effort is almost always involved in helping others.

TITLE: *The Patriotism of Popular Culture*
DESCRIPTION: The objective of this lesson to get students to understand that even popular culture is frequently a medium through which patriotism can be expressed. One way to accomplish this is to use popular music. *The America: A Tribute to Heroes* CD features a number of artists performing songs that may have forced each of us to redefine our idea of patriotism. The lesson should focus on why these artists were chosen (many of them, including U2 and Sting, are not American) and the meanings of the songs. The students should research the artists and attempt to discover whether they had any personal connection to the events of September 11th—U2, for example, hail from Ireland, which has certainly seen its share of terrorism—and how September 11th affected their lives. The students could even write a song of their own.

TITLE: *Heroes in the Community*
DESCRIPTION: Police officers and firemen and women are essential to any community. As the basis for this lesson, have students brainstorm or research the qualifications needed to enter one of these professions. After doing so, have a police officer or a fireman come to the class to share stories and experiences with the students. As a conclusion, have students write a reflective essay evaluating the contributions of these individuals. To take the activity further, try to arrange a ride with a police officer, or a tour of the local fire department.

TITLE: *A "Patriotic" Skit*
DESCRIPTION: This lesson is based on having students put on a small play or skit, which is a positive, interactive, and student-centered way to teach students about patriotism. Some ideas or themes are:

- A play about the signing of the Declaration of Independence.
- A skit that focuses on the anti-war movement of the Vietnam era.
- A play that re-enacts the heroism of Americans in tragic or disastrous situations.
- A simple play about the evolution of the American Flag.

- A musical that outlines the creation of the National Anthem or the Pledge of Allegiance.

Through methods such as this, students have the opportunity to think about and judge the patriotism of others.

TITLE: *Reflections on Election*
DESCRIPTION: This particular activity would be a nice addition to classroom instruction during election years. Assign students to research the platforms of various political candidates. At the conclusion of their research, students should evaluate the platforms of the various candidates, identifying the positive and negative elements of each, based on their personal perceptions of what is acceptable and what is not. Finally, ask students to evaluate the platforms of the candidates against what they believe the Founding Fathers of the United States would support and would not support.

TITLE: *Volunteering and Reaching Out to Others*
DESCRIPTION: This is a lesson that helps students see the effects and benefits of volunteerism. Using a clip from the movie *Patch Adams*, students learn that volunteerism is not necessarily only synonymous with things like helping at a soup kitchen. Begin by having students rank 5 citizenship values (patriotism, suffrage, volunteerism, military service, respect) on a "Value Continuum" and then defend those choices. Next, discuss volunteerism as a necessary and important component of a "good citizen." Brainstorm examples of ways students have volunteered, and have them discuss their feelings about volunteerism. After analyzing the *Patch Adams* video clip that illustrates volunteerism and public spirit, provide students with examples of diverse volunteer opportunities. Conclude the lesson by citing a number of social problems, having students write down ways that they could volunteer to help combat these problems in their own community.

TITLE: *American Flag on the Wall*
DESCRIPTION: Sometime early in the school year, ask students what they believe it means to be patriotic. After students have responded, explain that in addition to the items mentioned, patriotism also involves positive citizenship that entails "giving back" to others. It is

important to provide students with many different definitions for both citizenship and patriotism and not try to mold students to believe in one definition. Next, direct students' attention to the back of the classroom in the direction of an empty white wall, containing nothing more than a stenciled outline of an American flag, explaining that one of the year's objectives is to paint the flag. Every time that students engage in some type of community service, such as helping a teacher, assisting a senior citizen, or attend a community function, or anything they feel either resembles a form of patriotism or being a good citizen, they may paint a star or stripe, and appropriately label each with their contribution. The goal is to have the flag completely painted by the end of the year. This should get students thinking about the true meaning of being patriotic and being a good citizen. Then, when the flag is complete, students can look back and see all the good things they have done for the community and how each one represents the school and the class. Accomplishment such as this could be covered in the local newspaper and illustrate that students care and contribute to the community.

TITLE: *Artwork as a form of Patriotism*

DESCRIPTION: Assign a project in which students create a painting, picture, photograph, song, poem, or ceramic sculpture that represents an image of patriotism. It could resemble a number of different things, for example: a painted picture of a president, a famous civil war battle scene, any historical figure, a local community historical figure, a local map drawing, the American Flag, The Washington Monument or the White House. As a culminating experience, students would present their finished projects to individuals in the community, or to the community library, sheriff station, post office, court house, town hall, sports center or another place to reflect students' understanding of giving back to their community.

TITLE: *Fighting for American Virtue*

DESCRIPTION: Design a simulation game to help students create a sense of life without the basic rights that are guaranteed to United States citizens. For example, require that students pay for the use of a desk, or sit on the floor. Require that they do assigned work and give their credit to another student, or have them sit on a certain side of the room based on criteria that is obviously biased. After the game, discuss how these events and new rules made them feel. Afterwards, have students research a major war in which the US participated. Consider especially the American Revolution or Civil War from which Americans gained many special rights. Students should then write a reflective essay that includes the following:

- A list of rights for which Americans fought.
- What these rights mean to individuals today.
- How they think life would be different without these rights.

This should help students to develop a sense of pride in what their country is and how far it has come. This activity is a perfect opportunity to explore patriotism in times of war.

TITLE: *Tracing Local "Roots" Through Oral History*
DESCRIPTION: Send small groups of children to local nursing and retirement homes to interview elderly members of the community. Using tape recorders, students will make an audio record of local history. The elderly often have interesting genealogical information to share, as well as information about school, street, and city names. Photographs could be obtained in an effort to show students the history of their community and how it has changed in a lifetime.[9]

TITLE: *The United States as an Amalgamation of Many*
DESCRIPTION: The objective of this lesson is to help students discover the different kinds of people who helped make the United States a great country. Assign small groups of students to compile a list of ten prominent Americans from throughout history who, through one means or another, were recognized either by their contemporaries or through history as contributing toward the advancement of the United States. In this list, students need to represent three different races or ethnicities, a minimum of five nations or regions of the world, and at least two different world religions. Follow up with a class discussion in which students present their findings.

---

9. Betty Greathouse and Barbara Goldman Young, "'Roots' A Stimulus for Community Involvement," The Social Studies 70, no. 2 (1979): 75–80.

TITLE: *Guest Speakers from the Community*

DESCRIPTION: Guest speakers are an excellent way for students to become familiar with their community. Speakers from all walks of life and occupations could be invited to come into the classroom and share their personal views of what it means to be a patriot. Identify potential speakers by contacting various service organizations, local churches, local political parties, the Veterans of Foreign Wars, or the American Legion. The act of bringing community guests into the classroom allows students to feel appreciated by community members, and also permits community members to observe students in their school environments. Perhaps most importantly, students are subjected to a wider variety of perspectives and viewpoints than they normally see in the average school classroom. As a result, students will begin to see themselves as part of a greater whole rather than as passive observers of the world around them.

TITLE: *Local Election Night*

DESCRIPTION: Have students find the names of and learn about people running for office, by using the Internet, newspaper sources, and other primary source materials. They should look for information such as party affiliation, goals, campaign promises, e-mail addresses, phone, fax, postal addresses etc. Using this information, students can make posters with a photo of the candidates, a contact address, and other information to inform the community about candidates running for office in local and state elections. Presidential candidates may also be included.

TITLE: *Forcing Change through Letter Writing*

DESCRIPTION: Use the following story about the "children at play" sign, to inspire students to write a letter to a political leader voicing a concern.

A neighborhood boy was hit by a car while he was out riding his bike in the street. As a fellow ten-year old bike rider, I wrote a letter to the town council expressing my concern, and asked for a Children at Play sign to be put on our street. Two weeks later, a truck was parked out front installing a sign. The sign remains there to this day.

While it might seem rare that a ten year old would write a letter to the town council, that is the kind of responsible citizenship that all students need to display. Students should choose an issue that affects them directly, such as the town curfew, the legal state driving age, or federal spending on education. Students should do some preliminary research before writing their letters and justify their choice of official. Once students have handed in their background research, have them work in pairs writing and revising their letters. As replies are received, discuss what they think their letter writing campaign has accomplished.

TITLE: *History of the Church, Synagogue and Mosque in the Community*
DESCRIPTION: Throughout America, religious institutions and places of worship have shaped and influenced communities. A good way to incorporate this idea into the classroom is to have students explore a place of worship in their community. Students should focus on the relationship between the church, synagogue or mosque and the community, investigating what the relationship is, how the different places of worship have helped shape the community, how the community supports the religious institution, and what percentage of the community attends or visits each of these places of worship.[10]

---

10. Edwin Fenton, ed., A New History of the United States, 36.

10

Easy-To-Use Ideas for Teaching *New* Patriotism in High School Classrooms

~~~

What we need are critical lovers of America—Patriots who express their faith in America working to improve it.

HUBERT H. HUMPHREY

Teaching patriotism in high school classrooms need not be limited to the study of traditional definitions of patriotism. Patriotism should also include citizenship and character education. It is important that students experience first hand what it is like to care about, share with, and appreciate others. Often the best way for students to learn such qualities is either by direct community involvement or through association with those who have been previously involved. The closer people feel to their communities, the better they are able to interact positively with others and to offer assistance where needed.

The following collection of lesson plans provides a starting point for promoting patriotism through solid citizenship in the classroom. The activities may be used as originally designed, or modified to create a variety of additional activities. Depending on the maturity of the students, teachers may also find activities appropriate for high school in chapter nine.

TITLE: *NIFs, or National Issues Forums*
DESCRIPTION: Though it sounds more complex, a National Issues Forum is simply a student-centered, student-developed, and student-

147

directed discussion about important political issues and national interests. The role of the teacher is to direct discussion, making a conscious effort not to influence student choices. NIFs encourage students to develop their own perspectives, to see the views of the community as a whole, and discover where their own views fit into the common views of the classroom, school, and community.[1]

TITLE: *Public I or Private I: Pros and Cons of National Identity Cards*

DESCRIPTION: In this lesson students will explore the topic of national identity cards in the United States as a starting point in determining what types of information should be accessible to the government and private industry. Begin by reading an article on national I.D. cards as a class and follow up with a discussion of the reading. Have students form small groups to discuss and debate what information should be public and what information should remain private. Each group should then report its decisions to the class for continued large group discussion.

TITLE: *Encouraging Community Service by Peers*

DESCRIPTION: Students participate in a predetermined number of community service hours in a voluntary capacity during a semester-long experience. After the tasks have been completed the student should write an essay describing the location where they volunteered and how they feel this experience benefited them and helped the community. For example, students should explain whether or not their experience was fun, hard work, whether they would do it again, etc. Students may also choose to create a collage, brochure, or write a persuasive essay to influence other students to participate in a volunteer experience. It is important to provide a list of possible service opportunities, including contact numbers and email addresses of people the students can call for information. Students should do their own groundwork and preparation as a responsibility building exercise.

TITLE: *America: the Good Neighbor*

DESCRIPTION: Use the newspaper article titled *America the Good Neighbor* by Gordon Sinclair, June 5, 1973, to demonstrate how one

---

1. Lynden J. Leppard, "Discovering a Democratic Tradition and Educating for Public Politics," *Social Education* 57, no. 1 (1993): 23–26.

journalist sees and values the United States. Engage students in a discussion to illustrate that there are people beyond our borders who appreciate the US, and see the good works our nation does. This should help instill a sense of patriotic pride in our country.

This Canadian thinks it is time to speak up for the Americans as the most generous and possibly the least appreciated people on all the earth.

Germany, Japan and, to a lesser extent, Britain and Italy were lifted out of the debris of war by the Americans who poured in billions of dollars and forgave other billions in debts. None of these countries is today paying even the interest on its remaining debts to the United States.

When France was in danger of collapsing in 1956, it was the Americans who propped it up, and their reward was to be insulted and swindled on the streets of Paris. I was there. I saw it.

When earthquakes hit distant cities, it is the United States that hurries in to help. This spring, 59 American communities were flattened by tornadoes. Nobody helped.

The Marshall Plan and the Truman Policy pumped billions of dollars! into discouraged countries. Now newspapers in those countries are writing about the decadent, warmongering Americans.

I'd like to see just one of those countries that is gloating over the erosion of the United States dollar build its own airplane. Does any other country in the world have a plane to equal the Boeing Jumbo Jet, the Lockheed Tri-Star, or the Douglas DC10? If so, why don't they fly them? Why do all the International lines, except Russia, fly American Planes?

Why does no other land on earth even consider putting a man or woman on the moon? You talk about Japanese technocracy, and you get radios. You talk about German technocracy, and you get automobiles.

You talk about American technocracy, and you find men on the moon—not once, but several times—and safely home again.

You talk about scandals, and the Americans put theirs right in the store window for everybody to look at. Even their draft-dodgers are not pursued and hounded. They are here on our streets, and most of them, unless they are breaking Canadian laws, are getting American dollars from ma and pa at home to spend here.

When the railways of France, Germany and India were breaking down through age, it was the Americans who rebuilt them. When the Pennsylvania Railroad and the New York Central went broke, nobody loaned them an old caboose. Both are still broke.

I can name you 5000 times when the Americans raced to the help of other people in trouble. Can you name me even one time when someone else raced to the Americans in trouble? I don't think there was outside help even during the San Francisco earthquake.

Our neighbors have faced it alone, and I'm one Canadian who is damned tired of hearing them get kicked around. They will come out of this thing with their flag high. And when they do, they are entitled to thumb their nose at the lands that are gloating over their present troubles. I hope Canada is not one of those.

Stand proud, America![2]

TITLE: *The Patriotic Dissenter*

DESCRIPTION: Use figures such as Martin Luther King Jr., and Susan B. Anthony to point out the importance of dissenters in the creation of the American democratic system. It was the willingness of people such as these to question the social mores of their times that initiated major social changes in our history. Model appropriate questioning strategies and help students develop non-aggressive approaches to change to encourage appropriate and effective arguing techniques. Students should be encouraged to research and discuss the actions of people such as Martin Luther King Jr., Ralph Waldo Emerson, and Oliver Wendell Holmes, so they begin to understand the idea of the patriotic dissenter.[3]

---

2. Gordon Sinclair, *Letter to our Neighbor*, (Quebec, Canada: Published by Star Quality Music (SOCAN) A Division of UNIDISC Music Inc. 578 Hymus Boulevard Pointe-Claire Quebec Canada, H9R4T2, 1973)

3. Walter E. McPhie, "Dissenters in a Democracy: Patriots or Subversives?" *The Social Studies* 77, no. 5 (1986): 192–195.

TITLE: *Interweaving Patriotism and Citizenship*

DESCRIPTION: John F. Kennedy's quote "ask not what your country can do for you, ask what you can do for your country" can be used as an everyday classroom theme. Have students respond to the quotation in terms of what patriotism means to them. Then ask them what they have done to help their country either today or in the past. Explain that volunteerism and working to help others is a form of patriotism, and that they should try to do one such act everyday. By using examples from everyday experiences of one or two students they are reminded that more is expected of them if they are to be contributors to society. Students should focus on helping others. To facilitate this, set up weekly activities for students to demonstrate citizenship: for example shoveling snow, participating in can drives, tutoring or helping a teacher with something extra. Help them to see what their activities do for others and how they are personally impacted in positive ways.

TITLE: *Looking at Patriotism From a Different Perspective*

DESCRIPTION: The purpose of this lesson is to provide students with a "lens" through which they can view patriotism from a different perspective by watching a movie clip from *All Quiet on the Western Front*. The clip is an excerpt in which a German schoolmaster is urging his students to enlist in the German army to fight in World War I. Ask students to determine the quality of character being portrayed. Focus particularly on differences or similarities that exist in terms of patriotism and how it is defined and practiced in different countries.

TITLE: *Eyes on the Election*

DESCRIPTION: This activity helps students practice the skills of deliberation and data analysis, explore public opinion and determine their own stance on political issues by following the campaigns of several political candidates. Students should decide for themselves which issues the candidates represent and prioritize these issues. Next construct a poll for assessing public opinion, and develop a system for tracking the candidate's progress and positions on issues throughout the campaign. The poll data may be analyzed in conjunction with a math course, public opinion can be looked at from varying socioeconomic viewpoints, and the data can be arranged by region.[4]

TITLE: *Mock Elections*

DESCRIPTION: The presidential elections of 2004 provide an excellent opportunity to introduce students to the responsibilities of American citizenship. First, analyze why voting is an important part of being an American citizen and use segments from MTV's "Rock the Vote" for arousing student interest in the political process. Next, divide students into groups and have each group become part of a candidate's campaign. Students should research their candidate, using newspaper and magazine articles and the Internet to determine the candidate's stance on issues, including education, taxes, health care, etc. When the research is complete, students should present their candidate to the class by providing a packet containing fact sheets explaining the candidate's platform. Finally, after hearing the presentations and analyzing the fact sheets, students should determine who they would vote for in the election and why. Additionally, a discussion comparing current candidate platforms to the platforms of the nation's first presidents will provide insight into the changes that have taken place in public interest in the last 220 years.

TITLE: *Appreciating the Armed Forces*

DESCRIPTION: In order to help develop a sense of pride, understanding, and support of our military in students, invite veterans of the wars in which our country has been involved to the classroom to speak about the importance of supporting one's country and to relate their stories about their involvement in these wars. Hearing real-life stories of American heroes will help students understand the reality of wartime struggle and the personal sacrifices individuals have made for our freedoms in the past.[5]

---

4. G. Dale Greenawald, "Voting Isn't Enough," *Social Education* 60, no. 6 (1996): 333–335.

5. Andrea Billips, The Washington Times, accessed at *DADI, Dads Against the Divorce Industry*– "Teaching Patriotism: Retired Military Officers Working with Teen-agers to Teach Patriotism" [online source] (Washington: News World Communications, Inc., reprinted with permission from The Washington Times, 1999, last accessed May 13 2002), http://www.dadi.org/wt_patri.htm; Internet.

TITLE: *The Rock*

DESCRIPTION: Begin this lesson by having students write down their views of patriotism and compile a list of the people that come to mind when thinking of patriotism. Once the lists have been compiled, discuss these ideas with the class, including the ideas of patriotism within the context of the American Revolution, the Civil War, and modern military conflicts (Vietnam, and the burning of the flag), etc. Use these ideas to develop a class definition for patriotism. Once this is accomplished, watch the movie, *The Rock* and highlight potential patriots and non-patriots, (for example, the SEAL team attempting to rescue the hostages and take back Alcatraz, and the several soldiers who turn against Ed Harris in the end of the movie). Ask students to determine who the patriots are, then discuss different characters and the reasons why they could be considered patriots. Note that this film is R- rated.

TITLE: *Natural Resources Defense Council*

DESCRIPTION: To begin this activity, have students write letters to the NRDC for information on different regions in the U.S. that are being exploited, polluted, or likely to be harmed by business, chemicals, nuclear testing, oil drilling, etc. Students may also write letters to their state senators or congressmen if there are related bills being reviewed in the Senate or the House. Students should then attend local board meetings to bring the issues they have been working on to the wider attention of the village, county, or city.[6]

TITLE: *Morals and Mores*

DESCRIPTION: Conducting discussions centered on moral dilemmas helps students create their own schema of justice. In the cases of patriotism and citizenship, moral dilemmas force students to look at the larger picture of community and responsibilities to self and country. By looking at the "gray area," students must not only make difficult decisions, but be able to back up whatever course of action they choose. In this activity, first present the moral dilemma, then

---

6. National Resources Defense Council [online-source] (no publication information is available on this website, however the NRDC Regional Office may be reached at 1200 New York Ave., NW, Suite 400, Washington D.C. 20005, (202) 289–6868, last accessed May 13, 2002), http://www.nrdc.org; Internet.

have students discuss the dilemma and a series of possible solutions. In smaller groups, students should defend their decisions and their reasoning. To conclude, bring the class back together and discuss the reasoning strategies, focusing on analysis and closure. A possible dilemma may deal with a citizen of middle-eastern descent who knows of a relative planning terrorist activities in the United States. Should the individual turn in the name of his/her relative to the authorities, even if no crime has been committed?[7]

TITLE: *Civics and the Internet*
DESCRIPTION: As civics education and citizenship is the foundation of social studies, it is very important that students are educated to use the Internet in a responsible, respectful manner. There are many websites that can be used in order to imbue in our students the themes and concepts that are tied to patriotism in the United States. These websites can be used as a webquest activity for students to define and evaluate patriotism from a variety of viewpoints. Adolescents use computers and the Internet on a daily basis, and this activity enables them to use those technological skills constructively.

Some of the websites available include:

The Center for Civic Education—www.civiced.org
Close Up Foundation—www.closeup.org
Constitutional Rights Foundation—www.crf-usa.org
C-SPAN for the Classroom—www.c-span.org/classroom
Civics Online—www.civics-online.org

These websites provide primary sources, such as Congressional speeches and historical archives. In addition, professional development tools and interactive web-based activities are available for both teachers and students.[8]

---

7. Barry K. Beyer, "Conducting Moral Discussions in the Classroom," *Social Education* 40, no. 4 (1976): 194–202.

8. Frederick C. Risinger, "Teaching about Civics and Citizenship with the Internet (Surfing the Internet)," *Social Education* 66, no. 7 (Nov-Dec 2002): 425–428.

TITLE*: Different Definitions of Patriotism using American Figures*

DESCRIPTION: The purpose of this activity is to show that there are many notions of what patriotism is, and that over the course of American history, people have been considered patriotic for many different reasons. Organize students into groups and have each group discuss what it means to be patriotic. Next, assign groups an American Historical figure such as George Washington, Martin Luther King, Jr., or Andrew Jackson, who represents at least one aspect of being patriotic. Finally, students should address the question of patriotism today with regard to the wars in the Middle East by considering whether people who support the war are more or less patriotic than citizens who question their government.

TITLE: *A Letter to Congress*

DESCRIPTION: One way to encourage students to build citizenship is to have them research an American political or policy issue. Provide students with a list of topics and allow them to choose one that interests them. It is important to provide research topics that are controversial, such as the proposed drilling in the Alaskan Wildlife Refuge, or the legalization of gambling. When their research is complete, students should submit a position letter to the teacher, who in turn will send it to the appropriate lawmaking body.

TITLE: *Constitutional Rights as being Patriotic*

DESCRIPTION: One way to have students develop a better understanding of patriotism is to have them compare and contrast the United States government and culture with those of other nations. Other nations should represent a variety of governments and regions of the world that include Europe, Asia, Southeast Asia, Africa, South America, and Central America. To make this idea relevant to the day, students should research nations through newspapers, the Internet and newscasts dominating the current news. For example, in the year 2004 Iraq, Israel, Palestine, and Argentina would be good choices. Students should compare and contrast the rights, privileges, responsibilities and foundations of the United States with the other areas of the world. What freedoms do we possess that other people also have or do not have? What is the foundation for these freedoms? Considering this evidence, students can make informed decisions about their patriotic beliefs, where they originated, what they mean today, and what they will mean in the future.

TITLE: *Patriotic Quotations*

DESCRIPTION: This idea for teaching patriotism can be used two to three times a week at the beginning of class. Each day, post a quotation from an American somewhere in the classroom and have students copy it into a "quotation journal." The quote should come from anyone significant in American History that relates to the current period of study. For example, if the class is working on a unit about the Progressive Era, a quotation might come from President Theodore Roosevelt, or Upton Sinclair, author of *The Jungle*. Comment only briefly on the quote so that the students' interpretation is not influenced. Also, make certain to support the different definitions of patriotism by using a variety of quotations from a diverse group of Americans. In this way students can not only explore patriotism throughout the history of America, but also have the opportunity to analyze primary sources.

TITLE: *What does it mean to be a Patriot?*

DESCRIPTION: Patriotism can be defined in many ways. Does being patriotic only entail saying the pledge, volunteering for active duty, singing the national anthem before a baseball game, and verbally defending the President's policies? Is there more to patriotism than simply doing different "flag waving" activities?

Begin this activity with a discussion of patriotism. Introduce different—and often conflicting—views toward patriotism and ask students for their thoughts and opinions on the various perspectives. Some good examples include the following:

"I'm sick and tired of empty patriotism. You know the kind. Waving flags, singing "God Bless America" and cheering about everything in the good ol' USA, while at the same time becoming a mute robot and surrendering everything for which people have fought and died." —Ame W. Flones

"My own short list of what makes up patriotism certainly isn't exhaustive, but I don't see how it's possible to claim to be a patriot without these characteristics. A patriot: 'Is well informed . . . reg-

isters and votes...praises and criticizes the government. . . . Is active in his community'. . ." —Bill Tammeus

"*United we stand. Divided we will never be.*" —Bill Green

"*In the beginning of a change, the Patriot is a scarce man, Brave, Hated, and Scorned. When his cause succeeds however, the timid join him, for then it costs nothing to be a Patriot.*" —Mark Twain

"*It is both possible and moral, to love one's country and hate its government.*" —Dr. Walter Williams, George Mason University Economics Dept.

Have the students determine what their quotations mean and how they reacted to such differing viewpoints.[9]

TITLE: *The Patriotic Family Tree*
DESCRIPTION: This lesson for teaching patriotism includes making family trees or outlining family history. To begin, assign students to research their family histories. As part of data collection, students should conduct interviews with grandparents and parents, and use websites that focus on genealogy. This assignment will require that students explore different periods in history, including the point at which their ancestors came to the United States (if they did) and, more importantly, why they immigrated to the United States. At the conclusion of the activity, students should feel more of a direct connection to their ancestors. Also, by understanding the route that many chose while traveling to America, students should become more understanding of America as a "melting pot" of people and cultures.[10]

TITLE: *Evaluating Unpopular Views*
DESCRIPTION: Throughout the history of the United States, there have been many persons who supported unpopular views. Assign students

9. Politex, a non-affiliated U.S. Citizen, *Patriotism* [online source] (no other publication information is given, last accessed May 13 2002), http://www.bushnews.com/patriotism.htm; Internet.

10. Ellis Island Immigration Museum Site [online source] (New York: ARAMARK Sports & Entertainment, Inc., 2002), http://www.ellisisland.com/index.html; Internet.

to identify and compile a list of five such Americans. The list could be composed of politicians, social reformers, outspoken individuals, or "regular" citizens. Students should identify precisely what it was that caused each to be labeled as "unpopular." Next, have students evaluate the positions of each notable against the Declaration of Independence and the Constitution to determine the extent to which the individuals acted in a manner inconsistent with either of these two documents. Finally, involve students in a class discussion of whether or not history has done an injustice to these individuals by considering them "unpopular."

TITLE: *A Mock Dictatorship*
DESCRIPTION: In this lesson, the teacher becomes the dictator, and the students become the citizens in this new state. As citizens, the students have certain rights and privileges, and the teacher, as the authority figure, has control of these rights and privileges. An environment of this type could be set up where the students' rights within the classroom are severely restricted. For example, take away the students' right to leave class to use the bathroom without permission. Work within the confines of this situation can go on for a week or so, and then in a follow up, the students discuss and debate about how they felt having their rights taken away. Have the students read Orwell's *1984* concurrently, if possible. Tie this activity into discussions dealing with the plight of Jews in Europe during World War II, or some other persecuted group. Ultimately, the students should have a better understanding of what it means to be a citizen in this country and how it compares to living under different types of government regimes.

TITLE: *"Patriotic Websites"*
DESCRIPTION: A good way to teach patriotism is to use the Internet. Have students search the Internet for "patriotic" websites. Because patriotism can be defined in both traditional and non-traditional ways, students should have a substantial amount of freedom when searching (as with all Internet work, searches should be monitored). After three or four "patriotic" sites have been found, students should be required to justify why those sites illustrate patriotism and what elements or themes can be drawn from each site. Students should use this activity to explore the different definitions of patriotism and become familiar with the Internet in a scholarly way.

TITLE: Digital Citizenship

DESCRIPTION: Secondary education students are exposed to tremendous amounts of information through the various media outlets. At the same time, the Internet has allowed people of all ages to distribute messages throughout the world. The Internet is a medium that educators can use to explore the concepts of freedom of expression, freedom of information and privacy rights. Communication via the Internet is integrated with multicultural education, along with the values of citizenship and patriotism. Students are able to analyze, interpret, create, and evaluate information from many different cultures. Specifically, the Internet is an ideal way to integrate standards-based lessons, provide opportunities to develop new ideas of respect, empathy, tolerance and diversity, foster the study of world philosophies and religions and teach the critical thinking skills of media investigation and evaluation. Additionally, students are able to make connections between individual acts of patriotism and citizenship and global well-being.[11]

TITLE: *Teens, Let's Hear Your Smart Mouth*

DESCRIPTION: Students' abilities to express their opinions to their leaders are an important aspect of citizenship development. They should realize that by taking an active role, they have the power to help change the country. Students may use the Courier Journal's Internet site *Teens Let's Hear Your Smart Mouth* to voice their opinions on a current issue. The students choose an issue or event and write to their Senators or Representatives in Congress. When the public officials reply, allow students to analyze and discuss their replies in an open forum classroom discussion.[12]

TITLE: *Music of the Civil Rights Movement*

DESCRIPTION: Introduce this lesson by asking students to describe some of the things they do when they are feeling down and need some cheering up, directing students toward responses that refer to

---

11. Ilene R. Berson and Michael J. Berson, "Digital Literacy for Effective Citizenship. (Advancing Technology)," *Social Education* 67, no. 3 (April 2003): 164–168.

12. R. David Lankes, Director, *Ask ERIC Educational Information* [online source] (Syracuse: ERIC Clearinghouse on Information & Technolongy, Syracuse University, last accessed May 13, 2002), http://askeric.org; Internet.

music. Next, have students brainstorm times they might have seen or heard of music being used during the Civil Rights Movement. Following this, have the student listen to the song "We Shall Overcome" and write down some of the emotions or feelings they get from the music, and what meaning the song might have held for the activists. Discuss the students' responses as a class. Build on this by describing the scenario of the sit-ins at the lunch counter of Woolworth's in North Carolina. Have the students engage in a discussion of whether or not this song would have been appropriate to sing at the sit-ins. Then, play the song "Oh Pritchett, Oh Kelly" (or any other song not related to this particular sit-in). As before, have the students write down emotions, etc. as they listen to the song. Again ask the question of whether or not this song would be appropriate for the sit-ins. Finally, have the students determine in what context certain songs might be sung and why. This will enable them to understand the role of music during the movement and how it changed from one event to another. [13]

TITLE: *Appreciating Senior Citizens*

DESCRIPTION: Sometime shortly after the beginning of the school year, organize groups of student volunteers who would be interested in helping senior citizens with outdoor chores. For example, students could assist senior citizens with raking leaves and putting up storm windows in the fall, shoveling snow in the winter, and taking down storm windows and putting up window screens in the spring. In addition to directly helping senior citizens with their chores, this will bring together two different generations who sometimes misunderstand and/or mistrust one another. These newly opened channels of communication should provide a positive experience for both generations.

TITLE: *Using Newscasts and Newspapers to Develop Citizenship*

DESCRIPTION: Citizenship and tolerance are important aspects of character education that should be stressed in the classroom. One way to

---

13. Smithsonian Folkways recordings, *Lest We Forget : Sing for Freedom: The Story of the Civil Rights Movement Through Songs*, Vol. 3 (Smithsonian Folkways # 05488).

do this is to create lessons for students based on the national evening news such as the ABC *World News Tonight* with Peter Jennings, NBC *Nightly News* with Tom Brokaw, CBS *Evening News* with Dan Rather, CNN, FoxNews Channel and CSPAN. Over the course of two or three weeks, have students watch and summarize reports on these newscasts about national and global issues. Students may also use the Internet to read international newspapers and support their research. After the research is complete, students should present their findings to the class, focusing on topics such as war, famine, AIDS in Africa, the Israeli-Palestine conflict, the War in Iraq, and economic problems in countries like Japan. Students should examine why some of these issues, especially those found in international newspapers, are not reported by American News stations, and why the United States government does not provide support for some of these countries. In conclusion, students should offer ideas on how to help limit or stop the problems.

TITLE: *"Sitting" for Elections*

DESCRIPTION: Several weeks prior to local, state, and national elections, solicit student volunteers to work as babysitters in the vicinity of voting precincts, so that citizens are free to vote. Working in this capacity, students will provide a valuable community service and demonstrate their commitment to the community.

TITLE: Developing Good "Netizens"

DESCRIPTION: The term netizen refers to a citizen of the Internet. Teachers can use the Internet to help students explore the virtues of respect, responsibility, honesty, courtesy, and self-control.

Some questions to consider when evaluating citizenship on the Internet include:

Is downloading music a form of stealing from the musicians?
Does the use of webcams violate a person's privacy?
Are people and countries without easy Internet access at a competitive disadvantage?

These questions deal with the basic and fundamental rights proposed by John Locke. These same rights of privacy, freedom of speech and freedom of the press are ingrained in the history of the

United States by way of the Bill of Rights. An essential question to ask students is: "Does the Bill of Rights pertain to the Internet?"[14]

TITLE: *Service Learning Activities*
DESCRIPTION: Service learning connects classroom material to the cultural and social aspects of community life. Service learning is different from volunteering in that it involves the classroom and academic content. The focus of the experience should be on solving community problems, addressing environmental concerns, and challenging policies to promote the good of the whole. Service learning activities provide students with opportunities to experience the democratic process first hand, and should increase students' awareness of their community.[15]

TITLE: *"It's not what your Country Can Do For You . . ."*
DESCRIPTION: An important part of social studies is to teach students to be active citizens, and to address issues that society faces. This project is designed to teach students about the problems that occur in our communities by having them deal directly with the local problems. This lesson will take approximately one marking period, but can extend to an entire year. Begin the project by spending a day highlighting the different problems in the local community, such as education, homelessness, unemployment, medical care, welfare, drug problems, crime, etc. The students should create a list, categorize the problems, and brainstorm possible solutions to the problems. Contact local agencies (soup kitchens, inner city schools, inner city health care facilities, drug treatment centers, city hospitals and other local assistance programs) and set up days with each of these organizations when students can volunteer their time. Each student should be required to volunteer or observe for at least 10 hours. At the end of the semester, the students will be required to write letters to local representatives describing what they saw, what they did, and how they feel these problems could be best addressed.

---

14. Andrew J. Milson and Beong-Wan Chu, "Character Education for Cyberspace: Developing Good Netizens," *The Social Studies* 93, no. 3 (May–June 2002): 117–120.

15. A Position Statement of National Council for the Social Studies, "Service-Learning: An Essential Component to Citizenship Education," Social *Education* 65, no. 4 (2001): 240.

TITLE: *Universal Declaration of Human Rights Recognition Day*

DESCRIPTION: Schools (or school districts) could recognize December 10th, the anniversary of the signing of the United Nations' Universal Declaration of Human Rights, "a day of celebration and an affirmation of commitment to justice."[16] The day could be identified in the school or district calendar as a day of celebration set aside to honor students, teachers, and community members who acted on behalf of others and stood up for individuals whose rights were violated. Those who received the honor could be recognized as the "conscience for the community." If possible, invite the local media, award plaques, and inscribe the names of honorees on a Community Honor Role to be displayed in a conspicuous place. Such action by the school or district could send a message to the community that they value caring and advocacy for the protection of everyone's rights.[17]

TITLE: *An Act of Patriotism*

DESCRIPTION: This lesson incorporates a view presented in the movie *Memphis Belle* as one example of the variety of existing perspectives regarding patriotism. The pilot (Matthew Modine) is in the lead plane on a bombing run over Germany during World War II in 1943. The cloud cover over the target was too thick and the target was not in clear sight. Modine is faced with the decision of whether to simply drop the bombs and return home or sweep the formation around again for a better look at the target. At this point, stop the film and ask the students to make a list of the decisions that the pilot has to make and decide whether he should drop the bomb or leave the target. Then proceed with the film and follow up with a discussion of the type of leadership skills, decision-making, and patriotism the pilot showed.

TITLE: *The Four Stages of Citizenship*

DESCRIPTION: School shootings, terrorist attacks and ethnic conflict are often viewed through an emotional lens, which can lead to prej-

---

16. David A. Shiman, and William R. Fernekes, "The Holocaust, Human Rights, and Democratic Citizenship Education," *The Social Studies* 90, no.6 (1999): pp. 61–62.

17. Ibid.

udiced views and in some cases, more violence. Teachers should take advantage of the opportunity to explore the causes, actions, and effects of these events analytically. It is important that headlines be treated sensitively and analyzed with insight. Responsible citizens gather research, debate with others, and finally come to conclusions. The following is a description of this process.

1. Recall: Ask students to recall what happened. This should be based on fact and be unbiased. Students can list, count, name or define but should not analyze.
2. Infer: This is the stage in which students should infer and deduce what they can from the facts (e.g., the families of those killed in terrorist attacks mourn for their loved ones).
3. Analyze Values: Students think about the values in all parts of the world. Students should empathize and look at the situation from the point of view of the individuals directly involved.
4. Hypothesize: Ask students about the causes of the problem and different ways to solve the problem. This is where students have the freedom to propose solutions based on the previous three stages.

These four stages can be used in the analysis of propaganda, newspaper articles, political speeches, and primary source activities.[18]

TITLE: *The Combination of National, State, and Local Citizens*
DESCRIPTION: Being a citizen involves actively participating in national, state, and local affairs. At the national level, have students debate issues that are relevant and important to them, such as alcohol and drug abuse among teenagers. Students should have the opportunity to discuss these concerns and begin to work toward plausible solutions. In addition, guest speakers from the community should speak to students about the identified issues, explaining that students can have a voice in the broader political and social scene. At the state level, students from a number of different schools could attend statewide meetings to discuss and debate issues of concern on the

---

18. Douglas D. Alder, and Sherman J. Lindhardt, "World History: Building Conceptual Understanding for Citizenship," *Social Education*, 45, no. 7 (1981): 548–551.

state level, such as legislative bills and state budgets. At the local level, students could participate in a number of different activities, such as attending town board meetings or writing to local governmental officials to express concerns. Students should come away from such activities realizing that they have a political and social voice.[19]

19. Nancy C. Brown, "Student Citizenship Participation: Three Models," *The Social Studies* 76, no. 1 (1985): 12–13.

11

Using Historical Documents to Teach Secondary Social Studies Students Patriotism

If you want to be free, there is but one way; it is to guarantee an equally full measure of freedom to all your neighbors. There is no other.

CARL SCHURZ

Teaching patriotism through the use of historical documents in conjunction with traditional methods provides secondary students with ample opportunity for a solid academic experience, grounded in the philosophical foundations of the United States. Unlike teaching methods that rely exclusively on mindless memorization, recitation, and acceptance of patriotic pledges and songs, use of historical documents enhances student opportunities for understanding the complex meaning of patriotism. Ultimately, students are encouraged to develop more personalized and meaningful definitions of patriotism, definitions that they may more easily defend as products of their own discovery.

Learning Outcomes

As a result of working through the materials in this unit, students will be able:

To identify and list six characteristics of a patriot.
To construct a definition of patriotism that reflects a higher degree of intellectual imagination than simply "lovin' yer country."

To identify historical examples that can be used to support definitions of patriotism.

To distinguish historically defensible uses of the term patriotism from those that are not historically defensible.

To construct, act upon, and defend a definition of patriotism in a way that reflects a breadth of understanding and a depth of conviction.

To identify and/or challenge misinterpretations and/or misapplications of patriotism with defensible criteria.

To craft a coherent and arguable thesis statement and support it in essay form through the applied use of primary historical documents.

Using historical documents, the following options for the study of patriotism may be used in conjunction with the curriculum of any social studies course taught at the middle school or high school level. The teaching materials and activities are specifically designed to accommodate a wide range of teaching methods and/or curriculum requirements. Teachers may choose, for example, to use the teaching strategies and activities as presented below or use the same teaching materials and activities to create a number of additional options. The possibilities are limitless.

- Option One: Teachers may use the materials and activities presented in the unit description in conjunction with the curriculum for either a one-semester or a two-semester course of instruction. (When using this option, it is recommended that each level of the unit be followed precisely as it is presented in the curriculum.)
- Option Two: In this option it is recommended that teachers use the same activities and materials referred to in option one. Or, they may be used to teach an abbreviated non-integrated unit on patriotism.

NOTE: Teachers are also encouraged to use the research and discovery activities and materials presented in level four as many times as necessary to assure reinforcement.

To provide clarity, continuity, and impact, the unit activities are divided into six levels. To achieve optimum results from using the activities, it is suggested that they be used in the following order.

1. questionnaire
2. initial definitions
3. basis of judgment
4. research and discovery
5. debriefing
6. evaluation

By implication, two important teacher considerations are interwoven into each activity: (1) teachers <u>must </u>be fair in the selection of a true cross-section of personalities for study, and (2) teachers must refrain from directly helping students formulate their hypotheses on patriotism. The ideal teacher in this role is one who provides positive encouragement, but not specific advice.

Level One

Sometime early in the course, teachers will need to set aside class time to allow each student to complete the questionnaire on patriotism that is provided as Student Handout A. The purpose of this initial effort is to:

1. Prompt students to begin thinking about the meaning of patriotism.
2. Alert students to the complexities involved in understanding the meaning of patriotism.
3. Create within each student an interest in developing a personal definition of patriotism.
4. Encourage students to develop initial positions on the meaning of patriotism for use in discussion and comparison at some future date.

Subsequent to this first activity, it is important that teachers collect the completed questionnaires from each student for safekeeping and easy retrieval. In order to organize student writing samples, teachers will need to create an individual patriotism activity file for each member of the class. The activity folders will become the "Patriotism Depository" for the written work related to patriotism produced by each student. From time to time, the materials will be retrieved from the file and used for review and revision in conjunction with various class assignments. The same materials will also need to be retrieved for use during any debriefing that is scheduled to occur at the conclusion of the unit.

It is important that each student be apprised early in the course of the rules and expectations that will be enforced throughout the study of patriotism. The following list is intended to provide a beginning:

1. It is generally not acceptable practice to judge individuals from the past against currently accepted standards, but it is permissible to judge individuals from the past on the standards that existed during the era studied.

2. Although students may question other students on their views, it is unacceptable for any student to make disparaging remarks about the work, choices, or views of other students.

3. Students are encouraged to revise their definitions of patriotism or list of characteristics of a patriot on the Patriotism Revision Form (which will be distributed during a subsequent class session) as necessary.

4. Students are encouraged to expand their criteria for judging patriotism. The Judgment Revision Form (to be distributed during a subsequent class session) will be used for this purpose.

5. Since the design of the lessons involving patriotism requires that students be frequently called upon to make choices and/or take positions on certain issues, it is important that each student learn to defend his or her position with evidence drawn from history.

6. Since students are asked to participate in activities in which they have little or no prior experience, teachers should refrain from overly criticizing, suggesting, or recommending "correct" answers. Sometimes students experience their best learning through personal failures.

The remainder of the class period should be used to field and answer specific questions pertaining to the special emphasis being placed on the study of patriotism.

Level Two

At the beginning of the second level of the unit, furnish students with a copy of the Patriotism Form (Student Handout B) and a copy of the Patriotism Revision Form (Student Handout C). Form B provides space for defining patriotism and space for listing six characteristics of patriotism. Form C provides space for writing revisions of definitions and/or characteristics of what constitutes a patriot. Although the students will probably have little or no use for the Revision Form in Level Two, it is important they understand that the two forms play equally important roles in the forthcoming lessons.

After the forms have been distributed, teachers should give instructions for completing the tasks of defining the term patriotism and providing the appropriate number of characteristics for what makes a patriot. Teachers should also assure each student that the singular purpose of this exercise is to establish a starting point for defining and identifying characteristics of patriotism and that it is not necessary to feel pressure to produce a "correct" answer.

After students have completed the initial assignment, there should be a discussion focusing on the means that were used to arrive at their definitions and/or lists of characteristics of patriotism. Throughout this time of sharing, teachers should encourage student responses but avoid becoming judgmental. Every effort should be made to avoid stifling student participation.

At the conclusion of the exercise, forms should be collected and placed in the patriotism file for future use in a culminating activity at the end of the unit.

Level Three

At the beginning of Level Three, teachers should remind students that in order to pass judgement on whether various personalities were or are patriotic requires a base of judgement. The initial effort to establish criteria for judgment is based on any number of the documents identified in the Appendices, depending on the maturity and developmental level of the students involved. The first assignment in this phase of the unit will require that students complete the Judgment Form (Student Handout D) by identifying four criteria of judgment. Students who wish to work beyond identifying the four criteria required by the assignment may record their additions on the Judgment Revision Form (Student Handout E). For this first effort at establishing criteria, it is important that all students work on the same assignment. If some students encounter difficulty, it might become necessary to direct them to work on specific documents or parts of documents such as the theory of government paragraphs of the Declaration of Independence, or the Bill of Rights of the Constitution, etc.

A class discussion should follow completion of their assignments, with the focus on the criteria that different students selected for their beginning lists. It is important that students provide a strong defense for each criterion, justifying why the specific item was included. Throughout the discussion, it is important that teachers avoid being judgmental. It is also expected that students will undertake additional research to expand their personal criteria for judgment beyond the documents previously mentioned. In addition to studying the documents identified on the suggested list of documents in the Appendices, students may also be encouraged to cull information from available history books, newspapers, journals, and/or magazines, etc.

One of the primary benefits that students derive from working with the patriotism activities and materials is that they will become increasingly aware of the complexity of the concept of patriotism. As a demonstration of this complexity, the process of individually expanding the criteria for judging patriotism should prove productive for students. For this reason, it is recommended that students keep an accurate record of all changes in criteria. The form to be used for this purpose, identified as Appendix E (Judgment Revision Form), should be kept on file with the other forms.

Level Four

Level Four involves active inquiry into the historical support base of patriotism for each of the personalities investigated. This level may be repeated as desired; however, as a minimum requirement, each student should be expected to complete one activity in Level Four for each unit of social studies completed.

To spark students' imaginations a variety of historical personalities should be offered for investigation, analysis, and evaluation. The list should include extremes. Some names, for example, should be included on the list because they steadfastly adhered to the law, while other names should be selected because they "violated" the law. Some personalities on the list should be selected because they staunchly opposed government actions, while other personalities should be selected because they continually upheld the view of the government.

The following names are offered as examples of the extremes previously referred to: Benjamin Franklin, George Washington, Thomas Jefferson, Abigail Adams, Noah Webster, Robert Fulton, Andrew Jackson, Henry David Thoreau, John C. Calhoun, William Lloyd Garrison, Angelina Grimke, Abraham Lincoln, Robert E. Lee, Susan B. Anthony, Dorothea Dix, George A. Custer, Booker T. Washington, Carl Schurz, Andrew Carnegie, John D. Rockefeller, W.E.B. DuBois, Jane Addams, Theodore Roosevelt, Alvin York, Janette Rankin, Woodrow Wilson, Henry Ford, Charles Lindbergh, Ernest Hemingway, John L. Lewis, Jesse Owens, William O. Douglas, Joseph McCarthy, Aretha Franklin, Rosa Parks, Martin Luther King Jr., Barry Goldwater, Huey Newton, William Calley, Abbie Hoffman, Cesar Chavez, Jimmy Carter, Christa McAuliffe, Anthony Scalia, Louis Farrakahan, David Duke, Ronald Reagan, William Clinton, John Ashcroft, Barbara Lee, and George W. Bush.

Although the method of investigation, analysis and evaluation, including the questions used, could vary from personality to personality, it is suggested that the following questions be used as a starting point for studying each personality. As students progress through the various personalities, however, it may become necessary to develop additional questions for evaluation purposes.

1. What did he/she do that caused you to identify him/her as an example of patriotism? What was it about this person that he/she should be remembered and defined as a "Patriot?"
2. What did he/she do that would be considered unpatriotic?
3. On what basis was the judgment for question two made?

4. If there was a conflict between questions one and three, how was it resolved?
5. How did the subject fare when compared to the criteria for judgment that you stipulated?

Since this level of the unit requires that students become directly involved in research, it is recommended that a variety of teaching methods be used, requiring extensive student participation. The following strategies are offered either for actual classroom use or as springboards to prompt the discovery of additional and more creative teaching strategies. It may be necessary to devote between one and three class periods for each of the following assignments:

- Assign students to work in teams to research one or more (as is manageable) historical personalities to determine the patriotic status of each. Each team is expected to report its findings and/or conclusions.
- Assign students to work independently to research one or more (as is manageable) historical personalities to determine the degree of patriotism of each. Students are to report its findings and/or conclusions.
- Divide the class into two-student (or four-student, etc.) teams. Assign half the team to undertake research to determine how patriotic a personality (or several personalities?) is and assign the other half of the team to undertake research to determine how unpatriotic a personality (or several personalities?) is. A series of debates could be a follow-up activity for this assignment.
- Divide the class into teams of three to five students and provide each team with a list of personalities and the assignment to rank order the personalities from the most patriotic to the least patriotic. After an appropriate time period, each group should be asked to defend its choice of ranking.
- Assign students the task of researching a person who they believe best exemplifies the "ultimate patriot." Students should be required to defend their choices.

At the conclusion of each personality study, it is suggested that all four of the patriotism and judgment forms be retrieved from the files and offered to students as an opportunity to change and/or add to any definitions and/or criteria they had previously identified. Teachers may need to reassure students that it is okay to make modifications and that it is a sign of responsible citizenship and improved historical analysis to make such changes when research suggests that changes are appropriate.

Each personality analysis should prove revealing in terms of how students define the specific characteristics of the personalities as either patriotic or unpatriotic. Conceivably, the conclusions drawn from these investigations could serve as a benchmark of patriotism that could be applied to future patriotism searches.

Level Five

Toward the conclusion of the course of study—for the benefit of each student—teachers should set aside time for a personal "debriefing" of the unit. The time allowed should be recognized by both teachers and students as an informal opportunity to openly discuss feelings and/or attitudes that emerged as a direct result of the experiences encountered while working through the various lessons and/or stages.

As an initial step in the debriefing, the Questionnaire, the Patriotism Form, the Patriotism Revision Form, the Judgment Form and the Judgment Revision Form should be returned to each student. Students should be instructed to read carefully his or her "history" of participation in the unit. The actual debriefing should begin with a discussion focused on the following questions.

1. What changes, if any, would you make to your definition of patriotism as a result of your responses to the student questionnaire?
2. Why would you make these changes?
3. What changes, if any, did you make to your original definition of patriotism?
4. What had occurred that influenced your changes?
5. Did you make any changes to your list of characteristics of patriotism? How do you account for these changes?

6. What is the most creative item you have on your list of judgment criteria?

7. Why did you identify this particular item over the other items on your list of judgment criteria?

8. To what extent do you believe you have internalized the complexity of the beliefs, attitudes, and values offered by the unit?

9. To what extent do you feel your thinking has been impacted by your participation in the various activities of the unit?

10. To what extent have your abilities to research and analyze historical documentation improved? In what areas have you noticed advancement?

11. To what extent has your research permitted you to better support your opinions?

Although the ensuing discussion should focus on the previous list of questions, students should be permitted to take the discussion in any direction they desire as long as it relates to the general topic of patriotism. At some point, for example, students should be asked to identify what they believe to be the single most important lesson or experience gained by their participation in the unit. Shared experiences can often prove interesting and informative for both teachers and students. With the conclusion of the last activity, the action phase of the unit for teaching about patriotism is ended. Students who have participated in the sequence of experiences will have added one more dimension to their growth in citizenship. In today's society, perhaps more so than ever before, it is important that young people develop their analytical skills and become critical thinkers, in order to best defend against the various and manipulative elements that exist around us.

Level Six

If teachers are expected to use a formal evaluation, it should be based on the same spirit of openness that encompassed each of the previous activities. In essence, a high regard must be maintained for the views of each student. For assistance with the evaluation, the teacher might use one or more of the following options.

- Students may be required to analyze a specified number of person-alities to determine the extent each was patriotic. Ultimately, con-clusions will be tested to determine the extent to which students were consistent with their conclusions.
- The four collected forms could be used for a portfolio assessment of student experiences in the unit. For example, one approach might be to assess the student's advancement in terms of his or her comprehension of the central issues as evidenced by the maturity and complexity of student responses.
- A comparison could be made between a pre-test and a post-test of the questionnaire. Students might compare the "undecideds" with the "decideds." For example, fewer recorded "undecideds" might suggest an increased level of commitment to ideas.
- Student responses on the questionnaire could be evaluated against the responses of selected "authorities" in the field, such as the his-tory faculty of a nearby college or university.

As a culminating activity separate from level six, or as further means of assessment, teachers could create one or more patriotism-centered document-based essays. These would evaluate students' ability to analyze primary source documents and to use those docu-ments to apply their definitions of patriotism in writing. Following are a list of suggested essay questions and possible documents teachers may wish to use. Again, these are only a guide and the pos-sibilities are limitless. Teachers are also reminded that Appendix A of *Teaching New Patriotism in the 21ˢᵗ Century* provides a substan-tial list of significant American history documents.

Document-Based Assessments

Example A

Historical Context: In the years between the French and Indian War and the American Revolution, there were many matters of con-tention between the American colonists and the British govern-ment. Undercurrents of colonial self-rule accompanied by the mas-sive financial expense of maintaining the colonies, both financially and militarily, caused tension for both sides.

Question: Evaluating each player's level of patriotism, discuss the fiscal and legal policies of the English government between the years 1760 and 1776. In your discussion, be sure to define patriotism as well as compare the justification provided by King George and Parliament with the reactions of both loyalists and patriots in the colonies.

Suggested documents to excerpt:
1. The Navigation Acts of September 13, 1660.
2. Resolutions of the Stamp Act Congress, October 19, 1765.
3. Paul Revere's engraving of the Boston Massacre of March 5, 1770.
4. Captain Thomas Preston's account of the Boston Massacre, March 13, 1770.
5. The Coercive Acts (Intolerable Acts), March, 1774.
6. The Olive Branch Petition, July 8, 1775.
7. Thomas Paine's "Common Sense", January, 1776.
8. The Declaration of Independence, July 4, 1776.

Example B

Historical Context: Governmental decisions have had a great impact on the civil liberties of individuals and groups of individuals throughout American History.

Question: Discuss the impact of governmental decisions on civil liberties for individuals or groups of individuals living within the United States throughout history. Keeping in mind the values of varying time periods, evaluate the level of patriotism being displayed by particular individuals or branches of the government.

Suggested documents to excerpt:
1. The minutes of Cherokee Nation v. The State of Georgia, January term, 1831.
2. Painting titled "The Trial of Tears" by Robert Lindneux, found in the Woolaroc Museum, Bartlesville, Oklahoma.
3. The Enrollment Act, March 3, 1863.
4. Franklin Delano Roosevelt's Executive Order 9066, February 19, 1942.

5. Manuscript of William Calley's courts-martial beginning March 10, 1770. (Other personal accounts of the My Lai incident would also be excellent sources.)
6. George W. Bush's address to the nation on November 8, 2001.

Example C

Historical Context: Though only one of many causes for the Civil War, the existence of slavery in the United States, its justification, and its eventual demise raise some interesting questions about the statement "All men are created equal."

Question: In reference to American slavery, discuss the implications individual opinions of slavery had on what it meant to be a "proud American" in the years leading up to and during the Civil War.

Suggested documents to excerpt:
1. Frederick Douglass, "What to the Slave is the Fourth of July," July 5, 1852.
2. Abraham Lincoln, House Divided Speech, June 16, 1858.
3. John Brown, Address to the Court, October 16, 1859.
4. Charles Sumner, "The Barbarism of Slavery," June 4, 1860.
5. Jefferson Davis, Message to the Provisional Congress of the Confederate States of America, April 29, 1861.
6. Abraham Lincoln, Emancipation Proclamation, January 1, 1863.
7. Robert E. Lee, Letter to Andrew Hunter on Arming the Slaves, January 11, 1865.

The experiences that students encounter working through the levels of patriotism activities are intended to provide critical insight into the underlying complexities of defining patriotism. Used in conjunction with the more traditional trappings of patriotism, the experience of researching the historical foundations of patriotism will also assist in making patriotic songs, symbols, and pledges more meaningful. Ultimately, combining both traditional and nontraditional experiences will help educate students to be knowledgeable concerning relevant issues, committed to essential principles, AND patriotic.

12

Working to Make a Better America

The individual owes the exercise of all his faculties to the service of his country.

JOHN QUINCY ADAMS

L ending a helping hand to others and working toward a common goal has long been considered a cornerstone of the American way of life. From children collecting milkweed pods to help the war effort during World War II through young adults joining the Peace Corps to the current National "Make a Difference Day," Americans have made it their duty to provide help when help was needed.

Although there were a few exceptions, this propensity toward helping others was particularly evident in the days and months following the terrorist attacks of September 11, 2001. People all across the United States extended a hand to their families, neighbors, communities, cities, and country—it made no difference whether they were helping friends or strangers. Americans united as a single people while struggling to rebuild their shocked and violated nation.

The renewed sense of caring for and helping others that occurred after September 11, 2001 is presented in the following excerpts selected from newspapers throughout the United States. Arranged randomly, the articles clearly illustrate the newly energized attitude that swept across America. Even today people continue to reach out to help others in hopes that even the smallest of deeds will help promote a strong sense of community. It is this belief in caring for others, represented through action, that is endorsed in *Teaching New Patriotism in the 21st Century* as a critical element of the *New Patriotism*. The following excerpts also provide several additional ideas that teachers may adopt directly, or modify in some way, to create projects involving their students in positive community endeavors.

"Batson Helps Girl, 11, with Funds From Auction A Little Birdie Said"

Amarillo Globe News, Amarillo, Texas

(Sept 30, 2001) By Staff Reporter, Amarillo Texas

Paul Sutterfield was devastated to learn that his 11–year-old daughter, LuRae, has cancer and will need treatment in Houston. Thanks to the generosity of an Amarillo family, things will be a little easier.

Joe Batson, whose family estate auction began at Bentley & Associates Sept. 22–23 and will continue Saturday, heard about Lu-Rae from Neal Bentley. He decided to donate proceeds from the sale of a Hampton Court sterling silver coffee-and-tea set to the Sutterfields.

"The set brought in $3,500," Bentley said. "And Bentley's is donating our commission and buyer's premium, so the Sutterfields will be getting $4,200 to help with the medical expenses."

"The auction so far has been a huge success," Bentley said. "Batson wants people to know that the money isn't just going into a bank vault. It will be used to help people in the community."

"Many Grit Teeth and Shed Blood for Tattoos Showing Love of Country."

St. Petersburg Times, St. Petersburg, Florida

(Sept. 24, 2001) by Mike Brassfield

Millions of Americans are wearing their patriotism on their sleeves these days, but a select few are wearing it just beneath. They're getting patriotic tattoos.

In a sign of the times, an increasing number of people are marching into Tampa Bay area tattoo shops to have star-spangled banners or fierce-looking eagles inked onto their biceps and backs.

"Nobody can buy a flag now (because they are selling out), but they can get something that's forever. Now they can't forget," said Brent Cox, manager of a tattoo studio called Dynamite Dermagraphics in Crystal River. "This is the only thing that people can't take away from you. You can't lose it. It's not going to break. You take it to your grave."

"Geauga Will Bus Seniors to Hospitals"

The Plain Dealer, Chardon, Ohio

(March 15, 2002) By John Horton, Reporter

—The Geauga County Department on Aging will begin running its own bus next month to take seniors from the rural community to out-of-county hospitals, particularly those in downtown Cleveland.

Nearly 500 senior citizens are expected to use the service over the next year, said Sally Bell, who oversees the county agency.

"A service like this is particularly important in a rural community like ours," Bell said. "It ensures our senior citizens can get to the area's major medical centers for the treatment and care they need."

For the last several years, the department has arranged for seniors to be taken to regional hospitals three days a week by Geauga Transit, the county's public transportation system. Last year, 118 county residents used the service.

"Local Teen Aids Relief Effort"

The Marshall Democrat News, Marshall, Missouri

(October 4, 2001) By Chris Post, Marshall Missouri

The Sept. 11 terrorist attacks on sites in New York City and Washington, D.C., have kindled both patriotic and religious feelings in many throughout the country. One local teenager is giving area residents a chance to show both and to help those directly affected by the attacks as well.

Ashley McKay, who will turn 16 later this month, said that after seeing the destruction wrought by the attacks, she felt she should do something to help. The teenage entrepreneur already had a small business creating buttons and decided to use it as her means of helping.

McKay, the daughter of Mike and Shirley McKay of Marshall, said that her button business has become an assembly line operation with not only her parents but her brother and sister helping to make the buttons as well.

McKay has been selling the buttons, which bear a picture of the United States colored like an American flag with the words "In God We Trust" printed above and below, for $1 each. McKay said she wasn't sure how many of the buttons had been assembled to date, but that about 900 had been sold.

"People have been very supportive, very receptive," she said. "They want to help out."

In addition to letting people show their faith and patriotism, the buttons will also help those harmed by the attacks. McKay said she is setting aside 25 cents from each button to cover the cost of making them. The other 75 cents, as well as any money left over after paying for materials, will be given to service organizations for victim relief.

McKay said she would like to see some of the money go to help the firefighters who responded to the World Trade Center attack site, or to organizations set up to assist them and the families of emergency personnel who died in the rescue effort. She said she will also donate part of the proceeds to the American Red Cross to help the agency in its continuing relief efforts.

Ultimately, McKay said, she would like the money she is raising to help people get back to normal lives . . .

"Cookbooks Reflect America's Kitchens, From Sea to Shining Sea"

Arizona Daily Sun, Arizona, USA

(Oct. 17, 2001) By Joan Brunskill, *Associated Press Writer*

NEW YORK—How about baking a hearty loaf of Amber Waves of Grain? Patriotic cooks looking for a warm task in the kitchen to cheer chilly fall days have a wide range of evocative new cookbooks from which to harvest inspiration.

First off, there's this unbeatable name for a bread recipe—Amber Waves of Grain. . . . In the book Fertig [author] has collected "more than 150 recipes that celebrate the wonderful bounty that is the Heartland's claim to fame. From artisanal and small-town bakeries, the best home bakers and my own family's kitchen . . . they display the stunning diversity America's Breadbasket offers."

"Fireman's luck, quick action save carpet store"

The Floyd County Times, Prestonsburg, Kentucky

(April 1, 2002) By Loretta Blackburn, Staff Writer

ALLEN—A fire that could have been disastrous for Kentucky Carpet Factory Outlet at Allen—as well as the surrounding neighborhood—was interrupted by the quick thinking of a veteran volunteer firefighter.

On Thursday evening, Dennis Adams, a 30–year volunteer at Allen Fire Department, was leaving work at Mobile Oil when he noticed a fire outside of Kentucky Carpet.

Adams said that when he passed by he saw two flaming bags of trash against the side of the building. He used a two-by-four to drag the garbage away from the building and waited while a neighbor went to call the fire department. Freda Branham, part-owner of the store, said a neighbor informed her there was a fire outside the store and when she saw the smoke she called 911. Branham said that the store had three adjoining buildings full of carpet and she believed that if it had burned it would have burned more than the business. "I don't see how you could put out a fire with all this carpet," said Branham. Adams said he normally leaves work earlier than he did Thursday but he luckily happened to be passing by on a street that is normally vacant at that time of the evening and saw the fire.

"Fortunately I happened to be in the right place at the right time," said Adams.

"Hot Line Helps Stock Food Bank's Shelves"

The Nashville Tennessean, Nashville, Tennessee

(February 9, 2002) By Warran Duzak, Nashville Tennessee

A new hot-line system to encourage easy donations of money for food for Second Harvest Food Bank of Middle Tennessee has helped it reach a goal of securing 500,000 pounds of food for needy families and individuals in the Midstate.

Money to purchase even more food was collected by the non-profit organization in November and December and will help fill the Second Harvest pantry until late this spring.

"That is encouraging because the group," which assists 500 agencies in 37 counties, "needs all the help it can get during the economic downturn," Second Harvest spokeswoman Susannah Shumate said.

"In November, 45% of the people who came to us were first-time clients, and in December it was 44%," Shumate said.

"So almost half the people we saw in November and December were first-time clients, and that is staggering."

"We are experiencing a level of need that we haven't seen since the Gulf War, about 10 years ago. There are grandparents on Social Security raising grandchildren, and their checks aren't going far enough."

Second Harvest President and CEO Jaynee Day said that despite a "dire shortage of food" faced by the food bank and the agencies it serves, "the community rallied around us during the holidays."

"We are overwhelmed by the generosity of individuals and businesses and organizations that worked so hard to help their hungry neighbors," Day said.

"Students Meet Their Hero"

Times-News, Twin Falls, Idaho

(February 1, 2002) By Robert Mayer, Twin Falls Idaho

TWIN FALLS—Fourth-graders at Sawtooth Elementary School finally got to meet their pen pal: an Air Force pilot who just returned to Idaho from action in Afghanistan.

Since November, Nancy Hunter's class has been corresponding with Capt. Mike Ballek of the 391st Fighter Squadron while he was stationed in the Afghanistan region. Soon after coming back to Mountain Home Air Force Base, Ballek made a trek to Twin Falls Thursday to meet the kids who sent him homemade cards, school projects, Thanksgiving letters and e-mails.

The students, in turn, were thrilled to meet their pilot correspondent and enthusiastically raised their hands, eager to have their endless supply of questions answered.

Decked out in his green flight suit—not a jump suit as he corrected one mistaken student—Ballek patiently answered the students' queries for more than an hour.

"I got such a kick out of the letters they sent," he said. "It's nice to have people rooting for you back home."

"It was a great experience. We got to meet somebody who flew in a plane and flew for our country," said Terra Rushing. "I learned that pilots have leggings and vests and if you take off your mask, you might not be able to breathe."

While in Afghanistan, Ballek said he kept busy flying his F-15e Strike Eagle with sorties sometimes 12 to 13 hours in length. But, unbeknownst to him, he was also being used back in Idaho as teaching aid. Whether the subject was math, science or geography, it was always related in reference to Captain Mike, said Hunter.

"I wanted the kids to be thinking about their future, be it college or the Air Force Academy," she said.

But it was Hunter's desire to engage the class in a "random act of kindness" that really triggered the correspondence.

"If somebody is on the other side of the world protecting us, keeping us safe, so that we can drive to work every day and come to school every day and sit safe in our desk every day, the least we could do is write a letter," she said. "Little does he know he has touched all of our hearts."

"American Legion and VFW to Host Veterans Dinner with Key Club Sunday"

Chillicothe Constitution Tribune, Chillicothe, Missouri

(January 30, 2002) Chillicothe Constitution Tribune Staff, Chillicothe Missouri

In a deep spirit of gratitude, patriotism and appreciation, the Chillicothe High School Key Club invites all veterans (wartime and peacetime), their wives and widows to a Veterans' Appreciation Dinner at 1 p.m. this Sunday, Feb. 3, at the Vern R. Glick, Post No. 25, The American Legion home at 1400 North Washington Street in Chillicothe.

The American Legion and the Roy L. Burkett, Post No. 858, Veterans of Foreign Wars, of Chillicothe, are helping to host the carry-in dinner.

Last Veterans Day, the CHS Key Club wrote to local war veterans thanking them for their service to the nation. Dozens of World War II, Korean and Vietnam veterans wrote back to the Key Club members, many of whom stated that the Key Club's thank-you letters were the first time anyone had thanked them for their war service.

"Weather No Obstacle for Boy Who Wants a Cleaner Gillette"

The News-Record, Gillette, Wyoming

(January 24, 2002) By Kristy Gray, Gillette Wyoming

It was, put simply, cold. Winds blasted exposed cheeks and noses and turned fingers an unhealthy scarlet.

But even as bundled shoppers hurried to and from Wal-mart and Kmart, as car headlights circled the parking lots, one boy and his mother stayed outside clutching big, black garbage bags. They didn't leave until they picked up every piece of trash on the grass field between the town's discount stores.

"I feel proud of myself. It makes it look better and some people honk their horns. That makes me feel good," 12–year-old Michael Smart said. The Pronghorn Elementary sixth-grader has adopted the litter-spewed lot between Wal-mart and Kmart for a class environmental project. He's vowed to keep it as clean as possible through the school year and beyond. He'll keep doing it even after fulfilling his obligations to the class assignment.

Teacher Patsy Wirth made the assignment to fulfill a district requirement that all students should complete a project to improve their environment. Some have built bird houses, some volunteered with the Humane Society, others have monitored how much water they use. It raises the students' awareness of the world around them and what they can do to help. "They learn that one person can make a difference, and I think Michael has shown that," she said.

"It's just so wonderful that he took so much pride and initiative to go further than many students do," she said.

Smart figures that he's cleaned the field about five times—whenever he sees that it needs to be done and whenever his mother can drive him down there. She usually helps him, too, taking the pair about 30 minutes to finish the job . . . Now when Michael drives around Wal-mart or Kmart, he notices the lot.

"Wow, Mom. Look at how messy it is already," he'll say.

"I don't think they realize how messy it gets until they have ownership in it," Mary Lou Smart said.

"Watts and Heintzelman are Firefighters of the Year"

The News-Sun and The Evening Star, Cromwell, Indiana

(January 12, 2002) By Bob Buttgen, Cromwell, Indiana

Volunteer firefighters are hard to come by. Dangerous work, strange hours and no pay means there aren't a surplus of men and women who want this type of endeavor.

So when the Sparta Township Volunteer Fire Department finds a pair of good firefighters such as Taylor Watts and Jim Heintzelman, they like to make them feel appreciated. Last month the pair were named "Firefighters of the Year" for 2001 by their colleagues on the department, based in Cromwell.

Watts is beginning his 13th year as a member of the department, while Heintzelman has been a firefighter for 22 years. Both are graduates of West Noble High School.

When Watts isn't at the fire station, he's an engineer with Acadia Polymers in Ligonier and also serves as president of the Cromwell Town Council . . .

Both men say their department is a very tight fraternity of men united in the cause of helping others.

"It's a real family atmosphere," Watts said. "We're all tight and there's a lot of trust because you have to trust the guy who's backing you up."

Watts said the department is very family oriented. "That's a real tradition in Cromwell. We do a lot of family things together." . . .

For Heintzelman, being a firefighter is a family tradition as he is the third generation of his family to serve with the department. His father, Roger, and grandfather, Lawrence Heintzelman, both were longtime members of the department, which has served the Cromwell area for several decades. Heintzelman's brother, Jeff, also is a member and he has an uncle who served with the department for many years . . .

"I like to help people and it's an exciting job," he said of his second career. "You never know what you're going to go up against."

Like everyone on his department, Heintzelman takes his job seriously. "We're a brotherhood," he said.

Heintzelman said he and others have appreciated the renewed sense of recognition being shown to the nation's firefighters and other emergency workers following the Sept. 11 attacks and America's war on terrorism. "I feel we're a lot more appreciated and that helps a lot," he said . . .

"Homeless Given Free Flu Shots"

Leader-Telegram, Eau Claire, Wisconsin

(January 5, 2002) By Jennifer Schmidt, staff writer

Sarah Scott had never received a flu shot, and wasn't expecting to get one this year because she recently lost her job and had no permanent place to live.

But thanks to a free flu shot clinic brought Friday to the Beacon House, a homeless shelter operated by Interfaith Hospitality Network, Scott was vaccinated after all.

"I thought that it was nice that they offered it, because I definitely wanted to have it done," said Scott.

The project was prompted by the Healthcare Access Team of Healthy Communities 2000, an Eau Claire County effort to help build strong individuals, families and communities.

"Patriotic Duty"

The Burlington Free Press, Burlington, Vermont

(Nov. 27, 2001) By Keith D. Elston, Essex Junction, VT. Letter to the Editor

"We the people of the United States, . . . in order to . . . secure the blessings of Liberty to ourselves and our posterity, do ordain and establish this Constitution . . ."

One of the blessings of liberty is the ability to think for ourselves, not merely to walk in lock step with the current orthodoxy of ideas and opinions.

Patriotism comes in many forms. Displaying the American flag and singing "God Bless America" are certainly patriotic gestures, but there is little risk in either of these actions. True patriotism inevitably requires each of us to take risks for our country. Patriotism calls on each of us to learn and act: to learn about our history and act so that we don't repeat our mistakes; to learn about our government's actions and act to preserve our democratic values; to learn about the events and people who shape our government's policies and act to ensure that those policies are consistent and just.

When our leaders attempt to unravel our civil liberties, including the right to confidential communications between attorney and client, the right to judicial review of government action, the right to know what the government is looking for when they search your home, the right to a public trial, the right not to be held indefinitely without being charged with a crime—when our leaders, hoping to exploit the public's fears, move our country in a direction that is destructive of the constitutional rights that make our country the aspiration of most of the world community, then it is incumbent upon true patriots to publicly question their actions and demand the restoration of our rights.

True patriots are supportive of their government and their country, but will not hesitate to question their leaders' actions when they violate the basic tenets of our democracy. That is a blessing worth fighting for.

"Generation Gap Closing: Teens Helping Seniors to Safety-Proof Homes"

Las Vegas Sun, Las Vegas, Nevada

(December 21, 2001) By Rebecca Malone, Las Vegas Nevada

For people such as Evy Hannelius, living alone at 71 can often be dangerous. After watching a neighbor recover from hip surgery, a result of an injury incurred after falling off a ladder in her garage, Hannelius said she has learned not to try anything that may put her safety at risk.

"So far I have been lucky, but there are a lot of things like this that as you get older you won't be able to do," Hannelius said.

Starting in January, Hannelius and other seniors will be able to request help from a group of teenagers who work with the Volunteer Center of Southern Nevada. The teens are working with the Lowe's Home Safety Council to train teen volunteers to assess problems and help fix seniors' homes.

"High School Peer Mediators Take Their Message to Fourth Graders"

The Waterford Eccentric, Waterford, Michigan

(Nov. 7, 2001) By Carolyn Walker, staff writer

As peer mediators from Mott High School taught their message of non-violent conflict resolution to fourth graders at Haviland Elementary School last week they could only hope the lessons would have positive effects on the future as well as the present.

"I can't honestly tell you the last time I've seen a fight at school," said Mott senior, mediator Mike Smerczak, as he moderated a role-playing situation between learning elementary students. "It starts here. It starts with kids."

"Bush Makes a Pitch for Teaching Patriotism"

The Washington Post

(Nov. 2, 2001) By Dana Milbank, staff writer

"I am proud to be standing with the Patriots," said President Bush, the assembly's guest of honor, to a roar of approval from the suburban teenagers. "We're a nation of patriots. . . . We have a renewed spirit of patriotism."

That scene from earlier this week represents the sentiment the White House is seeking to spread among the nation's youth after the Sept. 11 terrorist attacks.

The administration has thrown its weight behind a mass Pledge of Allegiance by the nation's 52 million schoolchildren, a pen-pal exchange between U.S. children and Muslim children overseas, and classroom lectures by veterans. Far broader programs are being considered. The White House is considering legislation that would quintuple participation in AmeriCorps, the national service program, to 250,000.

"Committee Plans 'Day of Patriotism' Nov. 12 at Walter Sillers Coliseum"

The Bolivar Commercial, Bolivar, Mississippi

(Nov. 1, 2001) By Marcus Van Every, BC Staff Writer

The Bolivar Celebrates America Committee has planned a "Day of Patriotism" for anyone and everyone who wants to support the nation in this time of war. Bolivar County Chancery Clerk Jeanne Walker, along with the other members of the new committee, are excited about the scheduled event: "This will meet a need for people of the community to come together and be comforted and reassured that we are one nation."

"Fort Pierre Woman Saves Stranger's Life"

Rapid City Journal, Rapid City, South Dakota

(Oct 27, 2001) By Staff Reporter, Rapid City South Dakota

PIERRE (AP)—Pierre police were so impressed by a Fort Pierre woman's efforts to prevent a stranger from leaping from a bridge that they let her keep it up until they could get the suicidal woman to safety. Melody Hackett, a paralegal from Fort Pierre, had had a bad week. Her father-in-law had died after being taken off life support Monday and his funeral was Thursday. At about 10 that night, she saw a car stop on the Missouri River Bridge. A woman got out and crawled onto a ledge. She spun her car around and called 911, Hackett said, and then started talking to the woman. Police arrived three minutes later and slowly moved in as she continued to speak with the woman, who was identified only as being from Madison, Wis.

"She was doing such an excellent job of talking to her that they just stood by," Police Chief Allen Aden said. Hackett tried to maintain eye contact and told the woman she cared about her. When she learned the woman had a daughter, she used that to urge her not to kill herself.

"Somehow, I wanted to get it across to her how important life was, and she didn't want to end it," Hackett said. She begged the woman for a hug. When the woman reached out, officers moved in.

"They grabbed her arms as I was grabbing her neck, and we just pulled her in," Hackett said. The woman was taken to a hospital. Hackett has had no crisis-intervention training. She had to approach the woman in a non-threatening way.

"I'm an old cowgirl," she said. "I knew I couldn't just run at her and goat-tie her. . . . I feel like my guardian angel was helping me."

"Tickets Still Available for Seniors' 'Night Out'"

Daily Register, Portage, Wisconsin

(Nov 1, 2001) By Anne C. Zimmerman, Portage Wisconsin

A night of fun and socializing, starting at 4 p.m., has been organized by the TRIAD SALT (Seniors and Law Enforcement Together) for Nov. 4 at the Blankenhaus Restaurant in Portage.

It's a "Safe Night Out for Seniors" who will have the opportunity to play bingo and eat dinner, followed by a dance from 6 p.m. to 8 p.m. It's all part of a nationwide TRIAD effort to promote a night out for seniors who usually stay home after the sun goes down, or for those that don't go out at all.

The cost of the event is $5 with tickets available at the Blankenhaus, the Portage Police Department or the Market Basket. Officer Penny Kiefer, SALT coordinator, said those who have a problem getting a ticket should call her at 742-7950. The Portage Cab Co. has agreed to provide discounted fares to all seniors attending the event, and if they desire, will see to it that the driver accompanies the partygoers safely to their doors.

The cab company also has access to a wheelchair-accessible van. Those interested in using a cab, should make arrangements in advance by calling 742-6669.

All seniors in the area are welcome.

"Volunteer Program to Take on Lewiston School"

Daily Register, Portage, Wisconsin

(Oct 28, 2001) By Phil Rhein, Portage Wisconsin

Next spring, more than a hundred future teachers from around the state are planning to turn up at the Lewiston Elementary School and start painting, planting and generally improving the condition of the small rural school. The volunteer work will be performed by students in college education programs and is the result of Lewiston being awarded an Outreach to Teach grant that the school applied for last spring. Emily Shier, a master's student at the University of Wisconsin—Stout and student coordinator of the program, said they're expecting about 150 students for the April 14 work date, based on the number who turned out for last years project in Green Bay.

"We'll just squish in there and get the work done," she laughed, explaining that Lewiston is the smallest school to receive the grant in its four-year history.

"With the revenue caps and taxes, everyone is trying to figure out ways to help schools but not add to the expenses," she said. "There are all kinds of neat projects we haven't had the money to do." In addition to helping accomplish that, the grant also aims to give future teachers a chance to perform a valuable community service . . .

"There's more to teaching than just classroom prep and lesson plans," said Peter Gust, executive director of the South Central Education Association, one of the people who helped write the grant proposal. Shier isn't worried that future teachers, preparing to enter a field where many wind up feeling underpaid and overworked, will resent the challenge of doing volunteer work like this.

"People going into teaching aren't really out for the money," she said. "The future teachers I've met are very eager to get involved."

"It's kinda nice to help some teachers now, before we get into the profession ourselves," Shier added. "We can envision the looks on children's faces as they come in that Monday morning to see the changes made to the school."

"Community in Gear for Pumpkin Race"

The Idaho Statesman, Boise, Idaho

(Oct. 25, 2001) By Sandra Forester

Running has become a family affair for the Wrotens of Nampa. For the past three years, they have run in the annual Great Pumpkin Race.

"The pumpkin race is really fun because of the children's home," Kenny Wroten said. "That's what kinda got us involved in the first place." Proceeds from the Great Pumpkin Race benefit Northwest Children's Home, a private, non-profit organization that provides residential, therapeutic and educational services for troubled children and their families.

"Helping is Food-Bank Volunteer's Forte"

The Hutchinson News, Hutchinson, Kansas

(October 22, 2001) By Joyce Hall, Hutchinson Kansas

Mary Jo Vecchiarelli, Hutchinson, has worked around people all her life. After Vecchiarelli, a former home health aide, retired, she decided she needed something to do. For three years, Vecchiarelli has helped at the Food Bank of Reno County. She usually works on Tuesday afternoons. Her husband, Tony, helps on Friday mornings.

"I add perishable items to food packages," she said. "We keep real busy."

Vecchiarelli said there is much work to be done and she finds satisfaction in volunteering.

"It seems like it's so little that one can do," she said.

Vecchiarelli enjoys meeting and working with people. She also helps at Holy Cross Catholic Church's gift shop and with funeral dinners at the church. Food-bank manager Keith Marks said they have about 40 volunteers who help stock shelves and fill sacks with food.

"The volunteers are the backbone of the food bank," Marks said.

"Livonia Students Raise Their Voices for Patriotism, Funds"

Democrat and Chronicle, Rochester, New York

(Oct 15, 2001) By Joseph Spector, Staff Writer.

Students at Livonia Primary School have re-recorded a patriotic song, performed there in 1990, hoping to use proceeds from sales to help families of victims of the Sept. 11 attacks. The song, "We Are Free," was co-written by Mount Morris residents and composers Anne House and Van Walworth in 1976 to commemorate the U.S. bicentennial celebration. Livonia students sang it in 1990 as part of the celebration when the primary school was named a Blue Ribbon School for excellence in education. . . . School officials "'thought this was a good patriotic song to boost spirits.'"

"Kindergarteners Send Teddy Bears to NYC"

Lincoln Journal Star, Nebraska

(Oct. 21, 2001) By Jodi Fuson, School Notes

Karl Sawyer's all-day kindergarten class at Meadow Lane Elementary School found several ways to reach out to victims of the

Sept. 11 terrorist attacks and the people who helped with rescue efforts.

Students first brainstormed ways they could help. They decided to send a teddy bear and a toy to a child who lost a parent in the attacks on New York City, pack up cookies and juice and send them to a firehouse in New York City, compile a medical supplies package and send it to another firehouse, and draw pictures and write notes to firefighters, police officers, nurses and doctors in the New York City area.

Sawyer plans to send the letters for doctors and nurses, along with a box of approximately 20 teddy bears donated to the school by a Ventures in Partnership partner, to St. Vincent's Hospital in New York City.

"Patriotism Strong at Franklin"

Blytheville Courier News, Blytheville, Arizona

(Oct. 20, 2001) By Tena Furnish, Blytheville Courier News

Students at Franklin Primary School participated in a patriotic ceremony Friday afternoon that culminated in a release of red, white and blue balloons to show their support for the nation. Principal Ann Coleman said several factors came together at about the same time, leading to the ceremony.

"We wanted to help the children learn about patriotism. A teacher had the idea of a balloon release, and the music teacher had been teaching the children patriotic songs. We had asked for the new flags because our old flags were worn," she said.

"ROTC Cadets Run for Patriotism: Fire and Police Departments Join 'Unity Run' in Show of Solidarity"

Ka Leo O Hawaii, Manoa, Hawaii

(Oct. 14, 2001) By Erica Cordova, Ka Leo Staff Writer

A sea of more than 200 flags darted through campus last Friday as University of Hawai'i and visiting ROTC cadets ran to show their patriotism. "(The 'Unity Run') is an opportunity for cadets to show patriotism," said Capt. Gary Layne of the Army ROTC program. "You have people run for different causes—we do it for American pride."

"U.S. Flags Still a Hot Commodity"

Eastside Journal, Bellevue, Washington

(Oct. 11, 2001) By Patti Payne

HOW PROUDLY IT WAVES: Patriotism is way up, and so is Old Glory. Still. With flags hard to locate these days because of their renewed countrywide popularity, Costco received a huge shipment of American flags just a few days ago. Customer Bernadette Anne of Issaquah was surprised when shopping yesterday for other items.

"I had been looking for a nylon (American flag)," she said. "They were limiting one to a person and even had a Costco employee very pleasantly handing them out to whomever wanted to buy one. At $9.99, I have to applaud Costco for making these so affordable and they were already on an aluminum pole."

"Juneau Man Reaches Out to Kids . . ."

The Juneau Empire, Juneau, Alaska

(February 1, 2002) By Kathy Dye, Juneau Alaska

Chris Grisafe was reading a newspaper recently when he came upon a disturbing story about a teen-ager who was losing a battle with liver disease. The boy's grandmother had volunteered to donate part of her liver to save his life but doctors told her she was too old for the procedure, which carries some risk to donors. That's when Grisafe, 22, did something unusual. The Juneau man called to inquire about donating part of his liver.

"The bottom line is you're talking about a kid that hasn't lived much of a life," said Grisafe. He was told he could not donate a liver, because only family members are eligible to be donors.

"There's plenty of opportunity out there for him to take life by the horns, so why not help someone do that?" said Grisafe.

"Smith named unsung hero"

Brattleboro Reformer, Brattleboro, Vermont

(March 30, 2002) by Brattleboro Staff

BRATTLEBORO—Vermont Yankee Corporate and Community Affairs Representative Larry Smith has been selected as the 2002 Unsung Hero by the Retired and Senior Volunteer Program (RSVP) of Windham County. Larry will be honored at RSVP's annual Roast/Toast at the Brattleboro American Legion Hall on Saturday evening, April 6.

Smith has been one of Windham County's most active community volunteers for more than 30 years. He joined Vermont Yankee in February of 1997, and has received numerous national, state and local awards for his charitable and community efforts. He came to Brattleboro in 1967 and spent many years as a broadcaster, serving as General Manager and News Director of WTSA AM and FM. He is a former President of the Brattleboro Area Chamber of Commerce and remains a member of its board of directors. He is a graduate of Elkins Institute in Houston, Texas, where he earned a degree in Broadcast Management and Engineering. Smith, his wife Valerie and four sons live in West Chesterfield, N.H.

"Renewed Patriotism Boosts Banner Sales"

The Augusta Chronicle, Augusta, Georgia

(Sept. 24, 2001) By Robert Branch, Memorial News Service

The rush of buyers took Ms. Robinson by surprise.

"I didn't sell one American flag over Labor Day, and I had ordered extras for the holiday," she said. "And now that this has happened, the 1,000 American flags I had—from size 2-by-3 (feet) to 20-by-30 are gone."

One thing Ms. Robinson said she won't do is buy U.S. flags made overseas.

"I received a fax telling me that a large container was due in with flags made in China," Ms. Robinson said. "It said we could order as many as 10,000. I'm not going to do it."

"Kiwanis Flip Fluffy Flapjacks for Charity Saturday"

Dodge City Daily Globe, Dodge City, Kansas

(Nov. 7, 2001) By Anne Zohner Maxwell,*Dodge City Daily Globe*
The Kiwanis Pancake Feed is a familiar event for many in the area. The more than 75–year tradition that serves up fluffy flapjacks is certainly an annual ritual for Dale Hull. "It's interesting to meet people and to see old friends you haven't seen for a long time," he said.

"There's also the gratification of knowing that the group's efforts will help others in the community."

"A Dirty, Thankful Job"

The Oregonian, Portland, Oregon

(March 15, 2002) By Michelle Myers
TROUTDALE: Sweetbriar Elementary School fifth-graders spent this week shoveling out the foundation of a new wetland they helped designed. The muddy project unearthed passions for the planet in some students. "When I come back to visit, I'll feel like I helped the environment and I saved the world," said Emily Bargas, attired in rain gear from head to toe.

Led by teacher Len Otto, Emily and her classmates took on the wetland project after learning that mitigation was required to capture additional stormwater from a new covered play area with an impermeable blacktop surface. A new office is replacing the school's old covered play area.

Otto figured the project would be a practical application of the plant science curriculum he taught at the beginning of the year.

"But it's really taken on a life of its own," he said. "The kids have really come together on this and have taken real ownership."

In designing the wetland, the students learned about land surveying, native wildlife and pond construction, including mathematical problems such as determining slope and cubic yards. They learned new words and phrases such as "point-source pollution" and "mitigation."

"Patriotism Unfurled: Neighbors, Strangers Help Replace Stolen Flag"

The News-Times, Danbury, Connecticut

(Sept. 27, 2001) By Brian Saxton, staff writer

Whoever stole an American flag strung by two families across Flat Swamp Road stirred up so much neighborhood emotion, strangers sent replacements.

"It really warms your heart to see how supportive people have been," said John Doern, who helped his neighbor, Peter Borgia, hoist the flag . . . "How can you steal someone's patriotism?"

"Chamber of Commerce to Hold Fundraiser for Red Cross"

The Citizen, Beaver Dam, Wisconsin

(Sept 24, 2001) by Citizen Staff, Beaver Dam Wisconnsin

"Chamber Lights of Freedom," a fundraiser for American Red Cross Disaster Relief for New York City and Washington D.C., will be kicked off on Wednesday, Sept. 26, by the Beaver Dam Area Chamber of Commerce. The project chaired by Jane Schweiger of Jane's Added Touch/Bella, features patriotic luminaries consisting of a red-white-and-blue candle inserted in sand in a glass jar tied with a matching ribbon.

The chamber is asking members of the Beaver Dam business community and anyone wishing to participate to unite and show their support, not only in thoughts and prayers, but also by donating $5 or more for a Chamber Lights of Freedom luminary. Proceeds will benefit American Red Cross Disaster Relief. The luminary signifies your donation to the fund. . . .

In remembrance, the chamber is asking everyone to light their candles at 7 p.m. on Thursday, Oct. 11. All checks must be made payable to the American Red Cross Disaster Relief.

"Kindness Puts Theft Victim Back on Wheels"

The Saint Petersburg Times, Saint Petersburg, Florida

(Oct. 21, 2001) By Sheila Mullane Estrada

PINELLAS PARK—Thanks to an anonymous benefactor, Bonnie Foster has a shiny, green three-wheeled bicycle to ride in and around her mobile home park. Foster's last bicycle was stolen on her 77th birthday last month and she has since been virtually homebound.

Conclusion

*If we falter in our leadership we may endanger the peace of the world,
and we shall surely endanger the welfare of the nation.*

HARRY S TRUMAN

For over a hundred years, from the era of the American Revolution until the eve of the twentieth century, educators in the United States involved their students in patriotic ceremonies with an almost ritualistic passion. From one generation to the next, America's youth were instructed to honor flag, country, and God. The only interruptions were for purposes of modifying the tone of the message and/or incorporating significant changes in definition when it was deemed necessary. In most respects the period was almost devoid of change, at least where patriotism and its proper place in education were concerned. Traditional perspectives and practices were entrenched, and set the standard, almost without exception.

Beginning in the late nineteenth century, however, challenges to widely accepted traditional teaching methods occurred in increasing numbers, but they were generally of short duration and had little lasting impact. It was not until the Civil Rights movement and the anti-Vietnam War demonstrations, early in the second half of the twentieth century that a major assault on traditional views of patriotism and the manner in which it was taught was taken seriously. Many Americans, especially educators, began to question the beliefs and values that had previously been accepted elements of American pedagogy. Some suggested that new definitions of patriotism would be in order, or, at the very least, old definitions should be more liberally defined. There were also those who were so thoroughly turned off by the stigma associated with patriotism that they wanted nothing to do with it.

While it is true that the sixties, seventies, and eighties passed without answering all the questions related to patriotism and how it should be taught, one thing was certain, the period clearly produced a plethora of innovative options. Social studies journals and methods textbooks churned out an array of ideas for teaching non-traditional concepts. These ideas ranged from not teaching patriotism at all to requiring students to perform some sort of national service; no longer was it fashionable for students, especially those at secondary levels of education, to be taught traditional patriotism.

As the 21st century approached, many of the perceptions of patriotism and how it should be taught were still very much at issue. These differences were best illustrated through perusal of the *National Standards for Civics and Government* and the *National History Standards.* Although the authors of each claimed legitimacy for their respective documents as providing national standards in social studies education, they failed to reach agreement on the proper place of patriotism in the American classroom. As the century drew to a close, the problem was left to the next generation of educators to resolve.

The catastrophic events of September 11, 2001 brought a renewed interest in restoring patriotism to America's classrooms. The attacks on the World Trade Center, Pentagon, and Flight 93, and the subsequent public reaction emphasized the need for change from indifference to positive proactive instruction in what it means to be a patriot.

The research during the last half of the previous century left little doubt that teaching patriotism by engaging students solely in patriotic pageantry, especially at secondary levels, was simply no longer practical. The 21st century required that a spirit of patriotism be taught that incorporated a blend of traditional and nontraditional interests alike. This *New* Patriotism would include an effort to emphasize the glory of the flag and everything positive America stands for and to promote an understanding of the need to reach out and help those who were less fortunate, both at home and abroad.

The issue of patriotism and good citizenship does not end with American students, however. There is also a need for leaders in government, society, banking and business, as well as men and women on the street, to provide positive role models. The students that America's schools produce today simply have too much savvy to be deluded when they observe inconsistencies and contradictions. It is difficult for students to accept their teachers' rhetoric concerning the merits of demonstrating patriotism when they are made aware of too many Americans putting profits before patriotism. On one hand they see American corporations reap great profits, but elect to leave the United States and incorporate in Bermuda to avoid paying taxes, and, on the other hand, they see corporate executives plundering their own companies at the peril of their employees' future well being. And they are aware of oil companies manipulating prices for profits, at the expense—once again—of mainstream America. Instead, what is needed is the kind of corporate philanthropy promoted by the Bill and Melinda Gates foundation.

Unfortunately the problem doesn't end with corporate America. In recent years individual citizens in unparalleled numbers have elected to deposit untaxed earnings in offshore accounts in Switzerland, Hong Kong, and elsewhere, to avoid paying American taxes. Although the question of how many tens of billions of dollars owed in taxes to the United States government are lost annually through such devious practices is open to conjecture, it is apparently substantial.[1] Money that could go a long way toward assisting impoverished Americans, whose numbers are clearly a national embarrassment, could also help reduce suffering and the accompanying tension worldwide.

The United States is on the threshold of a new chapter in its history. It is more important today than ever before that educators teach their students to find personal meaning in the great documents that helped shape America as a nation, to be accepting, and to reach out and assist those who are less fortunate, in America and beyond. A revised Pledge of Allegiance could be introduced with its promise to *work toward* liberty and justice for all. This should give citizens, and the world, hope for a better future.

Admittedly, schools have an important mission, but to be truly effective, the *New* Patriotism must be practiced at all strata of society: social, political, and economic, as well as the educational. In the

---

1. Although the numbers vary depending on the sources consulted, some estimates of the amount of lost taxes range as high as $70 billion for 2001.

interest of the future, and to impart not just to ourselves, but to the world, a sense of optimism, the United States must strive for patriotism that reflects commitment to humanity. In this sense, the *New* Patriotism is unique, as it combines the best of traditional patriotism with the best of non-traditional methods. Educators need to teach that being a patriot means many things, that being a good citizen means many things, and that together the emotion of patriotism and the responsibilities of citizenship can produce a patriot with a sense of commitment to community.

Ultimately, the mission of *Teaching New Patriotism in the 21st Century* is twofold. First, to understand that respecting the flag, singing patriotic songs, and reciting the Pledge of Allegiance are important symbols of national unity, security, and faith in a better tomorrow. Second, and perhaps more importantly, these same symbols also provide an acceptance of diversity and a willingness to work for improvement in the quality of life for all people. Thus, when students recite the Pledge of Allegiance, sing patriotic songs, and wave the flag on commemorative holidays and other events, the experience will have a fuller, deeper meaning. And then, maybe, as former president Bill Clinton envisioned, the United States will be in a better position to set the stage for "the world you want for your kids."[2]

---

2. Teresa Watanabe, "Clinton Says U.S. Must Give More to End Terrorism," *Los Angeles Times*, January 15 2002.

Appendix
Table of Contents

Appendix A

Recommended Primary Source Documents For the Study of *New* Patriotism

The Declaration of Independence
In Congress, July 4, 1776

The United States Constitution
In Convention, September 17,
1787

The Bill of Rights
Ratified September 15, 1791

Declaration of Sentiments
Elizabeth Caddy Stanton
Seneca Falls, New York, July 19,
1848

Civil Disobedience
Henry David Thoreau
January, 26, 1848

The Emancipation Proclamation
Abraham Lincoln
January 1, 1863

Inaugural Address
John F. Kennedy
Friday, January 20, 1961

I Have A Dream
Martin Luther King, Jr,
August 28, 1963

Second Treatise of Government
John Locke
1690

Address before the Virginia
Convention
Patrick Henry
March 23, 1775

A Letter from Abigail Adams to
her husband, John
March 31, 1776

Letter from John Adams to his
wife, Abigail
April 14, 1776

The Federalist Papers
Alexander Hamilton, James
Madison, and John Jay
Late 1780s

On the Slave Trade
George Mason
1790

The Rights of Man
Thomas Paine
1790

On Woman's Right to Vote
Susan B. Anthony
various dates, 1873

Fourth Annual Message of
    Theodore Roosevelt
December 4, 1904

The World Will Always Remember
    September 11
George W. Bush
December, 11, 2001

Appendix B
Student Handout A

⌇

Opinion Survey

This is an opinion survey and there are no correct answers. Please be as honest as possible. Circle the appropriate choice that best reflects your feeling toward the statement made.

SA: *Strongly Agree*
A: *Agree*
U: *Undecided*
D: *Disagree*
SD: *Strongly Disagree*

1. SA A U D SD   The United States is unquestionably the best country in the world.*
2. SA A U D SD   Patriots unconditionally abide by what the United States government tells them.
3. SA A U D SD   Even though an individual circulates a petition against the government of the United States he or she could still be considered a patriot.
4. SA A U D SD   Any individual who is willing to wear a uniform and fight for the United States is a patriot.

---

* Robert S. Lynd and Helen Merrell Lynd, *Middletown* (New York: Harcourt, Brace and Company, 1929).

5. SA A U D SD A citizen of the United States should be allowed to say anything he pleases, even to advocate violent revolution, if he does no violent act himself.*

6. SA A U D SD A person who has participated in a demonstration, peaceful or otherwise, against the government of the United States could not be considered a patriot.

7. SA A U D SD Individuals can best show their patriotism by displaying the American flag.

8. SA A U D SD A person cannot be considered a patriot of the United States unless he or she could trace their heritage back to Europe.

9. SA A U D SD The white race is the best race on earth.*

10. SA A U D SD The individual who arms himself or herself with guns, becomes a member of a militia group, and trains to protect with force his or her rights against others, including agents of the government, is a patriot.

11. SA A U D SD An individual who defaces a recognized symbol of the United States, such as the flag, draft card, etc., could not be considered a patriot.

12. SA A U D SD An act that resulted in destruction of property and/or a loss of life could be considered a patriotic act as long as it was done in the name of a political cause.

13. SA A U D SD A patriot critically analyzes the activities of his or her government.

14. SA A U D SD A patriot understands his or her rights as provided in the Constitution, including the Bill of Rights.

15. SA A U D SD Patriotism and citizenship go hand in hand. A person would not be considered a patriot unless he or she also practiced good citizenship skills.

---

* Robert S. Lynd and Helen Merrell Lynd, *Middletown* (New York: Harcourt, Brace and Company, 1929), 200–2001.

16. SA A U D SD   A pacifist in war time is a "slacker" and should be prosecuted by the government.*

17. SA A U D SD   A patriot may disagree with some decisions of the government, but not with those that involve foreign wars when the United States is a participant.

18. SA A U D SD   It is possible for individuals who do not take issue with acts of government to be considered patriots.

19. SA A U D SD   A patriot always exercises his or her right to vote by voting in the various local, state, and/or national elections held in the United States.

20. SA A U D SD   The fact that some men have so much more money than others shows that there is an unjust condition in this country which ought to be changed.*

21. SA A U D SD   A patriot accepts the words of the Pledge of Allegiance as fact.

22. SA A U D SD   Every good citizen should act according to the following statement: "My country—right or wrong."*

23. SA A U D SD   People who do not recognize themselves as Christians cannot be considered patriots.

24. SA A U D SD   A patriot works toward the complete fulfillment of all the ideals and beliefs of the United States such as those expressed in the Declaration of Independence, and the Constitution of the United States, including the Bill of Rights.

25. SA A U D SD   A patriot feels a positive emotional connection to his or her country.

---

* *Ibid.*

Appendix C
Student Handout B

━━

Patriotism Form

Define the Term Patriotism:

_____

_____

_____

List Six Characteristics of a Patriot:

1. _____
   _____

2. _____
   _____

3. _____
   _____

4. _____
   _____

5. _____
   _____

6. _____
   _____

Appendix D
Student Handout C

◝

Patriotism Revision Form

From time to time, as more is learned about patriotism and related issues, opinions may be revised. As the need arises, please use the space provided below for that purpose:

Date: _____

Revision: _____

_____

_____

Date: _____

Revision: _____

_____

_____

Date:_____

Revision: _____

_____

_____

Date:_____

Revision: _____

_____

_____

Appendix E
Student Handout D

⥲

Judgment Form

To arrive at a fair and equitable means of judging "Patriotism," the two cornerstone documents of American history presented below will comprise the base of judgement. After that, as additional segments of the unit are studied, criteria will be expanded.

Declaration of Independence
Constitution of the United States

Criteria for Judgment

1. _____
   _____
   _____

2. _____
   _____
   _____

3. _____
   _____
   _____

4. _____
   _____
   _____

Appendix F
Student Handout E

~

Judgment Revision Form

As additional research uncovers information related to judging patriotism, the current criteria for judgment may need to be added to
or revised. As the need arises, please use the space provided below
for that purpose.

Date: _____

Revision: _____

_____

_____

Date: _____

Revision: _____

_____

_____

Date: _____

Revision: _____

_____

_____

Date: _____

Revision: _____

_____

_____

Appendix G
Patriotism and the Internet

America is much more than a geographical fact. It is a political and moral fact—the first community in which men set out in principle to institutionalize freedom, responsible government, and human equality.

ADLAI STEVENSON

With the increasing presence of technology in the class-room, teachers are faced with additional challenges, among them is the appropriate and efficient use of the Internet. Thanks to the vast number of resources available through the World Wide Web, teachers are able to bring history to life through the use of primary source materials, audio clips of famous speeches, and video clips of some of the more important events of our times.

The Internet also provides a wealth of information on the patriotic roots of the United States. To thoroughly understand the origins of the basic philosophical foundations of the United States, and of the many individuals who helped shape, and ultimately fought "to secure these rights," one needs to delve into early history. The following names, places, and events, should serve as a great starting place for an Internet search for finding out more about the origins of patriotism in the United States.

SUGGESTED SEARCH NAMES AND PHRASES FOR STUDYING EARLY AMERICAN PATRIOTISM

ABIGAIL ADAMS	*SAMUEL ADAMS*
JOHN ADAMS	*ETHAN ALLEN*

THE AMERICAN
REVOLUTION

BENEDICT ARNOLD

THE COERCIVE ACTS

CRISPUS ATTUCKS

SARAH FRANKLIN BACH

DANIEL BOONE

THE BOSTON MASSACRE

BOSTON TEA PARTY

BATTLE OF BUNKER HILL

GEORGE ROGERS CLARK

COMMON SENSE

THE CONTINENTAL ARMY

CONTINENTAL CONGRESS

WILLIAM DAWES

DECLARATION OF
INDEPENDENCE

THE DECLARATORY ACT

JOHN DICKINSON

BENJAMIN FRANKLIN

HORATIO GATES

GREEN MOUTAIN BOYS

NATHANAEL GREENE

NATHAN HALE

ALEXANDER HAMILTON

JOHN HANCOCK

PATRICK HENRY

THE INTOLERABLE ACTS

THOMAS JEFFERSON

JOHN PAUL JONES

HENRY KNOX

THADDEUS KOSCIUSZKO

MARQUIS DE LAFAYETTE

RICHARD HENRY LEE

BATTLES OF LEXINGTON AND
CONCORD

THE LIBERTY BELL

THE LIBERTY TREE

BENJAMIN LINCOLN

ROBERT LIVINGSTON

LOYALISTS

JAMES MADISON

FRANCIS MARION

JANE McCREA

THE OLIVE BRANCH
PETITION

JAMES OTIS

THOMAS PAINE

MOLLY PITCHER

SAMUEL PRESCOTT

WILLIAM PRESCOTT

PROCLAMATION OF 1763

PAUL REVERE

BETSY ROSS

BATTLE OF SARATOGA

THE SONS OF LIBERTY

SUGAR ACT AND STAMP ACT

VALLEY FORGE

GEORGE WASHINGTON

MARTHA WASHINGTON

BATTLE OF YORKTOWN

Acknowledgments

Researching and writing *Teaching New Patriotism in the 21st Century* required the assistance and suggestions of several students, friends, and colleagues. It is only proper that the contributions of those who gave so freely of their time be properly recognized.

A special thank you is extended to Dr. Katie Rommel-Esham for her advice, encouragement, and assistance in the early stages of the project that led to *Teaching New Patriotism in the 21st Century.*

Special thanks is also extended to Krista Anderson, Jenny Dietz, Becky Fox, Heather Robinson, Jennifer Smith, Ashley Wilson, and Rebecca Smith who wrote the majority of abbreviated lesson plans offered in chapter seven of the book.

Offering suggestions, criticism, a thought, an abstract for a lesson plan, reading a paragraph or chapter for content, typing manuscript, or simply providing some much needed encouragement, the following list of individuals also contributed in some way to the development and final completion of *Teaching New Patriotism in the 21st Century.*

Juliet Allen, Krista Anderson, Alicia Armstrong, Jennifer Armstrong, Brooke Ashe, Sarah Baggott, Linda Baxter, Kelly Blevins, Chris Blowers, Morgan Bossie, Colleen Coggins, Sherry Colman, Tom Crook, Morgan Denton, Emily DePorter, Stephen DePuy, Jenny Dietz, Carolyn Downing, Benjamin Esham, Carly Feenstra, Brenna Ferry, Kara Fitzgerald, Kelly Frind, Jill Garvey, Phil Gerhardt, Kim Guilford, Kristi Haun, Suzie Herman, Gretchen Hoag, Mark Huntley, Catherine Hurd, Brandon Herod, Eric Jacobsen, Robyn Jaffee, Katie Jordan, Aubre Jung, Matthew Ketterer, Matthew Klemann,

Rebecca Koch, Alanna Kramerson, Alison Langham, Ryan Lawler, Amie Lester, Sarah Lindner, Amy Lucas, Dan Mac-Donald, Kathy MacCracken, Jennifer Mansfield, Deb Maples, Greg Militello, Jenny Maj, Mary Lou Miller, Steven Nesbitt, Emily Nolan, Kate Parsons, Angela Patti, Nicole Pavan, Candace Perkins, Stephanie Peters, Dan Pike, Jessica Polito, Brian Powers, Andrea Prince, Tracy Przepiora, Pat Pugliese, Kim Putman, Mary Kay Osborn, Michael Rasmussen, Judy Recca, Robert Reed, Paul Resch, Matt Robbins, Becky Roffman, Katie Rommel-Esham, Kristine Schmit, Mark Scott, Jessica Sherrard, Ian Siepel, Mia Sinclair, Michelle Sloan, Kristen Smalt, Rene Smith, Andrea Storie, Becky Strathearn, Lynn Szczesny, Stephen Todd, Becky Trinder, Charles Trojan, Katie Warner, Cassandra Whalen, Jen Wrate, and Lisa Zeller.

Bibliography

Alder, Douglas D., and Sherman J. Lindhardt. "World History: Building Conceptual Understanding for Citizenship." *Social Education* 45, no. 7 (1981): 548–551.

Allen, Gay W., ed. *American Poetry*. New York: Harper and Row, 1965.

Ames, Herman V. "How Far Should the Teaching of History and Civics be used as a Means of Encouraging Patriotism." *The History Teacher's Magazine* 8, no. 6 (1917): 188–192.

Anderson, Howard. "The Social Studies, Patriotism, and Teaching Democracy." *Social Education* 5, no. 1 (1941): 9–14.

Associated Press. "Bush Praises U.S. Children's Generosity of Afghan Youth." *The Buffalo News*. 17 March 2002.

Baer, John W. "The Pledge of Allegiance—A Short History." [online source] (last accessed 11 May 2004) http://history.vineyard.net/pledge.htm.;Internet.

Ball, David. *Riding With Private Malone*. Nashville, TN: Dualtone Music Group, 2001. Audiocassette.

Banks, James A. *Teaching Strategies for the Social Studies*. White Planes, New York: Longman Inc., 1990.

Barr, Robert D., James L. Barth and Samuel S. Shermis. *Defining The Social Studies*. Arlington, Virginia: National Council for the Social Studies, 1977.

Bauer, Richard .H. "The Nazi Revolution and Its Influence on the Teaching of History in Germany." *The Historical Outlook* 24, no. 8 (1933): 421–430.

Bayles, Fred and Kevin Johnson. "U.S.: Shoe Suspect Linked to al Qaeda." *USA Today*. 17 January 2002.

Beadle, Gordon .B. "George Orwell's Meaning of 1984." *Social Education* 48, no. 3 (1984): 183–184.

Beatty, Jack J. "The Patriotism of Values." *New Republic* 185, nos. 1 and 2 (1981): 18–20.

Beinke, John A. "George Orwell and Education." *Social Education* 48, no. 3 (1984): 180–182.

Benitez, Helen. S.N. *Of Patriotism and Partisanship: The Sociological Effects of Secondary U.S. Curricula*. Washington D.C.: Georgetown University, 1995.

Beresney, Timothy A. "History in the Russian School before the Revolution." *The Historical Outlook* 22, no. 7 (1921): 324–328.

Bernier, Normand and Jack Williams. *Ideological Foundations of American History*. Englewood Cliffs, New Jersey: Prentice-Hall Inc., 1973.

Berns, Walter. *Making Patriots*. Chicago: University of Chicago Press, 2001.

Berson, Ilene R. and Michael J. Berson. "Digital Literacy for Effective Citizenship. (Advancing Technology)." *Social Education* 67, no. 3 (2003): 164–168.

Best, John. *Benjamin Franklin on Education*. New York: Teacher's College Press, 1962.

Beyer, Barry K. "Conducting Moral Discussions in the Classroom." *Social Education* 40, no. 4 (1976): 194–202.

Billips, Andrea. *The Washington Times*, accessed at *DADI, Dads Against the Divorce Industry*. "Teaching Patriotism: Retired Military Officers Working with Teen-agers to Teach Patriotism" [online source]. (Washington: News World Communications, Inc., reprinted with permission from *The Washington Times*, 1999, last accessed 13 May 2002). http://www.dadi. org/wt_patri.htm.; Internet.

Bingham, A. "Are Our Rights Insecure?" *Progressive Education* 25, no. 5 (1948): 67.

Bode, B.H. "Education and Social Reconstruction." *The Social Frontier* 1, no. 4 (1935): 18–22.

Bover, R.H. "The Nazi Revolution and its Influence on the Teaching of History in Germany." *The Historical Outlook* 24, no. 8 (1933): 421–430.

Bradford, Mary C. "An Appeal to the High School Young People of the United States." *N.E.A. Bulletin* 6, no. 3 (1918): 16.

Braun, Krysia and Jennifer Link. *Collaborative Thematic Unit: A Celebration of Diversity: Immigration and Citizenship* [online source] (Columbia: University of South Carolina, 1997–1999, last accessed 6 May 2002). http://www.libsci.sc.edu/miller/diversity.htm.; Internet.

Brinkman, Benjamin. "The Relationship between Indoctrination and the Teaching of Democracy." *The Social Studies* 35, no. 6 (1944): 248–252.

Brokaw, Tom. *The Greatest Generation*. New York: Random House, 1998.

Brown, Jordan and James Ciment. *Learning Adventures in Citizenship: The Melting Pot* [online source]. (pbskids.org, last accessed 7 May 2002). http://www.pbs.org/wnet/newyork/laic/lessons/e4_t4–lp.html.;Internet.

Brown, Nancy C. "Student Citizenship Participation: Three Models." *The Social Studies* 76, no. 1 (1985): 12–13.

Brubacher, Abram R. "A Formula for Citizenship." *The Social Studies* 29, no. 8 (1938): 339–342.

Bullard, Marcia. "Change the World." *USA Weekend*. 19–21 October 2001.

Burke, Mary. "Seatwork on Washington and Lincoln." *Instructor* 51, no. 5 (1942): 24–25.

Burns, Robert. "Rumsfeld: U.S. Must Prepare for More Attacks." [online source] (*Associated Press*. Last accessed 27 April 2002). http://www.cbsnews.com/stories/2002/02/20/attack/main501779.shtml.;Internet.

"Bush Tightens Leash on U.S. Aid." *Democrat and Chronicle*. (Rochester, NY). 23 March 2002.

Butts, R. Freeman. *A History of Education in American Culture*. New York: Holt, Rhinehart and Winston, 1953.

Butts, R. Freeman. *Public Education in the United States: From Revolution to Reform*. New York: Holt, Rhinehart and Winston, 1978.

Butts, R. Freeman. *The Revival of Civic Learning*. Bloomington, Indiana: Phi Delta Kappa Foundation, 1980.

Butts, R. Freeman. "The Revival of Civic Learning." *Social Education* 43, no. 9 (1979): 359–364.

Carpenter, Charles. *History of American Schoolbooks*. Philadelphia: University of Pennsylvania Press, 1963.

Center for Civic Education. *National Standards for Civics and Government*. Calabasas, California: Center for Civic Education, 1994.

Chase, Harold, ed. *The Guide to American Law: Everyone's Legal Encyclopedia*. New York: West Publishing Company, 1985.

Cheltenham Elementary School Kindergartners. *We are All Alike...We are All Different*. Photographs by Laura Dwight. (Scholastic Inc: USA., 1991).

Childs, John L. "Teachers and the Democratic Struggle." *Progressive Education* 25 no. 6 (1950): 116–122.

Cohen, P. "The Content of Their Character." *ASCD Curriculum Update* (Spring 1995).

Coleman, Charles. "The Schools and the War Program." *The Social Studies* 34, no. 6 (1943): 260–262.

Coleman, Ova L. "A Study of the Flag." *Grade teacher* 75, no. 6 (1958): 92–94.

Coles, Elisha. An English Dictionary Explaining the Difficult Terms that are used in Divinity, Husbandry, Physick, Phylosophy, Law, Navigation, Mathematick, and other Arts and Sciences. London: Printed by Samual Crouch, 1676.

Conaught, M., ed. *A Blueprint for Education Reform, Citizenship Education: Recovering a Lost Dimension* by Linda Chavez. Chicago, Illinois: Regney/Gateway, 1984.

Crabtree, Charlotte and Gary Nash, eds. *National Standards for United States History.* University of California, Los Angeles: National Center for History in the Schools, 1994.

Craf, John R. "General George C. Marshall." *The Social Studies* 35, no. 1 (1944): 13–15.

Craf, John R. "General James H. Doolittle." *The Social Studies* 35, no. 3 (1944): 111–113.

Craf, John R. "Lieutenant General Omar N. Bradley." *The Social Studies* 35, no. 8 (1944): 341–344.

Cremin, Lawrence A. *American Education: The National Experience 1783–1876.* New York: Harper & Row, 1980.

Cremin, Lawrence A. *The American Common School.* New York: Teacher's College, Columbia University, 1951.

Cremin, Lawrence A., ed. *The Republic and the School: Horace Mann on the Education of Free Men.* New York: Teacher's College Press, 1957.

Crowley, Geoffrey. "They've Given Away $24 Billion. Here's Why." *Newsweek.* 4 February 2002, 46–50.

Culea, Apostal. "The Teaching of History in the Elementary Schools of Rumania." *The Historical Outlook* 23, no. 1 (1932): 28–30.

Cummings, Ella. "The Flag." *Grade Teacher* 71, no. 10 (1954): 14–15.

Cunningham, Hugh. *The Language of Patriotism.* in *History and Politics:* Vol. 1. *Patriotism: The Making and Unmaking of British National Identity.* Edited by R. Samuals. London: Routledge, 1989.

Curti, Merle. *The Roots of American Loyalty.* New York: Columbia University Press, 1946.

Dalby, Bessie W. *"Mother Goose Helps Defense." Grade Teacher* 59, no. 10 (1942): 26.

Dawson, Edgar. *Teaching the Social Studies.* New York: The MacMillan Company, 1928.

Dees, Maurice. *Gathering Storm.* New York: Harper Collins, Publishers, 1996.

della Cava, Marco R. "All They Are Saying is Give Peace a Chance." *USA Today*. 2 October 2001.

Dewey, John. *Moral Principles in Education*. New York: Houghton Mifflin Co., 1909.

Dexter, Lewis A. "People, Patriotism, and Power Politics." *The Social Studies* 34, no. 8 (1943): 365–366.

Diamond, Larry. "Cultivating Democratic Citizenship: Education for a New Century of Democracy in the Americas." *The Social Studies* 88, no. 6 (1997): 244–251.

Diamond, Jared. "Keeping Panic at Bay." *The New York Times*. 21 October 2001.

Downey, Matthew T., ed. *Teaching American History: New Directions*. Washington DC: National Council for the Social Studies, 1982.

Durkheim, Emile. *Moral Education*. New York: The Free Press of Glencoe, Inc, 1961.

Dylan, Bob. *Masters of War*. New York: Columbia Records, 1964. Audiocassette.

Dynneson, Thomas L. "What Does Good Citizenship Mean to Students." *Social Education* 56, no. 1 (1992): 55–58.

Dynneson, Thomas L. "What's Hot and What's Not in Effective Citizenship Education." *The Social Studies* 83, no. 5 (1992): 197–200.

Eber, Jeffery. "Three Great Documents." *Social Education* 7, no. 5 (1943): 209–215.

Editorial. "Democracy Makes a Difference." *The Charlotte Observer*, 2001.

Editorial. "Safety, Liberty." *Detroit Free Press*. 20 October 2001.

"Educating for Patriotism." *N.E.A. Bulletin* 31, no. 8 (1942): 255.

Educator's Reference Desk. [online source] (Last accessed 5 May 2004). http://www.eduref.org.; Internet.

Ellis, Gwen, ed. *God Bless America*. Zondervan, 1999.

Ellis Island Immigration Museum Site [online source]. (New York: ARAMARK Sports & Entertainment, Inc., 2002). http://www.ellisisland.com/index.html.; Internet.

Elson, Ruth Miller. *Guardians of Tradition*. Lincoln, Nebraska: University of Nebraska Press, 1964.

Emmerich, Roland. *The Patriot*. Los Angeles, CA: Columbia Pictures. 2000. Videocassette.

Engle, Shirley H. and Anna Ochoa. "A Curriculum for Democratic Citizenship." *Social Education* 50, no. 1 (1986): 514–525.

Estvan, Frank.J. *Social Studies in a Changing World*. New York: Harcourt, Brace & World, Inc., 1968.

Europa World Yearbook, The. London: Europa Publications Limited, 1996.

Evans, Helen K. "A Unit on Flag Day." *Instructor* 50, no. 8 (1941): 16.

Faherty, William B. "A Neglected Objective in the Teaching of History." *The Social Studies* 33, no. 1 (1942): 27–30.

Farley, Chris J. "Patriot Games." *Time* 144, no. 2 (1994): 48–49.

Fenton, Edwin, ed. "A New History of the United States." *Carnegie-Mellon Social Studies Curriculum.* New York: Holt, Rinehart and Winston, Inc., 1975.

Finlay, Pauline. Holy Trinity Elementary School, Torbay, Newfoundland (Canada), Last accessed 5 June 2004. [online] http://www.education-world.com/a_tsl/archives/04–1/lesson006.shtml. Internet.

Fix, John. "Our Flag." *Instructor* 71, no. 10 (1962): 66–67.

Flagg, Ann. "Amazing Americans." *Instructor* 108, no. 1 (1999): 37–40.

Flagg, Ann. "Hail to the Chiefs." *Instructor* 111, no. 1 (2002): 37–42.

Flanigan, Robin L. "Generation X Hears, Heeds its First Call to Patriotism." *Democrat and Chronicle* (Rochester, NY), 21 September 2001.

Fleming, Thomas. *Liberty.* Hong Kong: Viking Penguin. 1997.

Fowler, Sara M. *Patriotic Heritage.* Idaho State Department of Education, 1–3, 1986.

Fox, M. *Whoever You Are.* (Scholastic Inc: USA., 1997).

Frost, Norman. "We Educate for Victory." *Grade Teacher* vol. 59, no. 9 (1942): 42, 53.

Friedman, Thomas L. "Ask Not What . . ." *The New York Times.* 9 December 2001.

Fritz, Jean. *Will You Sign Here, John Hancock?* New York: Coward-McCann, Inc., 1976.

Furumoto, Rosa, Luis Gamarra, Juith Iguina, Ignacio Reyes-Saldana, Adriana Rubalacva, and Phyllis Scadron. *Teaching Steps to Tolerance* [online source]. (Sharp Avenue, California, Museum of Tolerance, last accessed 6 May 2002). http://tst.wiesenthal.com/resources/talkinghands.html.; Internet.

Fussell, Cathy. "Idea Exchange." *Teaching Tolerance Magazine* no. 20 (2001): 6–9.

Gaalvez-Hijornevik, Cleta. "James A. Michener: Reaffirmations of a Permanent Liberal." *Social Education* 51, no. 4 (1987): 250–255.

Gaines, Addie. *Proud to Be Americans* [online source] (Seneca Missouri, geocities.com, 1997, last accessed 6 May 2002). http://www.geocities.com/Athens/Aegean/2221/america.html.; Internet.

Gagnon, Paul. "On Educating for Democracy: A Reply." *Social Education* 51, no. 6 (1987): 403–406.

Garrison, J. and A. Tubesing. *A Million Visions of Peace: Wisdom from the Friends of Old Turtle.* New York: Pfeifer-Hamilton: Scholastic Inc., 1996.

Gerges, Fawz A. "The Arab Tide Turns Against Bin Laden." *Los Angeles Times.* 2002.

Gideonse, H.D. "Non-partisan Education for Political Intelligence." *The Social Frontier* 1, no. 4 (1935): 15–18.

Grant, S.G. and Bruce A. Vansledright. "The Dubious Connection: Citizenship Education and the Social Studies." *The Social Studies* 87, no. 2 (1996): 56–69.

Greathouse, Betty and Barbara Goldman Young. "'Roots' A Stimulus for Community Involvement." *The Social Studies* 70, no. 2 (1979): 75–80.

Greenawald, Dale G. "Voting Isn't Enough." *Social Education* 60, no. 6 (1996): 333–335.

Greenberg, David. "Washington Diarist: Patriot Games." *New Republic* 213, nos. 3 and 4 (1995): 54.

Greenwood, Lee. *God Bless the USA.* Santa Monica, California: Music Corporation of America, 1984. Audiocassette.

Griffen, Alan F. *Freedom American Style.* New York: Henry Holt and Company, 1940.

Gross, Richard E. "Aims for American History in an Era of Crisis." *Social Education* 17, no. 6 (1953): 257–260.

Guthrie, Doug. "Boomers to Redefine Retirement." *The Detroit News and Free Press,* 4 July 2004.

Haggard, Merle. *The Fightin' Side of Me.* Los Angeles, California, Capitol Records, 1973. Audiocassette.

Halladay, Jennifer R. *Who are the Arab Americans?* [online source]. (A web project of the Southern Poverty Law Center, last accessed 6 May 2002). http://www.tolerance.org/teach/expand/act/activity.jsp?cid=155.; Internet.

Hallenbeck, R.L. "We sold stamps." *Grade Teacher* 60, no. 6 (1943): 29, 64.

"Hatred's just a click away." *Democrat and Chronicle* (Rochester, NY), 17 June 2004.

Heckel, Deone A.K. "Pure History and Patriotism." *The Historical Outlook* 16, no. 3 (1925): 106–110.

Heckman, M.I. "War Stamps Sale Organization." *Grade Teacher* 60, no. 1 (1942): 20–21, 97.

Hedges, Chris. "A Powerful Combatant in France's War on Terror." *The New York Times.* 24 November 2001.

Heindel, Richard. "American Influence on Japan." *The Social Studies* 33, no. 5 (1942): 214.

Hepburn, Mary A. *Democratic Education in Schools and Classrooms.* Washington DC: National Council for the Social Studies, 1983.

Hepburn, Mary A. *Educating for democracy in the United States.* Paper presented at the Conference on the Development of Democracy after World War II. Federal Republic of Germany, September 24–30, 1989.

Herford, Nancy Jo. "Hail to the Chief." *Instructor* 92, no. 6 (1983): 38.

Hicks, Kevin Bryant and the Associated Press. "Pledge Unites Nation's Schools." *Democrat and Chronicle* (Rochester, NY). 13 October 2001.

Hiestand, Michael. "Patriotic Super Bowl." *USA Today.* 10 January 2001.

Hoveneir, Peter J. "The Education of a Loyal Nazi." *Social Education* 47, no. 6 (1983): 391–395.

Howe, Samuel B. "The Basis of Historical Teaching." *The History Teacher's Magazine* 4, no. 3 (1913): 71–73.

Hurwitz, Howard L. "Teaching Patriotism . . . Not Nostalgia, but Necessity." *The American Legion* 109, no. 3 (1980): 14–16.

Iacocca, Lee. "Lady Liberty Needs You." *Instructor* 92, no. 6 (1983): 42.

Infoplease. "The Star-Spangled Banner" [online source] http://www.infoplease.com/ipa/A0194015.html.; Internet.

Javna, John. *50 Simple Things Kids Can Do To Save the Earth.* Kansas City: Andrews and McMeel, 1990.

Janger, Stephen A. "A Call for Innovation." *Social Education* 52, no. 6 (October 1988): 463.

Janowitz, Morris. "Toward a New Patriotism: Educating for Civic Consciousness." *Curriculum Review* 24, no. 4 (1985): 14–18.

Jarolimek, John *Social Studies in Elementary Education.* New York: Macmillan Publishing Co., Inc., 1980.

Johnson, David Cay. "U.S. Corporations Are Using Bermuda to Slash Tax Bills." *The New York Times.* 18 February 2002.

Johnson, Lynell and Robert Hess. "Kids and Citizenship: A National Survey." *Social Education* 48, no. 7 (1984): 502–505.

Jost, Kenneth. "Civil Liberties Debates." The CQ Researcher Online, 13, no. 37 (24 October, 2003): 893–916. http://library-cqpress.com/cqresearcher.; Internet.

Kamerman, Sylvia E, ed. *Patriotic & Historical Plays for Young People.* Boston: Plays Inc., 1975.

Kavett, Hymen. "How Do We Stand With the Pledge of Allegiance Today?" *Social Education* 43, no. 6 (1976): 135–140.

Kemsley, Sandy. *ABC Teach Network* [online source]. (ABC Teach Network, 2001, last accessed 6 May 2002). http://www.abcteach.com.; Internet.

Kerr, Selma A. "Here's a Way to Help Your Country." *Instructor* 51, no. 6 (1942): 17.

King, Barbara C. "Behind the Pledge." *Grade Teacher* 89, no. 1 (1971): 12–14.

Kisselbrack, L.J. "What About War Stamps?" *Grade Teacher* 61, no. 7 (1944): 28, 60.

Knoles, George H. "Thomas Jefferson: Crusader for Freedom." *The Social Studies* 33, no. 7 (1942): 297–304.

Kreigel, Leonard. "Boundaries of Memory: Liberals, Patriots, and Melting Pots." *The Virginia Quarterly Review* 71, no. 1 (1995): 19–35.

Krugman, Paul. "America's Press Has Been Too Soft on Bush," *International Herald Tribune*, 29–30 May 2004.

Kushner, Maxwell. "The Birthday of Our Flag." *Grade Teacher* 77, no. 10 (1960): 41–42.

La Morte, Michael W. *School Law: Cases and Concepts.* Boston: Allyn and Bacon, 1996.

Lankes, David R., Director. *Ask ERIC Educational Information* [online source]. (Syracuse: ERIC Clearinghouse on Information & Technology, Syracuse University, last accessed 13 May 2002). http://askeric.org.; Internet.

Lennon, John and Paul McCartney. *Give Peace a Chance.* Parlophone, London, England: 1969. Audiocassette.

Lent, J., ed. "Teaching During Wartime." *Instructor* 100, no. 7 (1991): 29–30.

Leppard, Lynden J. "Discovering a Democratic Tradition and Educating for Public Politics." *Social Education* 57, no. 1 (1993): 23–26.

Lesson Plans Page.Com. *How Communities are Different* [online source]. (EdScope,L.L.C., 1996–2002, last accessed 6 May 2002). http://www.Lessonplanspage.com/SSCommunityDifferencesVenn3.htm.; Internet.

Lewenstein, Morris R. "Some Current Projects in Citizenship Education." *Progressive Education* 29, no. 7 (1952): 249–252.

Lewenstein, Morris R. *Teaching Social Studies.* Chicago: Rand McNally & Company, 1963.

Lewis, Barbara A. *The Kid's Guide to Service Projects.* Minneapolis, MN: Free Spirit Publishing, Inc., 1995.

Lewis, Bernard. "What Went Wrong?" *History Matters* 14, no. 7 (2002): 1–3.

Lewis, Beth. *Elementary Educators: Veterans Day 2001* [online source] (About Inc. 2002, last accessed 6 May 2002). http://k-6educators. about.com/library/ weekly/ aa110101a.htm.; Internet.

Lewis, Sinclair. *It Can't Happen Here.* Garden City, New York: Sun Dial Press, 1935.

Limbert, Paul M. "What Children Think About War." *Progressive Education* 10, no. 2 (1933): 67–71.

Lindeman, Edward C. "Do We Need a New Approach to Democracy." *Progressive Education* 10, no. 2 (1948): 67–71.

Lowell, James R. *Political Essays.* Vol. 5, *Lowell's Prose Works.* New York: Houghton Mifflin Company, 1913.

Lubbers, Enbert. "Teaching Citizenship for Defense and War." *The Social Studies* 33, no. 6 (1942): 116–117.

Ludwig, Walter. "Ration Stamps and Salvage: A Tenth Grade Project." *Social Education* 7, no. 5 (1943): 205–208.

Lynd, Robert S. and Helen Merrell Lynd. *Middletown.* New York: Harcourt, Brace and Company, 1929.

Machacek, John. "Schumer, Clinton Give Thanks to Nation." *Democrat and Chronicle* (Rochester, NY). 16 September 2001.

Maloney, Richard. "They Made Our Country Great—Biographical series." *Instructor* 51, no. 9 (1942): 12.

Malveaux, Julianne. "Give Thanks With Some Exceptions." *USA Weekend.* 23 November 2001.

Mansfield, Brian. "Patriotism Revs 'Private Malone' into High Gear." *USA Today.* 2 October 2001.

Manzo, Kathleen Kennedy. "Education Experts Expect Resurgence of Patriotism in Nation's Classrooms." *Education Week.* 26 September 2001.

Martin, Asa Earl. "The Beginning of Japanese-American Relations." *The Social Studies* 33, no. 4 (1942): 153–159.

Martin, James A. and Mark E. Lender. *A Respectable Army: The Military Origins of the Republic, 1763–1789.* Edited by J.H. Franklin and A.S. Eisenstadt, *The American History Series.* Arlington Heights, Illinois: Harlan Davidson, Inc., 1982.

Martorella, Peter H. *Teaching Social Studies in Middle and Secondary Schools.* New York: MacMillan Publishing Co., 1991.

McCartney, Paul. *Freedom.* Hollywood, California: Capitol Records, 2001. Audiocassette.

McCutchen, S.P. "The Real Task of Social Studies." *Progressive Education* 12, no. 8 (1935): 543–551.

McPhie, Walter E. "Dissenters in a Democracy: Patriots or Subversives." *The Social Studies* 77, no. 5 (1986): 192–195.

Menacker, Julius and Wayne A. Wynne. "Helping Students to Serve Society." *Phi Delta Kappan* 63, no. 6 (1982): 381–384.

Mehlinger, H.D. and L.O. Davis, eds. *The Social Studies: Eightieth Yearbook of the National Society for the Study of Education.* Chicago: University of Chicago Press, 1981.

Metcalf, Lawrence and Maurice Hunt. *Teaching High School Social Studies.* New York: Harper and Row, 1968.

Metzger, Devon. "Young Citizens: Partners in Classroom Management." *Social Studies & the Young Learner* 12, no. 4. (2000): 21–23.

Michener, James A. "Reaffirmations of a Permanent Liberal." *Social Education* 51, no. 4 (1987): 250–255.

"Milkweed in the war." *Grade Teacher* 62, no. 1 (1944): 20–21, 89.

Milson, Andrew J. and Beong-Wan Chu, "Character Education for Cyberspace: Developing Good Netizens", *The Social Studies* 93, no. 3 (2002): 117–120.

Minkow, Rosalie. "We Pledge Allegiance." *Instructor* 84, no. 6 (1975): 22–23.

Morris, G. "Helping the war effort." *Grade Teacher* 61, no. 1 (1943): 30.

Morris, Jeffrey Brandon and Richard Brandon Morris. *Encyclopedia of American History.* New York: HarperCollins Publishers, 1996.

Morrison, Blake. "Passengers Turning into Air Police." *USA Today.* 17 October 2001.

Muessig, Raymond, and Vincent Rogers. "Teaching Patriotism at Higher Concept Levels." *Social Education* 28, no. 5 (1964): 266–270.

Murray, Thomas R. *Teaching Patriotism as a Moral Matter.* Paper presented at the annual meeting of the Comparative and International Education Society, 1993.

"Music, Music, Music." *Teaching Pre K–8.* (February 2002): p. 42–44.

Nash, Gary B. "Reflection on the National History Standards." *National Forum* 77, no. 3 (1997): 14–18.

Nash, Gary B. "The National History Standards and George Washington." *The Social Studies* 88, no. 4 (1997): 159–162.

National Council for the Social Studies Citizenship Committee. "Essential Characteristics of a Citizenship Program." *Social Education* 48, no. 6 (1984): 408–409.

National Council for the Social Studies Citizenship Select Subcommittee. "Service-Learning: An Essential Component to Citizenship Education." *Social Education* 65, no. 4 (2001): 240.

National Council for the Social Studies Task Force on Revitalizing Citizenship Education. "Creating Effective Citizens." *Social Education* 65, no. 5 (2001): 319.

National Education Association. "Preliminary Recommendations by the Committee of the National Education Association." *The History Teacher's Magazine* 4, no. 10 (1913): 291–297.

National Education Association. "Report of the Committee on Social Studies." *The History Teacher's Magazine* 8, no. 1 (1916): 4–25.

National Education Association. *Report of the Educational Policies Commission*. NEA, 1952.

National Franklin Committee, The. "Benjamin Franklin and Education." *The Social Studies* 35, no. 2 (1944): 79.

National Franklin Committee, The. "Benjamin Franklin the Patriot." *The Social Studies* 35, no. 3 (1944): 124–126.

National Monument and Ellis Island: Symbols of Liberty [online source] (National Park Service Education Specialist, last modified January 1, 2001. Last accessed 7 May 2002). http://www.nps.gov/stli/teachercorner/page8.html.; Internet.

National Resources Defense Council [online-source] (The NRDC Regional Office may be reached at 1200 New York Ave., NW, Suite 400, Washington D.C. 20005, (202) 289– 6868, last accessed 13 May 2002). http://www.nrdc.org.;Internet.

Newhall, David. "Civil Disobedience and Democracy." *The Social Studies* 64, no. 7 (1973): 307–312.

New York Times Daily Lesson Plan Page [online source] (New York: The New York Times, 2002, the New York Timeson the WEB Learning Network, last accessed 13 May 2002). http://www.nytimes.com/learning/teachers/lessons /archive.html.; Internet.

Newton, Jegge H. "Democracy or Super Patriotism." *Frontiers of Democracy* (April 16, 1941): 208–211.

Nietz, John T. *The Evaluation of American Secondary School Textbooks*. Rutland Vermont: Charles E. Tuttle Company, 1966.

Noel, M. "Getting in the Scrap." *Instructor* 53, no. 3 (1944): 33, 61.

Oakie, John H. "Japan's War Potential." *Social Education* 6, no. 2 (1942): 115–118.

O'Driscoll, Patrick. "Patriotic Could Become Name of These Games." *USA Today*. 22 January 2002.

O'Leary, Cecilia. "Americans All." *History Today* 44, no. 10 (1994): 20–27.

Orwell, George. *1984*. San Diego: Harcourt, Brace, Janovich, 1949.

Pablo, Petey. *USA Flag Remix*. New York, New York: Jive Records, 2002. Audiocassette.

Page, Clarence. "Here Comes the Patriotic Police." *Democrat and Chronicle* (Rochester, NY). 21 December 2001.

Parker, Kathleen. "Yet Another Spy Center Opens in Washington," *Democrat and Chronicle* (Rochester, NY), 12 June 2004.

Parker, Walter and J.Jarolimek. *Citizenship and the Critical Role of the Social Studies.* Washington D.C. National Council for the Social Studies, 1984.

"Passengers Take Back Bus in Utah." *USA Today.* 19 October 2001.

Paul, Richard W. "Ethics Without Indoctrination." *Educational Leadership* 45, no. 8 (1988): 10–19.

Pithenen, Allen M. "Strengthening Our Morale." *The Social Studies* 35, no. 2 (1944): 57–59.

Pohoska, Hanna. "The Teaching of History in the Secondary Schools of Poland." *The Historical Outlook* 23, no. 5 (1932): 235–238.

Politex, a non-affiliated U.S. Citizen, *Patriotism* [online source] (Last accessed 13 May 2002). http://www.bushnews.com/patriotism. htm.; Internet.

Polsky, Milton. "America the Dramatic." *Instructor* 92, no. 6 (1985): 32–33.

Postman, Neil. *The End of Education.* New York: Vintage Books, 1995.

Powell, Bill and Aparisim Ghosh, "Paul Bremer's Rough Ride." *Time*, 28 June 2004.

ProTeacher. [online source] (1998–2002, last accessed 6 May 2002). http://www.proteacher.com.; internet.

ProTeacher. [online source] (1998–2002, last accessed 6 May 2002). http://www.proteacher.com/090019.shtml.; Internet.

"Protect Patriotic Collections." *N.E.A. Bulletin* 6, no. 2 (1918): 16–17

Pullen, John J. *Patriotism in America.* New York: American Heritage Press, 1971.

Punke, Harold H. "Loyalty and Patriotism as Social Necessity." *The Social Studies* 47, no. 2 (1956): 61–69.

Purdum, Todd S. "California Census Confirms Whites are in Minority," *New York Times*, 30 March 2001.

Putman, Errol., ed. *Teach the Lessons, Make a Difference.* Houston: Holocaust Museum Houston, 2000.

Putman, Errol. "The Changing Tide of Professional Print Media and Teaching Patriotism: 1916–1956." *Theory and Research in Social Education* 32, no. 2 (2004): 366–80.

Quartermaster Museum, The. *Private George Watson Medal of Honor, World War II.* [online source] (last accessed 6 May 2002). http://www.qmfound.com/watson.htm.; Internet.

Quigley, Charles N. *Civitas.* (NCSS Bulletin no. 86). Calabasas, California: Center for Civic Education, 1986.

Quinn, Lynn. *My Country 'Tis of Thee* [online source]. (Boston: Massachusetts, Boston Teachnet.org, last accessed 6 May 2002). http://www.boston.teachnet.org/quinn/quinn.htm.; Internet.

Randolph, J.W. *Early History of the University of Virginia as Contained in the Letters of Thomas Jefferson and Joseph C. Cabell.* Richmond Virginia : J.W. Randolph, 1856.

Redefer, F.R. Democratic Education: "Suggestions for Education and National Defense." *Progressive Education* 17, no. 7 (1940): 452–479.

Redefer, F.R. "The School's Role in Winning the War and the Peace." *Progressive Education* 19, no. 6 (1942): 300–307.

Remarque, Erich Maria. *All Quiet on the Western Front.* New York: Random House, Inc., 1929.

Risinger, C. Frederick. "Citizenship Education and the World Wide Web." *Social Education* 61, no. 4 (1997): 223–224.

Roberts, Cokie and Steven V. Roberts. "Souls of Steel." *USA Weekend.* 12–14 October 2001.

Rodia, Becky. "Our Enriching Differences" *Teaching Pre K–8,* (October 2000): 44–47.

Rogers, V.R. "Teaching Patriotism at Higher Concept Levels." *Social Education* 28, no. 5 (1964): 266–270.

Ross, A. Franklin. "Has the War Taught American Teachers Anything?" *The Social Studies* 35, no. 6 (1944): 241–244.

Ross, A. Franklin. "Patriotism in an Upset World: Can it Survive?" *The Social Studies* 40, no. 1 (1949): 3–5.

Ross, A. Franklin. "Winning the War: A Job For The Schools." *The Social Studies* 34, no. 2 (1943): 51–53.

Roth, John. "History and Citizenship Training." *Social Education* 13, no. 7 (1949): 309–314.

Rover, Richard. "The Nazi Revolution and its Influence on the Teaching of History in Germany." *The Historical Outlook* 24, no. 8 (1933): 421–423.

Rowe, Benjamin. "On To Victory." *The Social Studies* 35, no. 7 (1944): 291–293.

Russell, William F. "The Early Teaching of History." *The History Teacher's Magazine* 5, no. 7 (1914): 203–8.

Ryan, Pam Munoz. *The Flag We Love.* Watertown, Maine: Charlesbridge Publishing, 1996.

Safire, William. "Terror Tribunals a Dictatorial Abuse of Power." *Charlotte Observer.* 21 November 2001.

Salisbury, Seward. "Positive Leadership." *Social Education* 4, no. 8 (1940): 545–548.

Samuelson, Robert J. "Tax Havens For One and All?" *Newsweek*. 8 April 2002. p. 33.

Sanderman, Alexa L. and John F. Ahern. "More Children's Literature to Promote Citizenship in the Upper and Middle Grades." *Social Studies & the Young Learner* 10, no. 2 (1997): 25–28.

Santoro, Cesare. *Hitler's Germany: As Seen by a Foreigner*. Berlin: Internationaler Verlag, 1939.

Santino, Jack. "Yellow Ribbons and Seasonal Flags: The Folk Assemblage of War." *Journal of American Folklore* 105, (1992): 19–33.

"Save coal, Save America." *Grade Teacher* 62 no. 6 (1945): 52–53.

Saxe, David W. "An Introduction to the Seminal Social Welfare and Efficiency Prototype: The Founder of the 1916 Social Studies." *Theory and Research in Social Education* 20, no. 2 (1992): 156–178.

Schaffner, F. *Patton*. Hollywood, California: Twentieth Century Fox, 1970. Videocassette.

Schmitt, Annalisa. Executive Summary: A Population Perspective of the United States. [online source]. (Filamentality, Pacific Bell, 1996–2002, last accessed May 6, 2002). http://www.prerdc.org/ summaries/uspopperspec/uspopperspec.html.; Internet.

Scholastic Books. *The Pledge of Allegiance*. New York: Scholastic Inc., 2000.

Schulof, Cathy. *Pursuit of Patriotism: an Internet Treasure Unit on Patriotism* [online source] (Filamentality, Pacific Bell, 1996–2002, last accessed 6 May 2002). http://www.richmond.edu/academics/a&s /education/projects/hunts/patriotism.; Internet.

Sedeen, Margaret. *Star-Spangled Banner*. Washington DC: National Geographic Society, 1993.

Shaver, James P. "Commitment to Values and the Study of Social Problems in Citizenship Education." *Social Education* 49, no. 2 (1985): 194–197.

Shermis, Samuel S. and James L. Barth. "Indoctrination and the Study of Social Problems: A Re-examination of the 1930's Debate in the Social Frontier." *Social Education* 49, no. 3 (1985): 190–193.

Shiman, David A. and Fernekes, William R. "The Holocaust, Human Rights, and Democratic Citizenship Education." *The Social Studies* 90, no. 2. (1999): 53–62.

Sims, Patsy. *The Klan*. New York: Stein and Day, 1978.

Sinclair, Gordon. *Letter to Our Neighbor*. (Quebec, Canada: Published by Star Quality Music (SOCAN) A Division of UNIDISC Music Inc. 578 Hymus Boulevard Pointe-Claire Quebec Canada, H9R4T2, 1973).

Singleton, Laurel R. *What makes a Good Citizen?: Models in Literature* [online source] (Boulder, Co: SSEC Publications, 1999, last accessed 6 May, 2002). http://www.ssecinc.org/less/Pg_ls_what. htm.; Internet.

Slackman, Michail. "Saudis Feel Unfairly Tarred With a Terrorist Brush." *Los Angeles Times.* 17 January 2002.

Smithsonian Folkways recordings. *Lest We Forget : Sing for Freedom: The Story of the Civil Rights Movement Through Songs,* vol. 3 (Smithsonian Folkways # 05488).

Snyder, Thomas, ed. *Digest of Education Statistics, 1996.* Washington DC: U.S. Department of Education, 1996.

Spielberg, Steven. *Saving Private Ryan.* Universal City, California: Dream Works Pictures, 1998. Videocassette.

Springsteen, Bruce. *Born in the USA.* New York: Columbia Records, 1984. Videocassette.

Stern, Jessica. "Terrorists' Own Words Can Help Us Stop Them." *USA Today,* 24 June 2004.

Stevens, Leonard. "Do We Need a New Pledge of Allegiance?" *Look* 34, no. 24 (1970): 19–21.

Stone, Oliver. *Born on the Fourth of July.* Universal City, California: Universal Studios, 1989. Videocassette.

Strauss, S.W. "Thrift, a Patriotic Duty." *N.E.A. Bulletin* 6, no. 1 (1918): 29.

Swarts, Elizabeth. "Keep the Beat." *Teaching K–8* 32, no. 6 (2002): 62.

"Teaching During Wartime." *Instructor* 100, no. 7 (1991): 29.

Teaching Tolerance Project. *Starting Small.* Birmingham, Alabama: the Southern Poverty Law Center, 1997

Temmerich, R. *Independence Day.* Hollywood, California: 20th Century Fox, 1996. Videocassette.

"The Return of Teach-Ins." *The New York Times.* 21 October 2001.

Thompson, Everett.L. "Your Flag and My Flag." *Instructor* 50, no. 8 (1941): 36–37.

Tippin, Aaron. *Where the Stars & Stripes and Eagles Fly.* Burbank, CA: Lyric Street Records, 2001. Audiocassette.

Toner, Robin and Janet Elder. "Public is Wary But Supportive on Rights Curbs." *The New York Times.* 12 December 2001.

Trudeau, Gary. "Doonsbury." *Democrat and Chronicle* (Rochester, NY). 4 November 2001.

Trumbo, Dalton. *Johnny Got His Gun.* Hollywood, California: Media Home Entertainment, 1982. Videocassette.

Tuttle, Harold S. "Drama for Democratic Citizenship." *N.E.A. Bulletin* 33, no. 1 (1944): 18.

United Nations International School [online source] (Contact information: United Nations International School, 24–50 FDR Drive New York, NY 10010, last accessed 7 May 2002). http://www.unis.org; Internet.; United Nations (New York: United Nations, 2000–2002 all rights reserved, last accessed 7 May, 2002). http://www.un.org.; Internet.

Unsigned Editorial. (1935). "Introductory Remarks on Education." *The Social Frontier* 1, no. 4 (1935): 8–9.

Wagoner, Kathy, ed. *A Salute to America.* New York: Sourcebooks, Inc., 2001.

Waldstreicher, David. "Rites of Rebellion, Rites of Assent: Celebrations of Print Culture, and the Origins of American Nationalism." *Journal of American History* 82, no. 1 (1995): 37–61.

Walker, Charles J. "Flag-Waving Fun." *Instructor* 92, no. 6 (1983): 44.

Washburne, C. "Indoctrination versus Education." *The Social Frontier* 2, no. 3 (1936): 212–215.

Watanabe, Teresa. "Clinton Says U.S. Must Give More to End Terrorism." *Los Angeles Times.* 2001.

Welter, Rosh. *Popular Education and Democratic Thought.* New York: Columbia University Press, 1962.

"What's Happened to Patriotism?" [*New York Times* advertisement] *Social Education* 35, no. 6 (1971): 653.

Wheatley, Christopher J. "The volunteers and the Rhetoric of Honor and Patriotism." *ELH* 60, no. 2 (1993): 397–418.

Whittaker, Mio L. "Objectives in the Social Studies." *Social Education* 1, no. 9 (1937): 625–628.

Wiley, George M. "The Social Studies—A Slogan or a Service." *The Social Studies* 30, no. 1 (1939): 3–6.

Williams, Dilafruz R. "Democracy and Civil Education." Unpublished Ph.D. diss., Syracuse University, 1987.

Willis, M. "The Real Task of Social Studies: Some Implications." *Progressive Education* 13 no. 4 (1936): 282–285.

Wilson, M.D. "My Country and My Flag . . . Their Story." *Grade Teacher* 79, no. 10 (1962): 50–52.

Winik, Lyric Wallwork. "We Have a Reason to Hope." *Parade.* 23 December 2001.

Wright, Robert. "Rumsfield's Moments." *The New York Times.* 20 January 2002.

Wright, Walter. "House Speaker Joins Mission to Revive Tourism." *The Honolulu Advertiser.* 7 January 2002.

Yardley, Jim. "Non-Hispanic Whites May Soon Be a Minority in Texas." New York Times, 25 March 2001.

Yeager, Elizabeth Anne and Diane Yendol Silva. "Activities for Strengthening The Meaning of Democracy for Elementary School Children." *The Social Studies* 93, no. 1 (2002): 18–22.

Young, Dean and Denis Lebrun. "Blondi." *Democrat and Chronicle* (Rochester, NY). 28 October 2001.

Young, Paul R. "Victory Gardens for School and Home." *N.E.A. Bulletin* 31, no. 3 (1942): 74–75.

Zakaria, Fareed. "The Good, the Bad, the Ugly." *Newsweek,* 31 May 2004, 33.

Zakaria, Fareed. "Tackle the Nuke Threat." *Newsweek.* 21 June 2004, 60.

Zevin, Jack. "Clashing Conceptions of Citizenship." *Social Science Record* 31, no. 2 (1994): 21–26.

Zick, Edward. *Courage Under Fire.* Los Angeles, California: 20th Century Fox. 1996. Videocassette.

Zimbalist, Alison and Javaid Khan. "Emblems of the Land I Love: Exploring the History and Impact of Patriotic Images." [online source] (New York: *The New York Times on the WEB Learning Network, New York Times Daily Lesson Plan Page* in collaboration with the Bank Street College of Education in NYC Monday October 29 2001, last accessed 13 May, 2002). http://www.nytimes.com/learning/teachers/lessons/20011029monday.html?searchpv=learning_lessons#standards.; Internet.

Zinn, Howard. *A People's History of the United States.* New York: Harper Perennial. 1995.

Zjawin, Sandy. "One Nation Indivisible . . ." *Instructor* 92, no. 6 (1983): 30–31.

Zjawin, Sandy. "The First Patriots." *Instructor* 92 no. 6 (1983): 28.

Index